Gerard ter Borch, *The Consultation*, 1635. Photo: Joerg P. Anders. Gemaeldegalerie, Staatliche Museen zu Berlin, Berlin, Germany. Photo credit: Bildarchiv Preussischer Kulturbesitz / Art Resource, NY.

Jacques-Louis David, *Portrait of Lavoisier and his Wife*, 1788. Oil on canvas, 102 ¼ × 76 ⅛ in. (259.7 × 194.6 cm). Purchase, Mr. and Mrs. Charles Wrightsman Gift, in honor of Everett Fahy, 1977 (1977.1). Art, New York, NY, U.S.A. Photo credit: Image copyright © The Metropolitan Museum of Art / Art Resource, NY (ART322961).

ALCHEMICAL MERCURY

A Theory of Ambivalence

Karen Pinkus

*Stanford
University
Press*

*Stanford,
California*

Stanford University Press
Stanford, California

Printed in the United States of America on acid-free,
archival-quality paper

Library of Congress Cataloging-in-Publication Data

Pinkus, Karen.
    Alchemical mercury : a theory of ambivalence / Karen Pinkus.
        p. cm.
    Includes bibliographical references and index.
    ISBN 978-0-8047-6032-4 (cloth : alk. paper)
        1. Alchemy in literature.   2. Alchemy in art.   3. Ambivalence.
4. Rhetoric.   I. Title.

PN56.A44P56 2010
700'.47—dc22   2008053119

Typeset by Westchester Book Services in 10.9/13 Adobe Garamond

Contents

Figures

Acknowledgments

Generous support from the University of Southern California College deans, the Early Modern Studies Institute at USC, and the Borchard Foundation made this book possible. My heartfelt thanks to the many libraries and collections where I researched, including the Biblioteca Philosophica Hermetica (Amsterdam), the Warburg Institute Library (London), The Huntington (San Marino), and the Getty Research Institute (Los Angeles), where David Brafman, in particular, shared his expertise. Colleagues at Cornell, University of Colorado, University of Oregon, University of Sussex, and USC asked challenging questions when I presented work in progress. Paolo Matteucci served as my research assistant, funded by a USC Provost's Strategic Theme Fellowship. Without his help this book might never have seen the light. Cecilia Boggio and Carolyn O'Neill also researched in the project's early stages. The students in my seminar on alchemy in Fall 2007 gave me ideas and energy. My parents took me to the Metropolitan Museum of Art so often that David's portrait of Lavoisier was imprinted in my brain and I couldn't help but write about it. Jane Winston and Sharon Achinstein read Marx with me. Francesco Adinolfi, Cristina Bartoccioli, Anna Camaiti, Roberto Diaz, Gabriel Giorgi, Maurizio Giuffredi, Bob Kaufman, Panivong Norindr, Sabrina Ovan, Tommaso Pomilio, John David Rhodes, Joy Sleeman, Peter Starr, and Bernard Yenelouis provided unconditional support and friendship. Orlando Bentancor, Richard Block, Tom Conley, Margie Ferguson, Peggy Kamuf, Natania Meeker, and Hilary Schor read all or parts of the manuscript and gave me amazing advice. I owe them jumbo loans, taken out, at times, on lousy credit.

ALCHEMICAL MERCURY

Introduction

Lead into Gold

A brand of Polish vodka recently ran a full-page advertisement featuring a blurred figure holding up a clear bottle of clear liquid, lit from an indicated source, a window on the left-hand side of the composition (Figure 1).[1] The text reads: "500 years ago, while others tried to turn lead into gold, Poland discovered a way to turn rye into vodka." The ad is printed in sepia tones, evoking the early years of photography. The image has been doctored with stains and blotches, perhaps meant to evoke vodka spills or signs that the photograph has been exposed to the elements, passed around, aged. A magazine reader would not need to be aware of the multiple visual and rhetorical precedents behind this clever advertisement to be an effective recipient of the message. Indeed, it could be argued that for an average consumer target, the advertisement signifies in a general mode something like "a mysterious transformative process of obscure, ancient origin." Inasmuch as a viewer may pass over an ad and only register its manifest form in an instant, an ad is most successful if it does call out the existence of some latent content (even if such content is not read explicitly). Of course the unstated signified in this advertisement is alchemy.

Alchemy is ubiquitous, multiple, and self-replicating. But what is alchemy? A practice? A theory? Some combination of both? A historical oddity or an atemporal spiritual mode? Is alchemy primarily about the production of gold from a base substance? If so, what does one do with the product? Display it like a trophy? Drink it in order to extend life infinitely? "Project it" in order to make more gold? And then what? Like a coin that is passed around so often it is clipped, sweated, and worn, "alchemy" has entered our rhetorical circulation, so that the original circumstances of its

FIGURE 1.   Belvedere vodka advertisement, ca. 2002.

minting, or its potential to radically disrupt a system of exchange, are no longer knowable. In our day, alchemy is common coinage. It is conflated with astrology or necromancy; overused as a rhetorical figure for "magic" or "magical transformation of materials." It has been conjured by contemporary critics and artists to describe work that involves material mutations or a certain disposition to experimenting with temporality.[2] It bears a privileged relationship to painting but also to photography, cinema, and, earlier, to printmaking. Tied to the realm of aesthetics, alchemy is not the normal business of either philosophers or economic historians.

For as long as the West has known of alchemy, debates have raged concerning the word's origins. While the *al* prefix is certainly Arabic, the root of the word may come from the Greek *Khem* or *Khamè*, meaning "dark" or "black" and linking suspect forms of transmutation with Egypt, as is found in the Decree of Diocletian (ca. 300). *Khemia* may later have been confused with the similar Greek word *khemeia* or *khumeia*, used to describe the arts of making tinctures or juices. Perhaps this word migrated into Arabic and was diffused in Spain and the rest of Europe (Latin *alchymia*).[3]

An early eighteenth-century source argues that chemistry itself is a purely Arabic word, from *chama* or *hama* (meaning "he hid or covered up"), stressing the fact that the knowledge (of chemistry) is passed down in secret; or from *kimya* or *kimyao* (burning, furnace), to which was added the prefix *al* (Barchusen 3). The great Renaissance alchemist-doctor, Paracelsus, claimed to have been taught the art by a Muslim in Turkey. This individual gave him the universal dissolvant or azoth—death, or that which putrefies; or the alcahest, the spirit, or sophic fire, which is key to "al-chemistry," a science named from the Arabic *chom*, and Hebrew *cham*, meaning "heat" (Barrett 51). Perhaps the word derives from the proper name Cham or Ham, son of Noah. This opens up several interesting patri-lineages: The biblical Cain, once a tiller of the soil, fathers Enoch, who disseminates secret knowledge of the angels to men. Enoch begets Lamech, father of Tubal-Cain, forger of bronze and iron tools. This line is an ambivalent one, revered and feared in later readings. The movement from farming toward a darker art could be seen as punishment for Cain's fratricide. Yet Genesis also describes an alternative line from Adam to Enoch to Lamech to Noah, whose sons are allowed on the ark and are saved with their father so they may repopulate the earth. After the flood, Ham is punished for seeing his father's nakedness, or as some have interpreted the passage, for having a sexual encounter with his father; for breaking proper father–son relations. His land—Canaan—is made subject to that of his brother Shem. If Ham is the "father" of alchemy, it is not because he moves from the land to metallurgy like Tubal-Cain, but perhaps because of his excessive curiosity or hubris. Tubal-Cain, taken up as an emblem by Freemasons, is, like Ham, a descendant of Enoch, an ambivalent figure standing at a moment of transition from agriculture to metallurgy. In any case, alchemy is generally believed older than Greek thought. It cannot be coincidental that almost all of the explanations displace alchemy's origins to an "other"—foreign, barbaric, exotic, sacred, or profane.

Scholars of alchemy tend to take up one of a number of possible positions toward their subject: Either alchemy is premodern chemistry; or it is a spiritual, ritualistic discourse or set of theories; or it is a practice that may or may not have succeeded in the remote past; it is a form of medico-pharmacological manipulation of elements; or it is some combination of the above. The problem of how to distinguish alchemy from (a prehistory of) chemistry is intimately bound up with the teleological view of the history of science as a progressive accretion of knowledge. As early as the seventeenth century, scientists who could not utterly dismiss the contributions of the alchemists favored adoption of the word *chymistry* to suggest a summation of both "old" and "new" ideas. Boyle specifically distinguished his work with the philosopher's stone (that is, with agents of metallic transmutation) as *chrysopoeia*. The term is derived from *chrysos* (gold) and *argyropoeia*, from *argyros* (silver) plus *poiein* (to make). Boyle also continued to use the word *spagyria*, from the Greek *span* (to draw forth or separate) and *ageirein* (to collect together). Spagyric chemistry referred to a particular process of separating a substance into its Essentials (that is, conventionally)—mercury, sulfur, and salt—and then purifying these ingredients and recombining them. Older terms, then, served in the "new science" to refer to embedded processes, coexisting with modern terms and methods. Over time, alchemy disappeared from the scientific realm, relegated to the (merely) aesthetic or to (mere) history. Yet nomenclature is not simply an awkward supplement to a grand problem (the Great Work). Rather, the persistent problem of terminology haunts alchemy, as it will haunt this book, always returning when it is least welcome or expected.

To take a stand on one side of the theory/practice debate, or even to attempt to say *what alchemy was* in a historical context, is already to be caught up in a form of ideology that structures both alchemy and writing.[4] Alchemy cannot be said to exist as a method or practice standing outside of or beyond writing. Like writing, or inasmuch as alchemy is writing, it is an admixture of opposites, dominated by the couple inside and outside, "the matrix of all possible opposition."[5] The question of what is "outside" of alchemy is fundamental. And ambivalence serves as a key concept to thinking alchemically.

Ambivalence, as Derrida notes in his famous essay "Plato's Pharmacy," is always already present in writing, from the beginning. Derrida's usage of the term might seem to convey a generic sense of ambiguity or "mixed feelings." But he employs "ambivalence" in the context of an essay that is profoundly structured by the relations of a series of binaries (poison/gift, inside/outside, son/father, sun/moon, and so on). Thus we are forced to recall that *ambi*-valence is not only a conscious sense of uncertainty, but also, more rigorously, the coexistence of *two* different and perhaps irreconcilable elements.[6] For Derrida, ambivalence, writing, and alchemy are intertwined and expressed in the figure of the *pharmakon*, a (mercurial) substance that is simultaneously remedy and poison:

> This charm, this spellbinding virtue, this power of fascination, can be— alternately or simultaneously—beneficent or maleficent. The *pharmakon* would be a *substance*—with all that that word can connote in terms of matter with occult virtues, cryptic depths refusing to submit their ambivalence to analysis, already paving the way for alchemy—if we didn't have eventually to come to recognize it as antisubstance itself: that which resists any philosopheme. (Derrida 70)

Ambivalence opens a way to undo the traditional "alchemical master narrative"—a narrative in which matter and man are finally redeemed and stabilized. Such a narrative is threatened by the specter of "reverse transmutation" that is normally disavowed or dismissed outright through the employment of logical or rhetorical strategies. Ambivalence, then, is not the same thing as dialectics, which might represent a forced and pacifying synthesis of (two) elements. In some alchemical traditions, to be fair, a third element—a glue or binder—is added to the solution. The title of Michael Maier's *Atalanta fugiens* covers alchemy under the narrative of resistant Atalanta (mercury) and persistent Hippomenes (sulfur), who throws down the golden apples (salt) in order to trap and fix his bride so that they can morph into dual lions. Salt is necessary, and it could be argued

Qui Rofarium intrare conatur Philofophicum
absque clave, affimilatur homini ambulare vo-
lenti absque pedibus.

EPIGRAMMA XXVII.

L *Uxuriat Sophiæ diverfo flore* ROSETUM,
Semper at eft firmis janua claufa feris:
Unica cui clavis res vilis habetur in orbe,
Hac fine, tu carpes, cruribus absque viam.
Parnaffi in vanum conaris ad ardua, qui vix
In plano valeas te ftabilire folo.

De

FIGURE 2. *Footless Man*, from Michael Maier, *Atalanta fugiens*, 1617. Research Library, The Getty Research Institute, Los Angeles, CA.

that this triadic variant (linked to the thought of Paracelsus) undoes ambivalence. A counterargument emphasizes that in Maier's text the Atalanta story disappears immediately after being invoked in the book's prefatory material. The mythogeme of Atalanta and the nonnarrative epigrams of the text exist together in the space of the *Atalanta fugiens* in a rather uncomfortable manner. Nor is ambivalence in alchemy reducible to formal "multiplicity" since even this term is vulnerable to totalizing. Bound to language as such, ambivalence serves throughout this book as a mode and a mood that continually reasserts itself.

Universalism and History

Alchemy is everywhere. Yet we might be surprised to find many texts that announce themselves as alchemical or are clearly recognized as such do not reference gold as a material object. Gold is not a universal equivalent in all of alchemy, in other words. Indeed, we could say that in its everyday circulation in the contemporary market, "alchemy" has been drained of gold—that is, of value. This implies that in some earlier, utopian moment, alchemy did indeed produce or at least have currency with gold. When could we locate this golden age? Is it a prehistorical moment, linked with tellurian gods, chthonic miners, hoarders, or proto-civilizations? Or is it a premodern moment, when men experimented on a small scale with the production of gold in interior spaces, making use of available technological means? Does alchemy have a history in which gold once reigned supreme, only to be gradually aestheticized, metaphorized? Has alchemy, over time, been dematerialized?

　　To be sure, alchemy's history is uneven. The popularity of alchemy in seventeenth-century Prague has been attributed, in part, to the patronage of humanist-sovereign Rudolph II. But alchemy is not necessarily tied to an absolute center of power, as it flourished in Northern Europe during the seventeenth century, an age of great expansion, mercantilism, and trade. And if post-Reformation Europe was alchemy's highest point, many of its tropes derive from the Christian Middle Ages. It enjoyed a revival in the age of Lavoisier, parallel to the so-called birth of modern chemistry. As late as 1782 the British Royal Society took the trouble to investigate a claim by James Price that he had transmuted metals into gold. Soon afterward Price committed suicide, suggesting that, at the very least, there was something ambiguous about his activities. Around Mannheim, during the formative years of Goethe, alchemy was all the rage. Strindberg mingled with an active group of alchemists during his absinthe-bingeing days in Paris in the 1880s. Should the history of alchemy be terminated at this point, such that from here on alchemy will be a melancholic attachment to the past? Marx asks in a famous passage: "Is the view of nature and of social relations on which the Greek imagination and hence Greek [mythology] based possible with self-acting mule spindles and railways and locomotives and electrical telegraphs? What chance has Vulcan against Roberts & Co., Jupiter against the lightning-rod and Hermes against the Crédit Mobilier?" (1857 110). Does alchemy end along with mythology with what Marx terms "the real mastery" over the "forces of nature"? Then why does alchemy bloom again in the early twentieth century, especially among the avant-garde and figures associated with radium and physics; or in the experimental dematerialized art of the late 1960s and early 1970s? Do these instances along the timeline bear anything in common?

Perhaps we could trace a (negative) history of alchemy based on juridical attempts to suppress it. For instance, by the end of the thirteenth century, Pope John XXII had issued a decree, *Spondent quas non exhibent*, declaring transmutation against nature. In 1404 a parliamentary act in Britain forbade the mutation of gold and silver. The law was repealed in 1689, and alchemy could be practiced legally, as long as the metals derived from it were deposited at the mint of the Tower of London, in exchange for their true value in "authenticated" gold and silver. The state thus tolerated some alchemy, as long the product was subject to regulation.[7] Scholars like Vilar, Braudel, and Flandreau wrote "histories" of gold (in its relation to money) over a *longue durée*. In particular Braudel mapped the global movements of gold in spatiotemporal terms such that we can visualize the intense mobility of gold in two dimensions. We might even place such a template over a similar "map" of alchemy, to see where and when these two histories converge. But even if such a graphic exercise were possible, it might not be particularly useful precisely since all that glitters in alchemy is not gold.

The universalism of alchemy is a problem without a simple solution. Any invocation of universalism might risk being perceived as an alliance with Jung, who did extensive work on the figures of alchemy as archetypes.[8] Even if some of Jung's disciples were, in fact, responsible for unearthing or translating some of the most interesting material on alchemy of the Middle Ages and early modern period, the Jungian archetype is easily dismissed, especially when confronted with the incomprehensibility of language.[9] Jung believed that the images of alchemy appear in dreams. He focused on the symbolic content of alchemical texts, but ignored their peculiar narrative logics and rhetoric. Barbara Obrist emphasizes that like Rudolf Steiner, Jung concentrated his scholarship on works from the seventeenth century—the apex of alchemical discourse. But both men tended to project the idea of alchemical practice as a religious quest back onto earlier texts where such a linkage would have been rare.

Almost every culture has some form of alchemy, from India to China to the West; and from antiquity to the present (or better, the future). Universalism sometimes serves as a legitimization for the very study of alchemy, as well as an underlying assumption grounding much of the scholarship on alchemy, even where this scholarship limits itself to the Western world. So, to cite Julius Evola (a philosopher, painter, mystic, and proto-fascist thinker; a character much more worthy of skepticism than Jung): "There is no question that alchemy is not simply a Western phenomenon. There are, for example, a Hindu alchemy and a Chinese alchemy. And anyone who is at all in touch with the theme can see that the symbols, the 'matters,' and the principle operations correspond inwardly and outwardly at the same time."[10] While Evola goes on to state that his work is not concerned with the implementation of these symbols within the culture of the East, it is impossible to ignore the powerful ideology that colors his specific investigations. So, when we speak of alchemy in general, are we speaking of it as a phenomenon that is spread through cultural transmission, or one that crops up in various geographical locales due to its fundamental coincidence with human nature in its essence? For an economic historian like Vilar, the essence is some form of exchange (although not necessarily money), as it is negotiated in relation to sexual reproduction. Saussure, revealing the inextricable ties that bind linguistic and economic values, would not disagree.

Alchemy should be distinguished from folkloric beliefs and from fields such as the apothecary mixing of tinctures and medicines that have been studied as early forms of (spagyric) chemistry. Peasants did indeed practice forms of mixing substances for all sorts of practical purposes. But alchemy was, and has remained, a theory/practice available to cultural elites that was not widespread enough among the populace to make it the object of a broad anthropological study. So are we left with no way out of the aporia surrounding the diachronic (long-standing transmission) and the synchronic (individual instances of usage)?

Such a question, obviously, can only emerge from examining many different examples from within what could be called the canon of alchemical literature. Once alchemy is understood to persist over a *longue durée*, and not simply at one spatiotemporal coordinate, it is essential to understand something other than gold as constituting alchemy at its base. The question is not unlike that asked by chemists when they examine a substance in order to determine its "intensive properties," those properties that will always be present in a sample of the substance, no matter its size, shape, form, state, or use. An intensive property might be thought as similar to the idea of a principal in seventeenth-century science. What is the intensive property of alchemy? By extending the idea of intensive property from chemistry to cultural production, we seek a least common denominator that may serve as a Law, providing a rigorous basis for alchemy that will help to transcend the Jungian notion of archetype.

Alchemy *approaches* universality, as long as we understand it in its most ample terms: as the production of a noble substance (most often gold) from the transformation of baser substances (most often base metals). But the trick will be to discover what, precisely, about alchemy is universal. If it is not gold, then is it greed? Marx teaches us that when money has become fully abstracted in capitalism, it is

> not only *an* object, but is *the* object of greed [*Bereicherungssucht*]. It is essentially *auri sacra fames* [the lust for gold]. Greed as such, as a particular form of the drive, i.e. as distinct from the craving for a particular kind of wealth, e.g. for clothes, weapons, jewels, women, wine, etc., is possible only when general wealth, wealth as such, has become individualized in a particular thing, i.e. as soon as money is posited in its third quality . . . greed itself is the product of a definite social development, not *natural*, as opposed to *historical*. (1857 222)

So greed develops alongside money in history, and it must, therefore, be considered in relation to alchemy to the degree that alchemy is a production (of gold) and gold is money. Greed is precisely what is disavowed by those more "spiritual" or philosophical forms of alchemy, and the typical early modern alchemical treatise includes disclaimers against the use of precious metals on the market. Even if the alchemist tried to exchange his product for commodities, he would not succeed. So greed must be considered crucial to alchemy, even when—or especially when—it is denied. Still, to posit greed as universal in alchemy would imply a facile materialism subject to being overturned by an equally facile mysticism.

So what is at stake in the universal? Perhaps when we are talking about early modern variants, nothing much more than the scholarly satisfaction of working on an "important" topic, one that reappears with periodic regularity and has gained particular currency in recent years. For instance, the ubiquity of alchemy as a topos in the Middle Ages and Renaissance opens up the field to an elaborate history of *transmission*, a key methodological term in the works of Warburg, Panofsky, Gombrich, and the other great iconologists who founded the discipline of (Renaissance) art history as we know it.

This study differs from iconology in its emphasis on tradition as both a handing down and a betrayal of language. This is not to say that texts trump images in the alchemical tradition, but rather, images do not constitute a separate or parallel tradition that could be thought outside of language. In his essay "Warburg and the Nameless Science," Giorgio Agamben underscores the importance of Warburg to "art history" in his withdrawal of the artwork from the "study of the artist's consciousness and unconscious structures."

> In Warburg, precisely what might have appeared as an unconscious structure par excellence—the image—instead showed itself to be a decisively historical element, the very place of human cognitive activity in its vital confrontation with the past. What thus came to light, however, was neither a kind of diachrony nor a kind of synchrony but, rather, the point at which a human subject was produced in the rupture of this opposition. . . . The greatest lesson of Warburg's teaching may well be that the image is the place in which the subject strips itself of the mythical, psychosomatic character given to it, in the presence of an equally mythical object, by a theory of knowledge that is in truth simply disguised metaphysics. (Agamben 1999, 102)

It is not a question of choosing between image and language, but of grasping "pure historical matter" (Agamben 1999, 103) that emerges from confronting transmission in history.

Uses and Abuses of "Alchemy"

Not surprisingly, in contemporary usage or common currency, the ambivalence of alchemy is generally suppressed. For instance, in a book on Rembrandt, the historian Simon Schama, discussing a self-portrait, writes: "Using a soft-bristled, precisely pointed squirrel-hair brush, the kind favored by seventeenth-century miniaturists, Rembrandt has taken one set of earthly materials (the builder's) and translated it into another (the painter's). It seems like alchemy" (Schama 13). On the other hand, Todorov, in an essay on Dutch painting, elevates the transformative power of the artist above the mere craftsmanship of the alchemist: "When Steen and Ter Borch, De Hooch and Vermeer, Rembrandt and Hals lead us to discover the beauty of [everyday] things in themselves, they are not acting as alchemists, capable of transforming any old mud into gold. They understood that a woman crossing a courtyard, a mother peeling a potato could be as beautiful as an Olympian goddess" (Todorov 180). In both of these examples, alchemy equals magical transformation, bearing some relationship to the work of the painter/artist, which is itself construed as ineffable and "outside" of writing.

Sometimes *alchemy* means "toxic chemistry," linked to the evils of capitalism. For instance, in a highly ironic passage from *The Jungle*, Upton Sinclair writes:

> They were regular alchemists at Durham's [a Chicago meatpacking plant]; they advertised a mushroom-catsup, and the men who made it did not know what a mushroom looked like. They advertised "potted chicken"—and it was the boarding-house soup of the comic papers, through which a chicken had walked with rubbers on. Perhaps they had a secret process for making chickens chemically—who knows? . . . "De-vyled" ham was made out of the waste ends of smoked beef that were too small to be sliced by the machines; and also tripe, dyed with chemicals so that it would not show white; and trimmings of hams and corned beef; and potatoes, skins and all; and finally hard cartilaginous gullets of beef, after the tongues had been cut out. All this ingenious mixture was ground up and flavored with spices to make it taste like something. (Sinclair 109)

Other critics extend the analogy of magical transformation into an economic sphere. In *Virtual Money*, Elinor Harris Solomon writes:

> A modern alchemy succeeds where the old failed. The ancients of the Middle Ages [*sic*] were never able to change lead into gold, but the medium of electronics turns magnetized particles (bits) into money-like value. Money seems for a time to be conjured out of nothingness, to be returned to nothingness either quickly or at an indeterminate moment. . . . Nor do we know, at this time, whether people will even want to do—and pay in this manner for— much significant business on the Internet. We don't yet have a do-it-yourself

money form, although a lot of people are trying to create a demand for one. (Solomon 85)

The author takes the commonsense position that alchemy was indeed a practice, albeit one that failed, precisely because it was based on faulty, "ancient Medieval" science. In the modern period, thanks to new technologies, it appears that alchemy has finally succeeded, transforming a base element (bits of digital code) into something of value. Like the aesthetic or painterly analogies cited above, this one works at the most basic level: transformation of something of little or no value into something of greater or noble value. Solomon's main point is to stress that e-money could potentially, in some not-so-distant future, represent a new money form, a homemade, cottage industry form of exchange or barter, but in any case, one that is not based merely on reserves of actual, material cash. We have not yet reached this golden age, since e-commerce today is still based on plain old dollars and cents. Solomon's casual analogy reveals that we cannot yet think outside of the money system. Moreover, she suggests that her alchemical e-money could potentially originate in a dematerialized state and return to that state ("to be conjured out of nothingness, to be returned to nothingness either quickly or at an indeterminate moment"). Solomon's "real alchemy" of the ancients was far from such a practice. For many alchemists, the work involved intensive engagement with material (lead or other ores, for instance). Had it succeeded, it would have resulted in the creation of a very real material that could be, in theory, freely exchanged on a market in which it had already established itself as the supreme value. This holds true in spite of the fact that a great deal of the alchemical literature either dissimulates or fails to mention gold as a product altogether. In a treatise titled *Introitus apertus ad occlusum regis palatium* (*The Open Entrance to a Closed Palace of the King*, probably written by George Starkey under the pseudonym Eirenaeus Philalethes), for instance, we learn that the silver and gold the author produced were so pure that they could not be traded. By bringing them to the market, the author would risk being unveiled as an alchemist and being persecuted by greedy adepts and nonbelievers. The author regrets the fact that he must keep his product to himself, not because he would like to spend gold for the purchase of other goods, but because he cannot share his good spiritual fortune. In any case, the production of gold is a highly anxious moment in alchemical discourse.

So gold is hypothesized in alchemy—gold that would be recognized as such (in modern chemical terms, that would have all of the intensive properties of gold, Au, such as good electrical conductivity, resistance to corrosion, the characteristic yellowish color, and a fixed density). This product should be understood as a mere potential exchange-value, but does not imply that any alchemists did, in fact, make their living by producing gold to exchange for subsistence or luxury. In such a (hypothetical) schema, alchemy would represent a subversion or shortcut around the usual ways that one acquires gold. But if we extend the analogy to the present, what would be the use value of Solomon's e-money if it had nothing to do with materiality? Isn't e-money, in theory, useful for the purchase of material goods over the Internet? Doesn't it ultimately result in the acquisition of some good or service for which a standard value is exchanged? Solomon's equation of alchemy to e-money adds a surplus value of "magic" to a transaction that, at least in the present, is simply a more high-tech or dazzling version of slogging through the mall in the money economy. Inasmuch as e-money is only a more apparently magical form of money, it is not at all revolutionary. Instead, it reinforces the established horizons of capitalism. Yet the alchemical analogy helps to blind us to the repetition inherent in the "new money," which tries to pass itself off as a dematerialized and futuristic form. Alchemy has often been considered in this way, wrenched out of its context in the economy, asked to fulfill an ideological function that would transcend the materiality of everyday life.

"Alchemy" appeared recently in a newspaper account of a complex experiment carried out by the Center for Human Reproduction in New York and Chicago. A group of American scientists created a hermaphrodite embryo by injecting cells from a male embryo into a three-day-old female embryo. The Y chromosome acts as a marker in the new embryo (XY XX), and this might provide an alternative to other gene therapies. Embryos that carry a defective gene could be cured by the injection of cells from another embryo with a good version of that gene (Bazzi). The combination of two different embryos in a test tube is explained for a general audience as "alchemical," meant not in the aesthetic or economic sense, but to describe the breaking of a powerful taboo in the laboratory combination of two elements that are brought together in nature only in the most abnormal or monstrous cases. The transformation is planned, rather than magical, and for all that such an experiment might violate principles of certain religious groups, for all that it may violate rights, it works, as science. It cannot be said to be a failure in the way that alchemy is perceived to be by modern science. We should keep this in mind, then, as we should also keep in mind the product of alchemy as hermaphroditic.

These various examples of the (mis)use of alchemy are important because they point to two powerful models that continually reemerge: (magical) transformation and the binary couple. The ambi-valence of transformation, and not, for instance, gold, emerges as a common denominator in alchemy over time. The dream of the (self-)production of gold or a noble substance from nothing, from shit, from whatever is readily at hand, is a powerful one, but "greed" cannot be the signified of all alchemical discourse. Or better, what we often find is a doubling back on greed—greed or accumulation, yes, but covered up with an alibi of (spiritual) transformation. This doubling back (greed/cover for greed) is another common signified of alchemy. It too is a couple.

What is at stake in establishing the couple as the foundation of alchemy? Julius Evola believed that alchemy was the *ars regia*, not merely sacerdotal or sentimental, but also metaphysical. He wrote:

> If you have followed our explanations up to this point, we trust you will have no need for specific arguments to be convinced that alchemy cannot be re-duced merely to chemistry in its infancy—unsystematic, superstitious, and overshadowed by modern chemistry. . . . Given the *synthetic* nature of this type of science, alchemy must of course include a chemical side, particularly as a basis for symbolic transpositions. In the same way that the art of construction, or masonry, could be used to express aspects of a spiritual, ritualistic, and initia-tory process (an echo of this has been preserved in Freemasonry), so the physi-cal understanding of the elements and certain operations involving the metals can be said to have a similar function. (196)

And he continues:

> So if in this special sector the objective of the production of metallic gold is sometimes pursued and sometimes even attained, it is a question neither of a sensational phenomenon nor a scientific discovery. It is a question, on the con-trary, of the production of a sign, that is, of something that Catholicism might probably call a miracle, particularly as opposed to a simple phenomenon. . . . The production of metallic gold was to alchemy a *proof of transfiguration given by a power*; the testimony of having realized the Gold *in oneself*. (197)

But over time, Evola continues,

> alchemy has deteriorated into pure greed, a purely material pursuit without spiritual dimension. It is necessary then to form "intermediate substances" or "androgynous" substances, both "spiritual and corporeal" (perception of the substance and perception of its "psychic" dimension, the one in function of the other): and thus has been established the first condition for the operations of physical alchemy. (202)

Cover-ups

The study of alchemy is, first and foremost, a problem of variants. Scholars must contend with, among others, issues of broken continuity (alchemy is often allied with an oral *traditio*, from father to son, a *patieralism,* to use a term from Jean-Joseph Goux), and with elaborate ruses, *Decknamen* (cover-names), alibis, and retractions, all meant to cover up the (practical) secrets of the Great Work. In fact, the distinction between theory and practice in alchemy is of little *value.* Or better, the reciprocal covering up of practice with theory and vice versa is not incidental to the rhetoric of alchemy, but rather, fundamental. *Decknamen* can function as mere analogies; that is, they may at times correspond to a particular element or ingredient in the alchemical experiment. At other times, however, *Decknamen* exercise much more complex linguistic or logical functions. They are covers that actually generate their own content. And rather than covering up something in particular, they may stand in a given text as ciphers of confusion, or they may actually cover up the lack of any deep meaning whatsoever. In other words, they may exercise a performative function, covering through their theatrics what is not there. Their merely mechanical function in a text is, like the automaton, revelatory of a certain moribund quality of writing.

Agamben explains that "the content of revelation is not a truth that can be expressed in the form of linguistic propositions about a being (even about a supreme being) but is, instead, a truth that concerns language itself, the very fact that language (and therefore knowledge) exists" (Agamben 1999, 40). He continues: "Revelation does not mean this or that statement about the world, nor does it indicate something that could be said through language; it concerns the fact that the word, that language, exists" (41). Or, put another way, "Every reflection on tradition must begin with the assertion that before transmitting anything else, human beings must first of all transmit language to themselves" (104). Agamben's writing on tradition serves as a basis to consider the peculiar defensive rhetoric of many alchemical texts. The alchemical writer typically promises that he is bound not to reveal secrets to the vulgar herd. So why write? Writing (alchemically) is always already a revelation of the secret, but only to those who know how to read. Alchemical writers are always claiming they write on the verge of excessive revelation, and with the utmost clarity possible. In the middle of his treatise on antimony, Basil Valentine writes: "It would not be right for me to set down the whole of this Art so plainly and clearly that any one, even the most ignorant, might, on its perusal, become a perfect adept; just as it is not well for a country bumpkin to eat the finest baker's bread" (Valentine 141). A 1685 English edition includes a note by a Dutch physician (and translator of an earlier edition of the work into Latin), Theodore Kerckring, "Yet Valentine has revealed the secrets of the Art more clearly than his successors, who have been busily employed in obscuring his light. . . . But of course, Basilius cannot describe the Art so clearly that any one, on taking up the book in an idle moment, may at once become a master of our noble Magistery" (Valentine 141). This rhetoric is entirely familiar once one begins to delve into the texts of alchemy. For instance, after a long list of instruments and ingredients common to alchemy, Paracelsus admits that such elements are "mere incumbrances of work."

> Someone may ask, What, then, is this short and easy way, which involves no difficulty, and yet whereby Sol and Luna can be made? Our answer is, this has been fully and openly explained in the Seven Canons [allegorical passages that appear prior to the list of items]. It would be lost labour should one seek further to instruct one who does not understand these. It would be impossible to convince such a person that these matters could be so easily understood, but in an occult rather than in an open sense. (Paracelsus 13)

Similarly, the *Introitus* admits that not everyone will grasp the meaning of the author's words:

> Yet because I did promise candor in this Treatise, something at the least is to be done, that I may not deceive the ingenious of their hope and pains: Know then, that our Regimen, from the beginning to the end, is only lineal, and that is to decoct and to digest, and yet this one Regimen in it self comprehends many others, which the envious have concealed, by giving them diverse names, and describing as so many several Operations: We, to perform the

candor we promised, will make a far more perspicacious manifestation. (Philalethes 90)

The implication here is that the virtuous reader, whom God has deemed worthy of the secret, will be able to read it in the text. Yet when I read the text, I do not come away knowing how to achieve the Great Work. So either I am the intended reader of this (that is, a reader who is not chosen), or I am not the intended reader of this text, and my failure is inscribed in the text itself. The text is impossible and infinite. Once again, Agamben's writings on language illuminate the paradox:

> The thing itself is not a simple hypostasis of the name, something ineffable that must remain unsaid, and hence sheltered, as a name, in the language of men. . . . The thing itself is not a *quid* that might be sought as an extreme hypothesis beyond all hypotheses, as a final and absolute subject beyond all subjects, horribly or beautifully unreachable in its obscurity. We can, in truth, conceive of such a nonlinguistic thing only in language, through the idea of language without relation to things. . . . The thing itself is not a thing; it is the very sayability, the very openness at issue in language. . . . The presuppositional structure of language is the very structure of tradition; we presuppose, pass on, and thereby—according to the double sense of the word *traditio*—betray the thing itself in language, so that language may speak about something (*kata tinos*). The effacement of the thing in itself is the sole foundation on which it is possible for something like a tradition to be constituted. (Agamben 1999, 35)

What is really at stake in alchemy is not so much whether it was (is) written or oral, but that as a *traditio* (from father to son, although the gendered line of inheritance is something that Agamben does not discuss), it has to be a betrayal of and in language. What does this mean, practically speaking, for alchemy?

Consider a rather typical example of alchemical rhetoric:

> In the green lions' bed the sun and moon are born; they are married and beget a king. The king feeds on the lions' blood, which is the king's father and mother, who are at the same time his brother and sister. I fear I betray the secrete, which I promised my master to conceal in dark speech, from every one that does not know how to rule the philosophers fire. When you have fed your lion with sol and luna lay them in an easy heat, enclose them like an egg; a long time will elapse before the king dies, after having eaten all the lion's blood; and at length he grows dark and dry like lamp-black. . . . But the secret

is to take the thing that began the work; join luna and the blood of the green lion as at first, and with it ferment the white or red, one to four, without cooling the matters, and seal the glass again until you see the black, white, and red. There is no better multiplication than to repeat the work of the ferment. (Abraham Andrews, cited in Barrett 300)

Buried, like treasure, in a passage on the green lion, the author has promised his master (father) to conceal the secret in "dark speech." So it would seem that the writing in this passage could be classified as twilight speech since it totters on the brink of comprehensibility. Dark speech, then, is the rhetorical mode of alchemy. This idea is echoed, to give just one example from among many, by the Polish alchemist Michael Sendovogius (Michał Sędziwój): "I wanted you to discover everything here and if at times you understand my meaning but not my words or syllables, I have revealed everything to you, principally in the first and second work" (48). The scholar who claims to know what is meant by the green lion and the philosophical fire, to translate these figures into "light speech," fails to see how his very translation is bound up with the tradition. The same goes for the female reader who expresses a certain righteous indignation at her exclusion from the tradition but then proceeds to rectify the injustice of history by demonstrating that she has seen the light. All readers should take Sendovogius at his word when he says, "I wanted you to discover everything here." And, we might add, in not revealing anything, he did in fact reveal everything: "What must be transmitted is not a *thing*, however eminent it may be; nor is it a truth that could be formulated in propositions or articles of faith. It is, instead, the very unconcealment (*a-letheia*), the very opening in which something like a tradition is possible" (Agamben 1999, 105). Is it possible that once we penetrate the dark speech, we will find precisely that dark speech was the thing itself, rather than a kernel of light matter enveloped in it?

Alchemy as a Dual or Ambi-valent Discourse

A typical alchemical treatise (this one from the early eighteenth century, but a revised version of a work from 1698) by a Dutch pharmacist and physician notes that iatrochemistry (medical alchemy) is divided into theory and praxis. The author acknowledges that Theory holds a higher place in his own writing. Yet Theory alone is useless unless married with Praxis.

("As things stand, some have argued that Theory in chemistry is of no use. Certainly, this is true for Theory alone, but when married to Praxis, it is of the greatest use in chemistry" [Barchusen 5, my translation].)

Perhaps one reason the author decided to revise his earlier *Pyrosophia* (Leyden, 1698) is that in the intervening years he witnessed Helvetius's gold ingots and crucibles and believed that alchemy was (practically) possible. Yet following upon the statement cited above, he does not offer any more "theory" in the sense that the modern reader might understand it. Instead, what he calls theory is a series of directives for the kinds of vessels to use in the process and a list of the medical uses of gold. His "theory" is *speculative* inasmuch as he does not tell the reader exactly what to do, step by step, to make gold. Yet he offers what we might call extremely practical advice. At no time does the author announce that he is moving from a discussion of theory to practice. Theory is what is written down so that practice may be accomplished, outside of the text. So theory and practice emerge in a relation to that exemplary couple "inside/outside." Basil Valentine writes:

> Contemplation is two-fold: one is called impossible, the other possible. The former consists in endless meditations, which can have no result because their object is intangible. Such problems are the Eternity of God, the Sin against the Holy Ghost, the infinite nature of the Godhead. They are incomprehensible, and necessarily baffle the finite enquirer. The other part of Contemplation, which is possible, is called *Theoria*. It deals with the tangible and visible which has a temporal form—shewing how it can be dissolved and thereby perfected into any given body; now every body can impart the good or evil, medicine or poison, which is latent in it; how the wholesome is separated from the unwholesome; how to set about destruction and demolition for the purpose of really and truly severing the pure from the impure without sophistic guile. (18)

He goes on to explain that the "practical experimentalist" will come to learn the meaning of the stages of alchemy, but if the process does not work: "Retrace your steps, learn the theory more perfectly, and enquire more accurately into the method of operation" (19).

Robert Boyle's writings suggest that the common denominator of alchemy is perhaps not one thing—not the English hermetic philosopher John Dee's *Monas Hieroglyphica*, for instance—but indeed a certain duality or a series of couples; ambivalence, as in the dual symbolic–real value of gold.[11] One of the couples in the alchemical—perhaps the dominant one—is the binary of male and female, but their ritual conjoining in a wide variety of different forms (wedding, bathing together, roasting in an oven) cannot itself be the common denominator of alchemy.

According to Jean-Joseph Goux, gold—as product or object—is univalent. A standard. In the modern era, this is where gold ends up. But before it does so, it undergoes a process of historical change that witnesses its excision (its castration, in the case of the phallus that Goux posits as analogous to gold in the realm of the symbolic) from a larger group as general equivalent. It is possible, perhaps even necessary, to assume that for gold to finally achieve its sovereign status, it must shed its hermaphroditic and ambivalent qualities, those very qualities that define alchemy. Goux's *Symbolic Economies* is not about alchemy per se, but we cannot simply say that the difference between gold in Goux's vision and in alchemy lies in the fact that he is emphasizing product rather than (alchemical) process, since embedded in the very fabric of alchemical transmutation is ambivalence about product. The product—gold—must be produced in order for the (alchemical) process to have validity (otherwise, it amounts to so many stabs in the dark). But in the very rhetoric of spiritual transformation that characterizes so much of the literature that we call alchemical, the product is simultaneously negated (it isn't gold we're after, it's enlightenment). Thus, at its very core, alchemy is intractably ambivalent.

Gold is not only an object of extreme value (perhaps equaled only by woman in its dual capacity for real and symbolic exchange); it was, and in some sense still is, a standard. For if gold is now traded on a market that is parallel to but not sovereign over other markets, it is referenced in economic culture as a fallback, a stalwart, always present in the background of newer and more volatile markets.[12] In contemporary culture, ads for gold bullion tend to feature spokespeople who look into the camera, dressed in highly conservative clothing, urging an investment in something that never loses its value. From a broader historical perspective, a standard is something that is held to be invariable. Thus, inasmuch as alchemy has been about the production of gold, it has been about the production of a kind of stability following a great deal of turmoil. The same cannot be said of woman.

In their essential book on the gold standard, Maria Cristina Marcuzzo and Annalisa Rosselli show that David Ricardo's contribution to economic theory was distinguishing between variation in the value of money and variation in price. In Ricardo's time, the Bank of England issued handwritten notes of credit. Merchants and bankers asked: Is gold increasing in value, or is paper money's value falling? Ricardo, an extremely wealthy man, suggested that any means of payment is money. International prices are expressed through the different purchasing powers of every national currency. Equilibrium is established through the exchange of bullion or coins. Metal = stability. There is, then, no danger of token money being multiplied. Rising prices and the premium of gold over other circulating currency were due to an excess of Bank of England notes.

In order to avoid dramatic fluctuations in the value of money, Ricardo believed, a political regime needed to tie the currency to the standard that tended to vary least of all. That standard, he reasoned, was gold. This theory would protect citizens from the random politics of institutions issuing paper money or notes, or the capricious will of individuals, and it would lend stability to England in the early nineteenth century. Within England, the level of prices depended on the amount of money (that is, paper money) in circulation. On the other hand, international prices were expressed by the purchasing power of given national currencies, and the exchange rate was established by the exchange of bullion or coins. It is in this sense that metal (gold, but not exclusively) equaled stability. In order to achieve stability within England, Ricardo argued, the bank should reduce the number of notes issued until it equaled the amount of gold in the vaults, thus restoring parity between domestic currency and internationally recognized metals. This was Ricardo's "currency principle" and it was opposed by Tooke, who espoused the "banking principle." Tooke's position was that banks were only issuing notes to meet demand, and as long as that demand existed, the bank had no obligation to curtail its work. Thus, Ricardo argued that by adopting the gold standard, England would return the pound to its "natural level"—that is, the value of money in terms of gold would remain constant. On the other hand, "in an unstable monetary regime, where the price of the standard is not bound, the task of holding the quantity of money at a set level is borne entirely by the monetary authorities" (Marcuzzo and Rosselli 5).

In his *High Price of Bullion*, Ricardo wrote, "Gold and silver, like other commodities, have an intrinsic value, which is not arbitrary, but is dependent on their scarcity, the quantity of labor bestowed in procuring them, and the value of the capital employed in the mines which produce them" (cited in Marcuzzo and Rosselli 42). This is somewhat different from the position taken by reason-of-state theorists of the early seventeenth century such as Gerard de Malynes. He argued that the value of gold was fixed by the mint and ratified by the king, who, by virtue of his godliness, was able to authenticate intrinsic value. But this position became increasingly difficult to sustain, as the king was thought to be apt to manipulate the relationship between the intrinsic value and the face value of coins that circulated in the realm (Poovey 73). Perhaps it is not unfair to see Ricardo in a logical progression from the reason-of-state idea. For him, gold and silver are comparable to other commodities, but they differ in the diminished degree of their variability; they are "tolerably fixed" with regard to their value over short periods of time. Value is the order of business of monetary experts, goldsmiths. *This* is what makes gold the standard rather than anything magical or vital in its nature as a metal. "As Ricardo once stated in parliament, if corn were the commodity with the least variable value, then banknotes should be convertible into corn" (Marcuzzo and Rosselli 43). In this, Ricardo differs from Adam Smith, who acknowledged qualities of "utility, beauty and scarcity" as the "original foundation of the high price of those metals" and hence their universal value. "This value was antecedent to, and independent of their being employed as coin, and was the quality which fitted them for that employment" (Marcuzzo and Rosselli 44). However, Ricardo was in a sense always looking for something even more stable than gold, and had he found it, he would have quickly discarded gold.

If we were to engage in an imaginative exercise and extend this logic further—and such an extension is certainly not indicated by Ricardo's writings—although alchemy (like gold-as-standard) may be tied to the production of gold, it may also, at some other moment in history, find itself allied with another product. In such a scenario, the hypothetical replacement for gold could be any product or raw material that is not only rare, but also difficult to extract from nature and therefore subject to relatively minor variations with regard to quantity.

Moreover, it might also be possible to hypothesize a form of alchemical practice related to a family-run business, not as profit-making, but perhaps as a form of resistance to primitive accumulation, understood as the (ruthless) movement to force workers into factories and wage-earning trades, leaving behind barter systems, cottage industries, or subsistence farming. Alchemy could, in this utopian fiction, be carried out in the commons, as opposed to private property. In this sense, we could consider alchemy as linked with rural life, as opposed to life in the city, as in the following description of expropriation:

> Simple dispossession from the commons was a necessary, but not always sufficient condition to harness rural people to the labor market. Even after the enclosures [in England], laborers retained privileges in "the shrubs, woods, undergrowth, stone quarries and gravel pits, thereby obtaining fuel for cooking and wood for animal life, crab apples and cob nuts from the hedgerows, brambles, tansy and other wild herbs from any other little patch of waste. . . . Almost every living thing in the parish however insignificant could be turned to some good use by the frugal peasant-laborer or his wife." (Alan Everitt cited in Perelman 14)

Naturally, there is nothing in this passage that explicitly refers to alchemy. Rather, the idea of a self-sustaining, forest-dwelling community is an interesting hypothesis to keep in mind, for whatever it is worth.[13]

The classical economists explained the prestige and movements of gold, not in relation to the general wealth of the country, but to the profit motives of individuals. They saw gold as any other commodity, and as long as it was profitable, it retained its value. However, Ricardo believed that export of gold from a country was always tied to overissue of (paper) money, whatever the cause; that an unfavorable exchange rate could be corrected by limiting the money supply (eliminating currency redundancy); that export of gold was not a necessary evil to help out in an emergency situation such as war or bad harvest, but rather, was the most economic means of making a payment. In short, gold was part of everyday life precisely because it transcended its materiality and because it was tied exclusively to money and to markets. Of course, the international exchangeability of gold remains a potentiality, a figure that looms over alchemy, since, as noted, the alchemist tends to hoard rather than exchange.

Hoarding, as Goux suggests, represents a solution, however temporary, awkward, and "unresolved" in a psychoanalytic sense, between this qualitative boundlessness of gold and its quantitative limits. The hoarder is one who refuses to allow gold to circulate. Before the stabilization of the gold standard, when coins were minted in gold, their exchange would cause them to become abraded, and their value would be literally worn away by fingers. Since gold became a standard, it has been flowing through the world in the form of bullion. It is also made into certain luxury goods or used in fillings or filaments (luxury accessories for the body), or it petrifies in the form of hoards. Mostly it flows between kings and nations. Bourgeois states actually try to limit hoards to a bare minimum, because they are dynamic and thrive on even flows and speeded-up circulation. Hoarding undercuts Keynesian dynamic national growth. Modern economies cannot tolerate the slow time of coffers and treasuries. If, in the time of a gold standard, everything is potentially convertible into gold, then the motive for hoarding comes from the fact that while gold (or money) is theoretically limitless in its power, we can only speak about gold or know gold in some finite quantity. At some point, for it to be actualized, spent, exchanged, it has to be weighed and measured.

Alchemy, Anomie, and Potentiality

Alchemists don't spend their gold. But this does not mean there is nothing to be said about consumption inasmuch as it is *potential* consumption. As Goux writes of the sovereign:

> In the very act of considering the labor of other men, the blood that is sweat by slaves or serfs, as the prey of his desire, he knows the men themselves as sacrificed, nullified beings and thus knows himself as one. . . . In contrast with this seigneurial existence, based on expenditure and maintenance according to social position, is the industrious entrepreneur or merchant of the rising bourgeoisie—sober, thrifty, prosaic, subordinating *jouissance* to production and finding it only through calculation in the economy of savings and earnings, of credit and debit, accompanied by an exact accountability of goods and a rational use of time. Thus, in opposition to the feudal nobility, which avidly devours more than it possesses, flaunting its luxury as the obligatory *sign* of rank, the bourgeois political economy must preach (with mounting hypocrisy, besides) postponement, the deferral of *jouissance*, patient retention with a view to the supplementary *jouissance* that is calculated. (204)

Gold, as Marx writes in the *Grundrisse*, "possesses all pleasures in potentiality" (222).

Some would undoubtedly argue that alchemy has nothing to do with production, at least if we agree with Marx that production is always consumption. Can we speak of alchemical gold as a product if "the production only obtains its 'last finish' in consumption"? (1857 91, "last finish" in English in original). If the gold produced by alchemy is not used (up), spent, passed around, or molded into objects or statues, then can it really be a product? An early modern courtier like J. J. Becher will argue that alchemy should (and indeed, does) serve to produce a product for consumption. Similarly, an alchemist explains:

> Even so it is with Gold, as long as it is in the form of a ring, a vessel or Money, 'tis the vulgar Gold, as concerning its being cast in our water, 'tis Philosophical; In the former respect it is called Dead, because it would remain unchanged even to the Worlds end; in the latter respect it is said to be living, because it is so potentially; which power is capable of being brought into Art in a few daies, but then Gold will no longer be Gold, but the Chaos of the Sophi; therefore well may Philosophers say, That their philosophical Gold differeth from the vulgar Gold, Which difference consisteth in the Composition. (Philalethes 42–43)

Real gold, having used up its potentiality, is dead. The alchemist is responsible for reviving gold (a process which means the death of alchemical mercury), but as long as gold is "philosophical"—that is, not yet material—it is alive.

In thinking, finally, about the slow temporality of alchemy, and about potentiality, it may be useful to invoke the idea of the "state of exception." One of Giorgio Agamben's concrete examples to define the state of exception in the temporal realm is the period called *iustitium*, which is derived from Roman law. Acts performed during this period of juridical *tempus mortuum* are characterized by anomie. He who acts during the *iustitium* "neither executes nor transgresses the law but *inexecutes [inesegue]* it. His actions, in this sense, are mere facts, the appraisal of which, once the *iustitium* is expired, will depend on the circumstances. But as long as the *iustitium* lasts, they will be absolutely undecidable . . . beyond the sphere of law" (2005, 50). The *iustitium* is a period of mourning, as for a dead king or pope—the nine days prior to the conclave to elect a new pope, for instance. During this time, in theory, nothing happens. But this very idea—nothing happens—is as paradoxical as it is impossible. *Anomie*, a term that is rarely used in English nowadays, comes from the Greek *anomia*, meaning "lawlessness, without a ruler, a-nomos." But anomie is not simply anarchy, it is also boredom and sloth in common usage. Durkheim suggested anomie as social instability resulting from a breakdown of standards and values; personal unrest, alienation, lack of purpose or ideals. Indeed, Durkheim is often credited with inventing the term, but this is, of course, a convenient fiction that might allow us to understand the social order resulting from the industrial revolution as something particular destined to disappear with new forms of production or new markets. Durkheim's anomie is interesting inasmuch as it results from a lack of order, but also an overdetermination of order. As social restraints are weakened, humans no longer have limits on their desires and aspirations. Whereas their goals were previously limited by morality, desire now becomes infinite in scope. What is needed is just the right amount of order.

In reality *anomie* is an older word, used in a variety of contexts prior to the "invention of modern ethnography." We could invoke what is a forgotten (and frankly, rather pedantic) text in the history of political economy, the *Elementi di economia pubblica* of Cesare Beccaria, an Italian *illuminista* best known for his influential *Dei delitti e delle pene*. Published posthumously in 1804, the *Elementi*, based on the author's lectures at the University of Pavia, outlines in great detail the relationship between precious metals and national and international trade. Writing about gold, Beccaria notes with some envy that a nation that produces precious metals is fortunate indeed, and such nations have always been "conquerors of the universe." But Beccaria consoles himself that the real politicians have always looked more favorably upon acquiring gold than upon possessing it as a natural resource; acquisition requires motion, action, and labor, which are the beating heart of any political body. Nations that possess gold as a natural resource can also be said to possess a drug that numbs all industry or productivity (175). Moreover, preferable to gold and silver is iron, "the metal of defense and conquest," which "serves to perfect all pleasures of life" (175).

On one hand this sounds like an elaborate apology for colonialism or a form of racist anthropology that supposes that those nations possessing mines will tend to be lazy, unproductive, or anomic, and require only a productive nation to stir up the native labor force from its torpor. Conversely, in Europe the political economists feared the withering away of desire as the market became flooded with goods, resulting in a listless population surrounded by valueless commodities. If agriculture is the foundation of all civilized life, for thinkers like Montesquieu developing "a certain idea of Europe," this does not mean that the most fertile areas are the most civilized: "The barrenness of the earth renders men industrious, sober, inured to hardship, courageous, and fit for war; they are obliged to procure by labor what the earth refuses to bestow spontaneously. The fertility of a country gives ease, effeminacy and a certain fondness for the preservation of life" (Montesquieu 273).

Following a similar logic, Montesquieu argued that the discovery of (colonial) mines could diminish the value of gold and silver in the countries of the colonizers: "The Spaniards raked into the mines, scooped out mountains, invented machines to draw out water, to break the ore, and separate it; and as they sported with the lives of the Indians, they forced them to labor without mercy. The specie of Europe soon doubled, and the profit of Spain diminished in the same proportion" (Montesquieu 370). In its greed, "Spain has behaved like the foolish king who desired that everything he touched might be converted into gold, and who was obliged to beg of the gods to put an end to his misery" (Montesquieu 372). However, in keeping with his broader ideas about the climate and law of Europe, he qualifies his general distrust of mines:

> My reasoning does not hold good against all mines; those of Germany and Hungary, which produce little more than the expense of working them, are extremely useful. They are found in the principal state; they employ many thousand men, who there consume their superfluous commodities, and they are properly a manufacture of the country. The mines of Germany and Hungary promote the culture of the land; the working of those of Mexico and Peru destroys it. (372)

In other words, mining did not necessarily in itself yield a great profit, but employment increased the wealth of nations. We see a similar idea in J. J. Becher's justification of alchemy in the *Physica subterranea*. In the hands of an honest prince, alchemy (like mining) is virtuous exploitation of one's own national natural resources. Becher asks: Why go abroad when you have what you need at home? "If Solomon could have made gold at home in Jerusalem he would not have had to cross the sea" (Becher 697).

The operative word for Becher's ideal prince is *honest*. The sovereign decides on the proportion of gold and silver in any monetary system, just as he guarantees the value of coins. Similarly, it is the sovereign who must take charge of overseeing mining. He declares the productive value of mining, making it his other, since "he decides on the state of exception." The sovereign is outside of the law (he can declare the value of currency only as he does not engage with it in exchange), but he is also inside the law, lawful. The picture of the sovereign is often inscribed on coins to signify that he guarantees value and takes on the fiduciary responsibility of coinage. He even grants his name to certain coins, such as the sovereign or the crown. The very word *crown*, as Ernst Kantorowicz outlines in *The King's Two Bodies*, a work that is of crucial importance to understanding the relation of money to the state of exception, refers to the royal demesne, the inalienable fisc that does not die with the death of the king. In modern, abstract terms the sovereign would seem to be he who protects us from the crash of the market by upholding the standards of monetary value by his very exceptionality.

But wait. As Marx outlines with great care in *Grundrisse*, money as a medium of circulation—that is, as coin—has lost its value as such. In order to be money, it has to be melted down, or demonetized—it has to shed its merely symbolic value. Coins have national or local characters, but not universal ones. In Marx's terms, "a coin acquires a political title, and talks, as it were, a different language in different countries" (1857, 226). If melted down, gold and silver are no longer symbols, but quantities, universal commodities. Money is the negation of the medium of circulation as such—that is, of the coin; but it holds the potential to be turned into coin. Money, as coin, inhabits a realm of anomie. As money, it has value only as gold and silver, but the face that the state impresses on it has no importance. In Marx's scheme of the coming to be of commodities, gold is the exception. It is placed outside of the circuit of commodities, yet it once was just one of the other commodities, so it is also inside. It plays the role of sovereign.

For the sake of an analogy with the monetary state of exception, we can say that alchemy involves production (of gold), but it is anomic production because little or no motion, action, or labor is expended in the process of its acquisition. Alchemy speeds up the natural processes of maturation of ores in the earth, and in that, it seems analogous to the stupefying narcotic that Beccaria writes about in his *Elementi*.

Not all thinkers of the early modern found alchemy to be morally suspect or anomic in this sense. A story circulated that Raymond Lull promised King Edward to supply funds to help convert infidels in 1307. He was given an apartment in the Tower of London and managed to transmute base metals into "nobles" of gold. J. J. Becher, who endeared himself to various courts of Europe, believed that good government depends, in part, on the ability of the sovereign to sustain the population and expand trade. Some say *alchemy* is a bad word, Becher notes, but worse are the following:

"contributions, taxes, seizures, interest, tolls, usury, the state treasury" (Becher 694). Alchemy is both natural and virtuous because it can improve the *salus publici*. As long as the prince is pure in his intentions, alchemy is good for society. It relieves Christian subjects from heavy head and ground taxes as it provides a potential new source of movable wealth. Naturally, the prince must regulate alchemy, because otherwise everyone would do it and there would be no one left for trades and other forms of production.

Many have written about alchemy, but few have balanced alchemy as a discourse about production (whether the product is gold or spiritual re-newal) with the facts of real conditions of production in the world. Yet, we recall that (the young) Marx did not hesitate to define man as *homo faber*.

> Labor—the faculty of producing—is what makes him man, and the con-sciousness he has of it is the import of his humanity. It transforms the simple biological belonging to the human species into consciousness of participating in humankind, and thus makes of all products of labor the privileged place of collective living. This is why the social relation is the essence of the individual as *Gattungswesen* (species-being), and why as well, in turn, all social relations are, in the last instance, reduced to relation of production. (De Duve 52)

Man brings his labor power to the market, and he is alienated inasmuch as the factory owner extracts his surplus labor from him. This is what makes man a social being. And this is precisely what most scholarship on alchemy suppresses. Perhaps the dream of alchemy is not so much about infinite riches or spiritual renewal, but autonomy from the labor market.

§ 1 Visibilia

Woe! Stuck within this dungeon yet?
Curse this dank frowsty cabinet,
Where even Heaven's dear ray can pass
But murkily through tinted glass!

　　　　— Goethe, *Faust* I, 398–401

Alchemy's relation to "visibilia" extends beyond the extremely rich field
of images that appear *in* alchemical manuscripts to embrace vision, transmutation, and ambivalence. Consider the Belvedere vodka advertisement
(Figure 1) with its prime signifier: alchemy. Isn't the introduction of such
a "low" image already a form of reverse transmutation or debasing of the
noble art? Any investigation of premodern iconology through a modern
advertisement must refer itself in some measure to Aby Warburg. His
unfinished project of a "universal pictorial Atlas" (his words—the geo-
graphic migrations of images seem crucial to maintain), Mnemosyne,
would have brought modern advertisements into proximity with images
archaic and antique.[1] Warburg's project (regardless of whether or not we
wish to interpret it as a symptom of his mental illness; as schizophrenic,
bipolar, or *ambivalent*) opens itself up to forward- and backward-moving
transmissions of ideas and affect.[2] His concept of *pathosformel*, or emotive
formula, can certainly be understood as duality. In its embrace of form
and content, of rational idea and irrational emotion, of ethos (interiorized
self-control) and pathos (unbridled self-loss) it is filled with a life force.
The conflict between ancient and modern makes a vivid formal imprint
(*Formegepräge*) on a viewer of an image.[3]

The vodka advertisement is most certainly inspired—even if
indirectly—by any number of early modern genre paintings, especially
from the Lowlands of the seventeenth century, the most intense temporal
and spatial confluence of alchemical visibilia. In particular, the two popular genres that the ad evokes are (a) a doctor (or, in some variants, a
quack) analyzing a urine sample of a patient, and (b) the alchemist in his

laboratory. In the first instance, a doctor may hold a clear vessel containing the urine of a female patient up to the light, as in the advertisement. Medical science of the seventeenth century (rightly) held that cloudy urine was an indicator of illness or pregnancy. Typically, the Dutch paintings in the uroscopy classification are said to contain a moral subtext. The woman patient may be pregnant by her lover, so the news delivered by the doctor is not exactly welcome. Or she may be suffering from lovesickness, and elements in the painting may highlight the vanity of impossible desire. Critics sometimes see these paintings as indictments of quack doctors with false credentials or of the gullibility of patients. The lover or husband is rarely present for the visit, so the "doctor visit" paintings normally portray an intimate interaction between a man and a woman who is not his wife. The scenes are usually highly dramatic, staging the moment at which visual proof of a yet-invisible truth is established. The mise-en-scène—and again, consider such paintings in general as a genre—does not develop in some abstract or theatricalized space, but rather, in the bedroom or sitting room of the woman; a room that is depicted in all of its bourgeois specificity with concentrated attention to the gleaming objects, paintings, furniture, and fabrics that belong to the woman, or better, to her husband or father. These are the real objects that surround her in daily life, and they form a mise-en-abîme, the inherited and accumulated wealth that will be passed on to her offspring, whose presence is perhaps signaled or negated in the liquid of the vessel itself.

Gerard ter Borch's *Consultation* (Figure 3) is both typical and atypical of the urine-analysis genre. The pose of the doctor who holds the glass up to the light constitutes the signature element. The office overflows with things—an overturned broken jug, a skull, mirror, dog-eared tomes, an hourglass—that reappear so often in alchemist paintings. Tiny white flowers are scattered on the floor, symbols, perhaps, of chastity undone. Where do they come from? They are fresh, as if they have just fallen from a plant, but the room is barren and dark. And what is written on the white piece of paper that lies next to the doctor's foot? Is it a name linked to the urine? A diagnosis? In some sense, the presence of *vanitas* objects on the messy desk cast suspicion on the doctor's capabilities. The suggestion that the doctor may be a quack is certainly not unprecedented in the larger classification of doctor-visit works from the period. Similarly, it is not uncommon to find a maid delivering the urine for her mistress, perhaps because the visit is to be kept secret from the husband. So far, then, ter

FIGURE 3. Gerard ter Borch, *The Consultation*, 1635. Photo: Joerg P. Anders. Gemaeldegalerie, Staatliche Museen zu Berlin, Berlin, Germany. Photo credit: Bildarchiv Preussischer Kulturbesitz / Art Resource, NY.

Borch has drawn on available conventions. But there are two rather atypical elements in this painting. First, the maid carries urine in an earthen-
ware bowl rather than a clear glass vessel. The doctor is busy with another
patient's urine when the maid enters the room. Ter Borch has introduced
narrative and serialization into what might otherwise be a fairly theatrical
and static pose. Perhaps the doctor will have to pour the urine from the
maid's bowl into a clear vessel in order to make his diagnosis. Various possibilities present themselves in what appears to be a rather mysterious interaction. The maid, we should note, is reflected in the urine glass, along
with the window itself—as a white dollop—which provides the light for
the doctor. Indeed, there are a number of reflective surfaces, including another glass vessel in a niche, the mirror (reflecting the white papers of the
doctor's books), and the hourglass. The room, however, is extremely dark.
In the left-hand corner—and this is the second surprising element—sits a
figure wrapped in red cloth with his or her back to the viewer. This ghostly
presence is literally marginal to the central interaction between the doctor
and maid. Yet inasmuch as no detail is insignificant in a work of this nature, the fact that this figure is sketched in, but not filled out, the fact that
his or her body occupies space without any particularity, seems notewor-
thy.[4] Perhaps this bodily mass in the corner is a gesture toward everyday
life (the individual just happened to be there when ter Borch came across
the scene), yet simultaneously, it hints at the shadowy nature of the doctor's work.

   Another variant of the urine-analysis genre, the "diagnosis of lovesickness," popular with middle-class Dutch patrons, links the domestic scene
to a long emblematic tradition: Only Love can cure Love. In *Amans
amanti medicus* from Otto van Veen's *Amorum emblemata*, Love stands in
the center of the composition, holding a "clear" vial—indicated precisely
by pictorial conventions of clarity—filled with urine. On the bed, a victim of lovesickness languishes. This emblem-type, then, while composi-
tionally similar to the diagnosis of pregnancy, engages immediately with a
unique symbolic register. Art historians have helped to refine the very notion of genre paintings, and sometimes to account for their popularity, on
the basis that they reflect the real conditions of bourgeois life, serving as
visual catalogues for the possessions of the very consumers of the paintings themselves, while they are simultaneously didactic, morally uplifting.
As Hal Foster writes in an essay on fetishism, "Even today, positioned rev-
erently before these gold chalices, fine porcelain pieces, and exquisite

glasses like so many worshippers before the Golden Calf, we might believe, as perhaps did the Dutch, that these things have a *mana* or power of their own—a *mana*, moreover, that redounds to the *mana* or value of painting" (Foster 255). Foster goes on to cite Goethe who praised a (copy of) Dutch still life depicting gold and silver vases with great skill. "One must see this painting in order to understand in what respect art is superior to nature and what the spirit of man lends to these objects when he observes them with a creative eye. For me there is no question: If I would have to choose between the golden vases or the painting, I would choose the painting" (cited in Foster 256).

Recent art-historical work has brought to the fore a debate about Northern painting as descriptive, as opposed to (Italian) narrative. Mieke Bal, among others, has explored how these two modes work together. The dual "purpose" to genre paintings is based on an assumption, widely shared by art historians of the Northern Renaissance and Baroque, that the consumption of paintings is pleasurable in and of itself, but that consumption has to be tempered by an underlying alibi, a justification, provided precisely by the moral emblems or traditions evoked as subtext. This leads us, however, to a more troubling query that cannot be fully addressed here: Should we assume that the desire to consume, the pleasure of seeing one's possessions reflected in the painting-as-object is primary, and the moral subtext merely adjunct? Or is the moral subject primary, and the faithful representation of daily life an added "bonus" to soften a hard lesson, the carrot before the stick, the sweet honey on the cup, like eloquence for rhetoric? This question may seem to be a digression, but it is actually essential to pose it, if only to trouble the apparently seamless account of Dutch genre painting that is offered by a certain scholarly trend. For why should we assume that the Dutch *needed* morality to justify their "base" greed? And why should we assume a collective desire for *having* that dominates over, say, a collective pleasure in *economizing*?

All Rubbish

The so-called moralizing subtext is not buried, but rather, quite evident in many depictions of the alchemist. Like the urine-analysis genre, the alchemist in his laboratory is a popular theme in Dutch seventeenth-century art. In general, various elements of this type engage in "the art of describing [the everyday]," in Svetlana Alpers's influential terms, and yet

FIGURE 4. Philippe Gallé, *The Alchemist,* 1558. Etching, after a drawing by Pieter Brueghel the Elder. Photo: Jörg P. Anders. Inv.: 45-1964. Kupferstichkabinett, Staatliche Museen zu Berlin, Berlin, Germany. Photo credit: Bildarchiv Preussischer Kulturbesitz / Art Resource, NY.

symbolic elements are also often present. A well-known example of this generic type is an etching by Philippe Gallé (after a 1558 drawing by Brueghel) (Figure 4). The scene takes place in an extremely disorderly room populated by an extended family and a scholar. First, we should note that the engraving is based on a drawing, hence the original was reversed. It is specious, therefore, to make any arguments based on the lateral disposition of objects in the scene. On the right a scholar sits at his desk and points with one hand to an alchemist (presumably the father) and with his other hand to a volume open to the chapter heading *Alghe Mist* (All Rubbish).[5] Indeed, the scholar consults several different books at once: there is no single authority for the intellectual trash that is alchemy. Various implements are scattered around the floor, including scales for weighing gold (does this imply that real gold was/is produced, or is it simply a sign of greed?), bellows (the implement of the puffers or *souffleurs*), a sack marked "drogery," various pots and pans, an hourglass, and so on.

In the midground, two witchlike women (presumably mother and grand-mother) work. The father—the alchemist—tries to work at his desk, while one can vaguely make out the word *misero* on the paper pinned precariously above his head. The parents ignore their children, who climb inside a cupboard. One of the children has a pot lodged on his head. He wears it into the "next" scene, viewed through the window: the family is being led off to the poorhouse. The foreground scene, then, depicts a miserable family at work under the spurious supervision of a scholar. The composition is overcrowded, entirely antithetical to the moral ideal of the ordered Dutch (Calvinist) interior. All of the characters are completely absorbed in their respective activities, so they do not see the potentially ruinous consequences of their actions.

The moralizing text in this image can be said to emerge from the certain emblematic elements (the chapter heading in the book, for instance, or the overturned vessels, or the children at play), but, more significantly, by the coexistence in the same pictorial space of two temporally different events. Engravers (like painters) borrowed the use of a window or doorframe from emblematics to delimit a secondary space where a "moral" unfolds itself, cordoned off from the rest of the composition. In this regard, the Gallé engraving is quite typical for the period in question. We normally consider the insertion of emblematic codes in paintings of everyday life or genre scenes as nonnarrative. But perhaps it is already incorrect to speak of "insertion" as if the scene existed in some real spatiotemporal dimension, onto which the emblems are merely stuck (or better, etched) like so many appliqués. Could one say that the moral content associated with emblematics is always already inherent in the very conception of the everyday? The assumption that the foreground scene represents "life" and the framed background scene represents a static, lifeless moral, may indeed appear obvious given what we know of generic conventions surrounding depictions of alchemy; that is, it is an assumption that could achieve wide consensus among interpreters. But the real question is not just what we think is happening, but how we seem to know what is happening.

In his *Groot schilderboek*, first published in 1704 (thus appearing considerably later than the Brueghel drawing and the Gallé engraving), Gerard de Lairesse specifically details how secondary spaces should be used in narrative development: "The outcome or ending of a story must always be set in the principal place in the composition, and the beginning of it in the background. Just as a cannonball, shot from a distance, hits a nearby bulwark and scatters everything in its path, by this means the gist of the matter will appear at first glance" (cited in Hollander 46). Based on his accounting of actual painterly practices, Lairesse noted that background or secondary scenes, which generally depict an earlier moment in narrative development, tend to clarify or explain foreground scenes. They may also provide irony, parallels, or resolution to the principal scene. Indeed, the frontispiece to Lairesse's treatise (Figure 5) can be considered exemplary in that it includes a number of discrete spaces: In the foreground the (blind) painter, Lairesse himself, works, guided by the muse. A secondary space is revealed behind a curtain (lifted by Fame), where a painter (possibly Apelles) works diligently by candlelight. Lairesse probably adapted this detail from Cesare Ripa's *Iconologia* (Gaskell 16). In a third arena, an emblematic crowning of painting occurs in a roundel, surrounded by palettes, brushes, and other attributes. Convention teaches us that whatever appears front and center is most important, most "present" in a temporal sense. Hollander explains: "Lairesse's concept of the *bywerk* is clearly exemplified by the ancillary views in seventeenth-century paintings. The associative, explanatory function of the ancillary view reflects its heritage in medieval and Renaissance narrative expansion" (46).

Initially, then, it may seem that the Gallé etching contradicts Lairesse's notion of temporality in that the background scene apparently takes place after the foreground scene. That the family goes to the poorhouse after attempting alchemy is not what is important so much as that this secondary scene, or *bywerk*, clarifies the status of alchemy, like a cannonball that "scatters everything in its path" and resolves the entire composition. In coming after, as a result, and in being smaller, this scene asserts itself as primary in a sense, overtaking the scene that is larger, grander, and foregrounded. The secondary scene is not only important in terms of its content, but it also accomplishes a compositional function—it directs the eye back in space. "The *doorsein*, which invites the eye to peer through a 'hole' in the picture while providing a secondary motif for scrutiny and contemplation, accomplishes two things: the penetration of the picture's imaginary space, and the elaboration of its surface" (Hollander 46). In this regard, *doorsein*, the Dutch variant of (Italian) linear perspective, is also a rhetorical mode, to allow for a "studied discontinuity" within a composition.[6] We can agree, then, according to convention, that the poorhouse scene is meant to come after the foreground scene. We have already established that for Lairesse, as for various painters of the Lowlands, background

FIGURE 5. Title page, Gerard de Lairesse, *Het groot schilderboek*, 1704.

scenes more commonly appear prior to foreground scenes. There is no aesthetic code in the engraving that instructs us to read the two discontinuous images in any particular order. In fact, we might be tempted to begin reading from the highest point (which is also the back) downward. If we did so, we might arrive at the following: A family is led into the poorhouse. Once inside, they perform disorderly alchemical operations under the supervision of a scholar, perhaps as a way to arrive at independence from alms, or to free themselves from a state of quasi incarceration. We know that this interpretation, while plausible, is probably incorrect.

Assuming, then, that the secondary scene occurs later than the primary scene, what happens to the scholar? Does he remain in the laboratory, perhaps attaching himself to another gullible family or waiting to receive a luminous rune like Rembrandt's Faustus (Figure 6)? Does he disappear into the ether as the family is brought down to earth? If the framed scene, the *doorsein*, takes place after the foreground scene, the scholar is the figure who slips through the cracks. His status—like theory itself in the ambivalent alchemical couple—is indeterminate in the moral "ending" to this tale.

Extending beyond Brueghel/Galle's particular image, there is a crucial link between the materiality of engraving and alchemy itself. An exemplary figure in this link is Albrecht Dürer. As a young man Dürer was apprenticed to his father to be a goldsmith, but he rebelled and decided to pursue art. Still, his experience with the etched templates used for goldworking would prove useful for his work as a printmaker as well as a painter. In fact, copper engraving grew directly from goldsmithing in the fifteenth century, spreading from the Upper Rhine throughout Europe (Anzelewsky 19). Although several of his most famous engravings—for instance, *Melancholia* (Figure 7) and *St. Jerome in His Study* (Figure 8), both from 1514—were done using a more traditional technique, Dürer's legacy to printmaking depends, in part, on his invention of *"aqua fortis."* This technique has significant parallels with alchemy itself, as Maurizio Calvesi explains: "We have a metal plate, a corrosive acid (just as mercurial water dissolves the 'prima materia'), we have a fire that burns and smokes metal, we have a series of phases, waiting, mysterious passages from matter to 'form.' It is most unlikely that an artist like Dürer who was interested in the processes of alchemy, as demonstrated by a correct interpretation of *Melancholia*, would not have thought about these parallels."[7]

FIGURE 6.   Rembrandt, *A Scholar in His Study*, ca. 1652, Rijksmuseum, Amsterdam.

FIGURE 7.   Albrecht Dürer, *Melancholia*, 1514, Inv. B.74–II. Photo: Jörg P. Anders. Kupferstichkabinett, Staatliche Museen zu Berlin, Berlin, Germany. Photo credit: Bildarchiv Preussischer Kulturbesitz / Art Resource, NY.

FIGURE 8.   Albrecht Dürer, *St. Jerome in His Study*, 1514. Inv. 401–2. Photo: Jörg P. Anders. Kupferstichkabinett, Staatliche Museen zu Berlin, Berlin, Germany. Photo credit: Bildarchiv Preussischer Kulturbesitz / Art Resource, NY.

And he notes: "There is an even more eloquent testimony of this link: among the alchemical synonyms or equivalents of mercurial water, also called *aqua nostra, mercurius vivus, argentum vivum, succus lunariae*, we also find *acetum fontis*, which Jung defines as a 'powerful hard water that dissolves everything that it becomes; and so gives birth to the most durable of all formations: that is, the mysterious *lapis*'" (Calvesi 1993, 67; translation mine).[8] In a number of treatises from the fifteenth century, *aqua fortis* refers to a highly acidic liquid (perhaps nitric acid) that is capable of dissolving all metals except gold. In 1514, the year of his "master engravings," Dürer also began experimenting with new techniques. In this regard, etching, the wearing away of a plate by toxic liquid to yield (golden) images, stands as a compromise between the desire of the father that the son should continue in his tradition (working with gold) and the deviation chosen by the son (working with images, exchanged for capital).

The Clear Vas

A similar duality—nonnarrative emblems/narrative—may be said to underlie what is perhaps the most famous, albeit idiosyncratic, example of the urine-analysis genre, *The Quack Doctor* by Gerrit Dou (Figure 9). This work was exceptionally large for Dou, and this has led critics to surmise that he granted it a great deal of importance. Specifically, in this work, the underlying moral has to do with an audience's visual gullibility rather than the wasting of time on vain pursuits. Dou has moved the urine analysis from the controlled confines of a drawing room out to the public space of a market. He has also added a second male protagonist, a painter, that is, Dou himself, who leans on a window ledge just behind the doctor and looks out at the viewer.[9] The painting suggests that doctor and artist both engage in forms of deceit, although painterly deception is certainly less dangerous, and indeed, is praiseworthy. The rather motley bunch of townspeople who are drawn to the dais appear to undertake the activities of daily life. They engage in bartering, conversing, playing. Closer study of the painting, with a handbook, reveals that each one of these activities corresponds to a popular emblem. A boy tries to trap a bird (based on an emblem by Jan van Veen: "The lust for gold is a scourge"); a pancake seller wipes her baby's bottom (a common emblem of the period links shit and "production"); a woman is so caught up in the quackery that she allows her

FIGURE 9. Gerrit Dou, *The Quack Doctor*, 1652. Museum Boymans van Be-
uningen, Rotterdam, The Netherlands. Photo credit: Kavaler / Art Resource, NY.

pocket to be picked; and so on.[10] A dog sniffs at the ground. The figures also seem to be different sizes, as if something is amiss here. Although the sky is cloudy, the sun breaks through somewhere on the left-hand side of the composition, since the figures are in light, and a glimmer of light hits the glass vessel. In such a context the painter's ability to depict a clear vessel in an illusionary manner stands as the positive analogue to the deception of the quack doctor. The vessel is a masterful chimera.

But the link between painterly illusion and the clear vessel is not merely casual, and we can trace it back at least to fourteenth- and fifteenth-century images. In the narrative of the Annunciation, God casts his shadow on Mary. The clear vase—or, for our purposes, the (alchemical) *vas*—signifies, in Dutch painting, the purity of Mary. Light penetrates the glass as God penetrates her womb (sometimes called *vas clausum*). Millard Meiss explains:

> Fascinated by light, some of the leading Flemish painters of the late fourteenth and early fifteenth centuries adopted a striking symbolic image that was current in mediaeval thought. Theologians and poets often explained the mystery of the incarnation by comparing the miraculous conception and birth of Christ with the passage of sunlight through a glass window. . . . Her [the Virgin's] virginity was not affected by this mysterious insemination and she remained intact even giving birth to Christ and forever after. (Meiss 176)

The *vas* motif traveled to Italy, as in the *Annunciation* of Fra Filippo Lippi's altar in San Lorenzo, circa 1440 (Figure 10).[11] The vase in the foreground that casts a slight shadow illustrates a hymn in which light enters a vase but does not destroy it. Filippo Lippi's *vas* is placed at the limit of two spaces, one interior, one exterior. In its highly sophisticated use of shadow at the edge of transparency and opacity, reflection and refraction, the painting thematizes the very impenetrability of the mystery in the vessel.[12] The vase cuts into the floor, as if dematerializing the stone. The lily held by the Angel is tilted so that it might fit right into the glass itself. Lippi was immersed in a Baconian culture of physics: the visual rays are supposed to enter the eye at right angles to the "glacialis" or "crystallinus"—scientists believed that the center of the eye was the glassy focusing lens (not the back of the eyeball, as we now know). The Virgin does not feel the heat of sexual passion, but rather the coolness of the shadow that falls on her resulting from a body of light: "The holy spirit came upon her

FIGURE 10.   Filippo Lippi, *Annunciation and Predella with Scenes from the Life of Saint Nicholas* (attributed to Pesellino), 1440. S. Lorenzo, Florence, Italy. Photo credit: Scala / Art Resource, NY.

in a manner analogous to the way light passes uncontaminated through a transparent medium" (Meiss 105).

Later, Paracelsus wrote of the vessel in his *Coelum philosophorum*:

> All things are concealed in all. One of them all is the concealer of the rest— their corporeal vessel, external, visible, and movable. All liquefactions are manifested in that vessel. For the vessel is a living and corporeal spirit, and so all coagulations or congelations enclosed in it, when prevented from flowing and surrounded, are not therewith content. No name can be found for this liquefaction, by which it may be designated. (Paracelsus 5)

He clearly extends the nature of the vessel beyond its materiality, to a potential realm where inside and outside are no longer distinguishable. The trope reemerges in *The Chemical Wedding of Christian Rosenkreutz*, where the narrator helps incubate forms containing tiny, nearly transparent images, male and female.[13] Form and figures are so fused that, as the narrator notes, "I thought they [the homunculi] were meer christal" (204).

Read against the background of this iconology and Paracelsian material immateriality, Dou's painting provides a symbolic matrix in which painting and alchemy find themselves absolutely intertwined around the clarity of the glass. The clear glass as womb is the place of alchemical transformation, and sometimes it is the material of the transformation itself— that is, the glass is not simply a container.

The Laboratory

Compared with the urine-analysis works, the alchemist in his laboratory is more closely associated with other low-life genres, such as drinking in taverns or playing cards.[14] The alchemist works in a dark and dusty space, often with a window on the left side of the composition, repeating the pattern of the artist in his studio and so many other Dutch interior compositions, including a number of famous works by Vermeer.[15] In Dutch painting light is of paramount importance. The portraits of saints, artists, and alchemists in their studies play on the tension between the light entering the room from outside the picture plane and the transformation of such "real light" into paint.[16] The transformation is not something hidden or suppressed. Rather, it seems to be a key theme that is being worked out—alchemically, if we wish—in the interplay between paint, canvas, and perception.

Goethe must have had the alchemist's laboratory in mind when he wrote the lines cited at the beginning of this chapter, and he chose one of Rembrandt's scholars (referred to either as Faustus or an alchemist in the eighteenth century) for the title page of *Faust* (Figure 6). Like the saint in meditation, another figure central to Rembrandt's oeuvre, the alchemist may sit at a desk, poring over a tome of secrets.[17] Adepts (or perhaps the alchemist's wife), if present, may do the actual labor. If present, children play at frivolous games or blow bubbles. The alchemist, like the saint, is apparently caught unawares by the painter. He is so fully absorbed in the theory of alchemical transformation that he loses all track of time. Inasmuch as the depiction of the alchemist can be considered a portrait, it is like those of individuals who do not pose knowingly, but are instead involved in some activity that collapses the durational process of applying the paint to the canvas into the blink of an eye.

Paint and Tincture

If we explore these two genres—the doctor-quack and the alchemist in his laboratory—in the broadest possible terms, we should keep in mind that we are talking about painterly genres, not merely about representations *tout court*. Painting has a particular status not only vis-à-vis patronage and ownership of the image, but also in relation to the illusionary nature of the (clear) vessel and in the application of tinctures to a canvas.[18] This is especially important in the context of the Lowlands. For instance, Gerard ter Borch's prowess in depicting satin (in the context of genre paintings for the Dutch burghers) came to define a "modern" style that fuses form and content. Because of its peculiar weave, satin was difficult to reproduce. Traditionally, painters began with a layer of relatively inexpensive tinctures known as dead coloring, on top of which were layered other colors, perhaps more expensive to obtain. Yet ter Borch rejected this traditional method in favor of a more modern approach, applying fewer layers of paint in a more simultaneous manner. Ter Borch's method was rejected by many of his contemporaries as it was considered too "loose." Gerard de Lairesse suggested that it would be best to avoid this loose method in which "the paint would run down the piece like shit." Admittedly, the surface of the work would appear "smooth and mellow so that the objects seem round and in relief," but this was achieved by artists of the modern method "only through artifice and through smudging" (cited in Wheelock

38). Lairesse's terms, as he derides the modern manner of Rembrandt, ter Borch, and others—dead colors, feces, and the temporality of the drying paint—are central terms in alchemy. Painting boasts a long and privileged relationship to alchemical thought and practice. Critic James Elkins has gone so far as to suggest that we can truly understand the materiality of paint—an ineffable combination of wet and dry substances—only in relation to alchemy. The "wet way" was preferred by many alchemists (in their writing, at least). The "dry way" was faster, but more dangerous and likely to give rise to explosions (see Figure 11, for instance).

More specifically, the very dual quality of gold—as a color or tint and as a metal (both potentially applicable to a canvas)—forms the basis of various alchemical logics. In his *Sceptical Chemist*, a text that has been widely misread as a purely anti-alchemical diatribe, Robert Boyle refers to the ambi-valent nature of gold in its capacity for separation into a "sulfuric" essence and a "mercurial" essence:

> Tis not, that after what I have try'd myself I dare peremptorily deny, that there may out of gold be extracted a certain substance, which I cannot hinder Chymists from calling its tincture or Sulphur; and which leaves the remaining Body depriv'd of its wonted colour. Nor am I sure, that there cannot be drawn out of the same Metal a real quick and running Mercury. But for the Salt of Gold, I never could either see it, or be satisfied that there was ever such a thing separated, *in rerum natura*, by the relation of any credible eye witnesse. (Cited in Principe 43)

In this passage Boyle is not expressing a generic distrust of alchemy, at least as far as its use of sulfur and mercury as *Decknamen* or analogies. Instead, his polemic is against the Paracelsians who favored a triadic (admitting salt as one of the primary or universal elements of all matter) instead of a dyadic model. It is not that gold is the only element that can be separated into two elements, but rather, as it undergoes this potentially universal process, it simultaneously reveals the process to the eye, hence gold emerges as exemplary for its sensory, aesthetic yield. Gold (and so alchemy) is intermixed in painting like a pigment with a binding substance. This mixed quality is brought to prominence in the problematic of how to depict gold, especially in sumptuous fabrics worn by wealthy patrons during the early modern period, for instance. Because gold is both a color or tint (and as such, it bears a merely nominal relation to a certain admixture of other tints) and an actual mineral substance, it can be used,

FIGURE II.   Hendrick Heerschop, *The Alchemist's Experiment Takes Fire*, 1687.
Courtesy of the Chemical Heritage Foundation Collections.

for instance, as gold leaf, applied to a canvas, or painted over and then revealed through *sgraffito*.[19] The use of gold leaf is a gesture that is both in-
dexical (as a reference to gold) and material (it increases the value of the
painting as object). Nevertheless, the application of gold to the surface of
the canvas decreases with the advent of linear perspective and painterly

illusion. So, Leon Battista Alberti, in his treatise on painting of 1435–36, affirms:

> There are some painters who make excessive use of gold, because they think it lends a certain majesty to painting. I would not praise them at all. Even if I wanted to paint Virgil's Dido with her quiver of Gold, her hair tied up in gold, her gown fastened with a golden clasp, driving her chariot with golden reins, and everything else with resplendent gold, I would try to present with colours rather than with gold this wealth of rays of gold that almost blinds the eyes of spectators from all angles. Besides the fact that there is greater admiration and praise for the artist in the use of colors, it is also true that, when done in gold on a flat panel, many surfaces that should have been presented as light and gleaming, appear dark to the viewer, while others that should be darker, probably look brighter. (Cited in Edgerton 107)

Elkins notes that both painting and alchemy are messy practices watched over or critiqued by theorists unwilling or incapable of dirtying themselves with the materiality of the substances involved. He writes:

> In alchemy as in painting, there are people who prefer to live antiseptically, and think about the work instead of laboring over it. In alchemy, those are the "spiritual" or "meditative" alchemists, the ones who read about alchemy and ponder its meaning, but try not to go near a laboratory; and in painting they are the critics and art historians who rarely venture close enough to a studio to feel the pull of paint on their fingers. (Elkins 2)

Certain art historians who have been accused of failing to look closely or engage with the viscosity of oil paint are likened to the critics who write about alchemy without actually trying to transform base materials into gold. The contradictions within this analogy will become apparent throughout the course of this book. Elkins sees his analogy as a symptom of another deep similarity: as in alchemy, the relationship between the painter and the paints is one of "blind experimentation" (Elkins 9), inspired and unpredictably magical. Monet, as an example, layered paint on the canvas "without premeditated method until the paintings reached the magical point where it became impossible to tell how they had been painted" (Elkins 14). The unfathomable "secret" of Monet is a sublime admixture of "the precariously balanced viscosity of the pigment, and a nearly masochistic pleasure in uncomfortable, unpredictable twists and turns . . . [the paintings] are about that beautiful moment when the dull oil paste, squeezed from the lead tube, becomes a new substance that is neither liquid, solid, cream, wax, varnish, or vaseline; and they are about the body's turning against itself, and within itself, to make shapes that the eye cannot recognize as human marks" (Elkins 18). Apparently this kind of work cannot be written down or taught, and it is extremely difficult to imitate. This is the same language we find repeated in early modern alchemical treatises. Elkins writes of years of trial and error that a painter has to undergo in order to grow into the tradition of painting. It might be possible to paint like Monet, and his works may certainly be reproduced in posters and prints, on umbrellas and handbags, so that they are identifiable, and even so that the clumps of paint on the canvas are represented. But in order to forge a Monet painting for the art market, a counterfeiter would not be able to take technological shortcuts. He would have to immerse himself radically in the paints and brushstrokes, and were he to succeed in doing so, there could be significant financial rewards, although Elkins has no interest in foregrounding this aspect of forgery. "Alchemy is the old science of struggling with materials, and not quite understanding what is happening: exactly as Monet did, and as every painter does each day in the studio" (Elkins 19). Alchemy is invoked to explain the combination of magical transformation of materials and the physical, bodily, gestural struggle of applying paint to the canvas, but with gold/money completely evacuated from the scene.[20]

Chemical Bath

It should be clearer now why the vodka advertisement that opens this book is so important. It refers to painting indexically, or better, it is caught up in an iconology of the history of genres and in materialist considerations of the nature of paint as a medium. We should recall, however, that the advertisement is a photograph, and so we witness another level of transformation—from painting to photography—that is, like photography itself an analogue to alchemy.[21] Photography, as we well know, involves the immersion of plates fabricated from precious metal (and later paper) in a (noxious) chemical bath, yielding a transformation into "nobility," that is, the nobility of the image. It is a victory over time, a preservation of an image, by light, which makes the photograph possible in the first place. Photography is, as Barthes insisted, closer to chemistry than it is to painting (Calhoon 1998, 626). It is a transmutation of matter. This position takes the focus away from the object that is being represented—the "imagery" or iconology of the photograph—and turns it to the organizational pattern of energy that causes the image to emerge before the eye. However, photography is not *mere* transformation in that silver, the medium on which light is recorded, is, like all metals, alive (in contrast with the "dead colors" used by Dutch painters to undercoat their works). Like photography, alchemy "aims at the same 'dematerialized materiality' by means of which gold coins purportedly conveyed the unique translocality of the royal body" (Calhoon 1998, 629). Kenneth Calhoon notes that the movement, in the history of photography, from silver to paper could be seen to repeat the advent of paper money as it came to replace precious metals. It is a short distance from photography to cinema, and the gold of cinematic capital.

Considering the various images in this brief chapter, we feel, intuitively, that the effect—in terms of both form and content, rational and irrational—appears in the realm of ambivalence, that is, dual, bipolar, doubled, and inextricable. To speak of alchemical images as content without considering the materiality of their forms, is to strip them of a vital life force, as we learn from Warburg. This force is not something ineffable, but rather, something at the limit of language, in the realm of the *pathosformel*. The next chapter addresses ambivalence more directly, again, not to diagnose (or cure) Warburg, but to explore the relationship of ambivalence to bipolarity, schizophrenia, multiplicity, value, and reason.

Excursus: Ambivalence

The term *valence*, of which ambivalence is not merely a variation, but a decidedly new and separate concept, derives from chemistry and atomic physics. Valence can refer to an extract or tincture, usually from an herb. In this connotation, it has obvious ties with the field of "medical alchemy," or iatrochemistry.[1] In the mid-1800s, valence theory began to be used to signify the normal number of bonds that a given atom can form with other atoms—a register that links valence with philosophical materialism, matter, and Epicurianism. In recent scientific work, valence refers specifically to the number of electrons in the outermost shell of atoms. It is not provisional or occasional in its relation to the atom. Valence *is* atomicity. It defines a given chemical element, perhaps not in its essence, but in its capacity to combine with other elements—its potentiality. Valence is denoted by a simple number, and elements are said to be monovalent, bivalent, trivalent, quadrivalent, and so on. About one-fifth of all elements have a fixed valence (sodium is always 1, or monovalent; calcium is always 2, or bivalent; and so on). Many elements have valences that are variable, depending on the other elements with which they are combined.

As in the word *ambidextrous*, the prefix *ambi* (or *ambo*) might imply an element whose combining capacity is equivalent not to the number two, but rather to "both" of something in a class of two—and only two—possible elements. "Both of what?" we might well ask, since "both" requires a referent, a predicate, or a genitive object, and cannot stand on its own. It is possible to imagine a scenario in the field of chemistry in which an element were to be placed next to, or have the capacity to combine with, "both" elements in a given field, and only with "both" elements. That is, in this linguistic (hypothetical) game, ambivalence would not seem to threaten the scientific grounding of chemistry. In any case, the designation of "both" rather than the more general "two" or "more than two" is generally used in reference to hands, gender, coins, and to the analytic relationship in psychoanalysis. In alchemical discourse, the figure of the bipedal hermaphrodite cosmopolite stands with his feet on two (both) mountains (that is, he has a foot in the worlds of both genders).[2] (See Figure 12.) He may also be biheaded, or his (ambi-valent) gender may be indicated by his genitalia. All of these cases normatively involve pairs: both (of two) hands, both (of two) genders, both feet, both heads, both sides of the coin, both actors, and so on. It could be argued, then, that the *ambi* prefix actually forecloses the possibility of multiplicities or differences beyond two.

The Sign of Three?

In contrast, however, consider an episode from Francesco Colonna's *Hypnerotomachia Poliphili*, published in Venice in 1499. The protagonist, Poliphilo, undertakes a pilgrimage (understood as an alchemical process by many Renaissance readers). At one point he confronts three doors that lead to the realm of the high queen Telosia (from *telos*, or *causa finalis*), a woman so beautiful that no mortal can behold her (Colonna 115). Two nymphs will help him make the right decision—Logistica (Logic) and Thelemia (Pleasure). The three doors bear the titles *gloria dei* (*theodoxia*), *mater amoris* (*erototrophos*), and *gloria mundi* (*cosmodoxia*). Poliphilo first decides to open the door on the right, *gloria mundi*, made of a mottled green-red metal (*di metallo di verdaceo rubigine infecte*) (127). Logistica helps him reject the vanity of earthly pleasures, represented by a wanton woman. Next he opens *gloria dei* on the left. He is greeted by a woman with a gold sword (*una matrona chyrsaora*), but it quickly becomes apparent that this choice is too difficult and would require great sacrifice. Finally he opens the middle door (*mater amoris*), made of bronze, where he is greeted by Philtronia (Seduction). This is the door that will lead him to his beloved, Polia. Logic flees, leaving the protagonist with Pleasure, since she is primarily responsible for the choice. They embrace, and Poliphilo continues on his journey.

The choice between *three* paths (illustrated in the text by a woodcut showing the three doors carved into a craggy hillside and surrounded by

EMBLEMA XXXVIII. *De secretis Naturæ.*

Rebis,ut Hermaphroditus,nascitur ex duobus montibus,Mercurii & Veneris.

EPIGRAMMA XXXVIII.

R *Em geminam* REBIS *veteres dixêre , quod uno*
   Corpore sit mas hæc fœminaque , Androgyna.
Natus enim binis in montibus HERMAPHRODITUS
  Dicitur , Hermeti quem tulit alma Venus,
Ancipitem sexum ne spernas , nam tibi Regem
  Mas idem , mulierque una eademque dabit.

SO-

FIGURE 12. *Like the Hermaphrodite, the Rebis Is Born of Two Mountains, of Mercury and Venus,* from Michael Maier, *Atalanta fugiens,* 1617. Research Library, The Getty Research Institute, Los Angeles, CA.

dangerous boulders) is in no way crucial to the narrative or the pilgrim's progress, and nothing in the episode would appear to directly reference the practices of the alchemist. Nevertheless, the choice of three doors brings us to alchemy through a circuitous path that leads from the medieval *Gesta romanorum* (where a woman has to choose between caskets of gold, silver, and lead to win the son of the emperor), through Shakespeare's *Merchant of Venice*, to Freud and Sarah Kofman, who analyzes Freud's essay "The Theme of the Three Caskets" in a short book. Kofman compellingly argues that the apparent "choice" in various narratives masks the fact that metals are, materially, ambivalent; that is, they are subject to transformation so that gold itself actually derives from and could actually revert back to the "base" metal—lead—that it would seem to supercede or outshine. It is all very well, Kofman explains, that a subject might be ineluctably driven to "choose" the casket of death. Ambivalence here is not primarily about "both" or "one of two" in this case.[3] It is fully imbricated in—or better, alloyed with—the way we think about alchemy, and hence, the way we might read a text and its figures alchemically, even when alchemy does not present itself manifestly on the surface of a text.

Common Senses of Ambivalence

Ambivalence, as we use this term in everyday speech, has no place in modern science. Even premodern science seems troubled by ambivalence. For if gold can be transmuted from base metals, this must mean that it can be transmuted back into base metals. The Renaissance philosopher-critic Benedetto Varchi cites Aristotle on the generation of species as an argument against the truth of alchemy:[4]

> Anything that is generated is generated by a single thing, that is, from like, and from something of the same species: so mice generated from putrid matter are not, they say, of the same species as those generated by coitus, and the same goes for all the animals, and so they do not generate, nor are they distinguished with regard to sex, even if they seem the same, and share all other characteristics (*accidenti somigliantissimi*) . . . so gold produced by nature and that produced by art, having been generated in different ways, are not of the same specialized species. Therefore alchemy is not true. (Varchi 13–14, translation mine)

Varchi explicitly notes: "It is easier to unmake something than to make it. Gold cannot be unmade, therefore it cannot be made either" (43). Yet at the end of his treatise, Varchi turns the tables, concluding that alchemy is indeed possible, even though he himself has never witnessed a successful transmutation. For while Aristotle is correct, if gold is corrupted it can change form just as some insects change form and undergo metamorphoses. Moreover, Varchi engages in a common form of (specious) argumentation: those writers worthy of esteem who say alchemy is false are probably talking about sophistic alchemy, not real alchemy.[5] The only way to accomplish the "true" alchemy, then, is to corrupt the species ("corrompere la spezie" [21]) so that it is reduced to the *prima materia* of metals. In this way, it is not the alchemist or the art that makes gold, but rather Nature herself, as aided by the alchemist. For Varchi, the "true" alchemist is analogous to the doctor, who heals the sick, facilitated by nature; or the farmer who grows crops. Varchi upholds the Aristotelian ideal of like generating like, while still leaving open the possibility of alchemical transformation. What he does not resolve in his treatise is the fundamental anxiety about gold's derivation, in nature, from the same base origin as other metals. He does not close off the possibility, then, of a reverse transmutation. The fundamental ambivalence of metals haunts this philosopher's text and remains suspended.

Valence is derived from the same root as the Latin verb *valedicere*, meaning "to have power, force, or effectiveness." In relation to money, this term means "to be worthy, to have or add up to the value of something else." *Valedicere* requires at least two terms that are valued in relation to each other, but if one wishes to signify that a sum of money is, in absolute terms, a great sum, there are other ways of saying so. Moreover, *valedicere*, as should be clear to speakers of the Romance languages, also refers to the value of a word or words to signify, to "add up to the value" of, a particular thought. The realm of meaning and value around *valedicere* nicely fits with the pair signified and signifier. It lends itself, we might say, to a binary linguistic system. In any case, on its own, without any prefixes or suffixes, *valence* means "strength," pure and simple.

(Ambi)valence operates, then, between chemistry, economics, and psychoanalysis in the realm of value. So Marx writes: "By virtue of being value, [capital] has acquired the occult ability to add value to itself. It brings forth living offspring, or at least lays golden eggs" (cited in Macy 131). At stake is a definition of *value* itself, a controversial and complex topic within economic thought, to say the least. Long before the political economists, the Scholastics took up Aristotelian commutative justice, asking about the (hidden) universal equivalents that allow us to know that two things are of equal value. The Thomist idea has been called a proto-labor theory of value, inasmuch as Thomas Aquinas recognized that to some degree the value of an object should be determined by the amount of labor that went into its production. Extending such an idea into the realm of alchemy, we come to realize that Thomist thought is clearly more theological-ethical than it is economic. The hoarding of gold, the false and vain pursuits of the magician, the lust after gold, as pure avarice, do nothing to serve to meet the needs of human beings. For this reason they are to be morally condemned.

William Petty argued that the two universals that help determine value are land and labor. Smith and Ricardo move value theory toward the position that "labor and labor alone is what gives commodities their power of exchange" (Macy 132). Where Thomas Aquinas had been concerned with a moral foundation of prices, the labor theory was about removing obstacles to economic growth. Growth is moral in its very nature, as it is good for the nation. Nevertheless, there are some elements of Aristotle that remain embedded in the writings of the political economists: (1) The primacy of production over exchange, and (2) "The Aristotelian search for the innate substance within commodities which makes possible commutative exchange" (Macy 133). Smith believed that exchange value represented the costs of production. Labor is important in his equation, but it is only one factor in determining value. Only with Ricardo does value theory become fully wedded to the labor embodied in commodities. Of course, this does not mean that in Ricardo's scheme laborers are entitled to the full value of their products. Nor does it lead to something like a utopian labor money system in which individuals are paid with chits equivalent to the time spent in working that would allow them to purchase goods or services of "equal labor" value. Instead, in Ricardo, production can help increase the wealth of nations, not the individual laborer. "Ricardo never claimed that labor was exclusively the creator of *wealth*, which he was careful to distinguish from *value*" (Macy 134).

Moving from this basis we can consider Marx's notion of surplus value. Let us assume that it takes a worker six hours to reproduce the conditions for his subsistence. The Owenites might suggest that he could cease working at this point, and that he could, in fact, exchange his earned labor money for necessities. But as Marx notes, in reality the worker continues to work for another six hours. The last six hours result in profit, the "golden eggs" that capital lays, magically (alchemically?) for itself. The results of this "second" six hours on the worker's body might be tangible. Yet the golden egg is always mere metaphor, since according to Marx, the one common element that acts as a universal or standard is not gold. This common element "cannot be a geometrical, physical, chemical, or other natural property of commodities" (Marx 1867, 36). It is labor. More recent theorists, even those sympathetic to Marxism, have said that labor is arbitrary in this equation, in that other basic commodities could serve equally well as the value standard (Macy 138). Marx doesn't say trading partners consciously reduce quantities of their goods to this common element. "Rather, the process occurs behind their backs through the 'laws of motion' of the market." "In short, the claim is not that labor is simply the *measure* of value, but that it is the immanent *substance* of value, the *werkliche Kost* to society (real social cost) that ultimately limits (directly and indirectly) the quantity of abundance" (Macy 138). This is the subject of debate among economists, but for now, what is important is that the very capacity to exchange anything, and so the capacity for a valuation, depends on *some* universal or standard that is like gold, but is not gold.

Leaving aside value, when we look up *ambivalence* in a general-use dictionary, the physical-chemical register characteristic of *valence* has disappeared. We do *not* find a definition in which two (or "both") charges exist around an atom. So while valence is necessarily or originally univalent— inasmuch as it means strength prior to any notion of equivalency or contingency we must keep in mind that ambivalence is not merely the doubled or bipolar version of valence. Instead, it refers to affect, general fluctuation, or, as in the third of three entries in *Merriam-Webster's Collegiate Dictionary* (Tenth Edition), "uncertainty about which approach to follow."

In the linguistic realm, the addition of the *ambi* prefix does not, then, appear to increase the output of valence. More crudely, ambivalence does not double the force of (a given) valence. On the contrary, where valence represents a potentiality, once it has been expanded with a prefix, *ambivalence* appears rather degraded, or better, abraded, to invoke a term from chemistry, to mean something like indecisiveness or ambiguity (a word that is often commonly exchanged for ambivalence). The dictionary entry mentioned above suggests ambivalence as a (merely) intellectual problem that can be solved by rational thought. A similar notion will emerge in a definition of the uncanny put forward by one of Freud's predecessors, Ernest Jentsch. He writes of ambivalence as an effect that can be produced in subjects in a variety of different conditions, even as a willful aesthetic choice. However, for Freud, everything about the castration complex that he is bent on sustaining depends on defining the uncanny as something that *cannot* be consciously created, rationalized, or resolved by mere intellectual force of will.

Bleuler and Schizophrenia

In 1910 Eugen Bleuler discussed ambivalence as a sine qua non of schizophrenia, directly linked to the *Spaltung*, or splitting, that the pathological subject undergoes. It essentially means the simultaneous coexistence of any two (or possibly more!) opposing tendencies such as love and hate. Defined as such, however, ambivalence would seem to allow itself to be easily taken up in a general context, as a neurotic problem that is not specific in any way to schizophrenia. For Bleuler, what distinguishes genuine ambivalence (in schizophrenia) is its simultaneity, understood, though, in a very particular sense. He writes:

> For the healthy subject, everything has two sides. Roses have their thorns. But in ninety-nine percent of cases the normal subject balances the negative against the positive. He loves roses in spite of their thorns. Schizophrenia, with its faulty associations, is not necessarily able to reconcile the two sides: he loves the rose for its beauty; and at the same time he hates it because of its thorns. The same holds true for numerous other ideas, both simple and complex, which have for him two affective valences which show themselves side by side or alternate one after the other. (cited in Grilliat 174, my translation)

As Denis Grilliat points out, this passage would seem to suggest that for Bleuler, the side-by-side manifestation of two valences is the same thing as their succession, or at least, both of these temporal schemes are possible in the case of the schizophrenic patient. There appears to be a unique grammar of the schizophrenic.[6] In short, in the schizophrenic patient, the two conflicting ideas are not merely simultaneous, they are truly linked in the same temporal sphere of the utterance, as a temporal short-circuit. "The *Spaltung* unveils itself here by barring discourse in its dialectical, articulable function" (Grilliat 174). It is closed unto itself and resistant to metaphorization or paraphrase. Bleuler further broke the term down into three distinct elements: affective ambivalence—that is, the simultaneous existence of love and hate for the same object; ambivalence of will (or ambi-tendency)—that is, the coexistence of two incompatible desires; and intellectual ambivalence, the simultaneous (or alternate) existence of an idea and its opposite as posited by a given subject. It is this latter element that most closely ties ambivalence to a certain notion of schizophrenia, but again, we need not necessarily view the symptom in such a drastic or profound form.[7]

Freud

A key question in the evolution of Freud's thought is whether ambivalence can be considered something "originary" in a subject, or whether it derives, instead, from the relationship between ego and object. Ambivalence makes an appearance in Freud and Breuer's *Studien über Hysterie* (Studies in Hysteria). Freud meets Emmy von N. on May 1, 1889. She suffers from hysteria and sleepwalking, and Freud makes his first attempt at hypnosis with her. Emmy's desire to remain silent is contradicted by her act of making noise. That is, her idea is overpowered by an "antithetical" action that overcomes resistance.

Later, Freud integrates ambivalence into his concept of the drive, with, for instance, the coexistence of sadism and masochism. In Freud's neurotic, the two opposing drives of ambivalence are not present on the same plane, but rather, one may exist as a consciously expressed wish while the other may be repressed in the unconscious. Thus, the difference between the schizophrenic and the neurotic comes into clear light when considered as a difference between Bleuler's and Freud's conceptions of ambivalence. In later writings, Freud suggested that "emotional" ambivalence (two conflicting feelings toward the same [love] object) could result in a narcissistic withdrawal into the self. He also linked conflicting feelings with the two conflicting drives described in *Beyond the Pleasure Principle*. Love and hate regularly accompany one another, and

> in human relationships hate is frequently a forerunner of love, but also . . . in a number of circumstances hate changes into love and love into hate. If this change is more than a mere succession in time—if that is, one of them actually turns into the other—then clearly the ground is cut away from under a distinction so fundamental as that between erotic instincts and death instincts, one which presupposes physiological processes running in opposite directions. (Freud, 1923 43)

It is not necessarily clear if the relation between the two is analogic, structural, or more profound.

Freud wrote in "Mourning and Melancholia" (1917) about the ambivalent way in which the mourner internalizes the object that is both loved
and hated. Is Freud's interest in binaries (such as Thanatos and Eros) a
phenomenon that we can locate in his broader philosophy, in his relation
to certain other thinkers, or is it empirically a quality of instinct? To what
degree is the intrinsic link between the couple love/hate and the couple
male/female (or even lover/beloved, if we want to leave open the possibility that all love relations could be ambivalent) grounded in the early appearance of ambivalence in the Oedipal conflict (which Freud referred to
as an *Ambivalenz Konflikt*)? What kind of secondary unpleasure is produced by living with or in ambivalence, especially if the subject is not able
to solve the problem during the primary stages of libidinal evolution (say,
through a Kleinian child analysis)? Not only is ambivalence intolerable, it
is shameful, a sign that the subject wears to indicate that she or he has not
yet "solved" the problem of the object. "Depression, like mourning, con-
ceals an aggressiveness toward the lost object, thus revealing the ambivalence of the depressed person with respect to the object of mourning"
(Kristeva 1989, 11).

Intolerable Ambivalence

Ambivalence is intolerable for a variety of reasons. In chemistry, ambivalence is unnecessary, since bivalence expresses the idea of a force of two,
trivalence a force of three, and so on, in a much more unambiguous manner. When attached to an object that is lost, ambivalence necessarily prolongs the process of mourning (as it prolongs or deepens some forms of
psychosis). This provides a clue, then, to the status of ambivalence when
detached from its context in relation to the unconscious, as it circulates in
discourse of pop psychology or common usage in contemporary life. La-
planche and Pontalis note the tendency to use ambivalence in a very broad
(we might say popular) sense. Ambivalence is particularly, though not exclusively, linked with the object that is the spouse, the Other of the couple. One is ambivalent about one's partner, a state that psychotherapy
might try to fix. What is interesting about this popularized figure, to rise
above the level of its banality, is that in such a case, the very structure of
the symptom—ambivalence—mirrors the duality of the cause. Ambivalence, being the coexistence of *two*, and not more than *two* (would *polyvalence* be schizophrenia?) opposing affects, manifests itself with particular

regularity in relation to the problem of the couple. Ambivalence exhibits a symptomatic consistency in its form and content. It is binary, and stubbornly so. It refuses to open itself up to multiplicities just as resolutely as it refuses to reduce itself to one.

What if ambivalence is never overcome, but remains a fundamental quality that the subject feels some need to preserve in order to preserve his very self? This suggests that ambivalence is rightly and even necessarily linked with defensive drives. And in turn this could be quite suggestive for alchemy inasmuch as the alchemical may be as much defined by a set of images, practices, rhetorics, and fetish-objects, as it is by the goal, the finished product, gold. Like psychic conflict, chemistry (and alchemy) employs a rhetoric of solutions. An (al)chemical solution is a bath, a state of suspension in which various elements (often two, perhaps more) exist together. Once the transmutation has taken place, there is no more solution (and there is no more problem). Perhaps it is the case that in all couple-relations, when they are subjected to analysis, ambivalence is always present but is overshadowed by a practical solution. When ambivalence is "resolved," this means the death of difference by burial or burning. In the next chapter I will discuss, precisely, the alchemical wedding, in order to address some of the questions raised here.

§ 2 Chemical Nuptials

In the 1998 Dutch film *The Vanishing*, a young couple goes on a summer road trip to a "*bois vieux*" (an old woods, an alchemical locus par excellence) in Southern France.[1] As the film opens, Rex Hofman (an alchemical name par excellence) is driving, while Saskia (a Rembrandtian reference?) applies her makeup in the rearview mirror.[2] After a brief, quasi-flirtatious squabble, Rex and Saskia enter a long tunnel. Saskia's mood turns dark, and she relates a recurring nightmare in which she is trapped inside a golden egg, floating through space. Or rather, as she corrects herself, the last time she had the dream there was another person, trapped in another *vas*, but the two eggs could never meet or they would rupture. It is a dream about loneliness, or at least that is how she interprets it. Just then, the car runs out of gas, the couple is trapped in the tunnel, and the twin lights of an oncoming truck strike Saskia as a foreboding representation of the frightening double eggs in her dream. Terrified, Rex and Saskia argue, and he storms off to get gas, leaving her alone in the tunnel. The ambivalent scene figures dualities of light and dark, male and female.

Cut to daylight. Rex and Saskia drive on through the countryside, arriving at a service station. It is a banal place, crowded with summer travelers. The conversation between the lovers is also banal. Saskia practices her minimal French, laughing at her mistakes. They stretch their legs, play Frisbee, and Saskia buries some coins in the dirt under a tree. It's a silly, superstitious gesture. After requesting some change for the vending machines, Saskia vanishes (hence the film's title). The Tour de France is being broadcast on the radio. And as it turns out, Saskia is wearing a yellow jersey when she disappears. Rex searches the service station. When he returns to the car, someone has stolen the couple's bicycles.

After the requisite waiting period, Rex files a missing person's report. Police investigate, but to no avail. Years pass, and although Rex has a new girlfriend, he continues to be obsessed with Saskia's disappearance. In the meantime, the viewer learns through flashbacks that she was abducted by a bourgeois chemistry professor with a nice family. The professor prepares draughts of ether in the shed of the country home, a makeshift laboratory that seems a throwback to earlier times, filled as it is with antique containers and apparatuses. He also sends clues to Rex, unable to restrain himself from taking risks. In fact, the film gives a kind of etiology for what the professor terms "a slight abnormality in [his] personality": We see him as a boy, seated on a chair on a small balcony overlooking a town square. He opens a (facsimile) copy of the *Mutus liber*, one of the most famous works of alchemy, although the viewer probably has no chance to register the title without a pause button. The boy opens to the frontispiece with its image of a ladder. Next he runs his fingers along an image—the book is without text, hence *mutus*—of a couple holding a glass vessel between them. The vessel contains a homunculus. But the boy soon loses interest, or perhaps he is inspired by the book, and he climbs out onto the balcony ledge. We note a washing service just below the apartment, a *blancherie*. The adult chemist explains in a voice-over that he decided to jump, precisely because he knew he was not predestined to do so. His *salto mortale*, he explains, was a holy experience. He survived with only some broken bones. And so, he is addicted to risk-taking.

Finally, Rex simply has to know what happened to Saskia, so he travels with the professor to the service station. The professor puts him to sleep with ether, promising that he will have exactly the same experience as Saskia. When Rex wakes up, he finds that he has been buried alive— perhaps the most uncanny event possible, as Freud says.[3] Of course, this burial refers the audience back to Saskia's prophetic dream of the twin eggs. The film ends as Rex's butane lighter gives out: he has learned the truth, but at the price of his life.

Various narrative or scenographic elements of the film bring alchemy "into the present." In other words, *The Vanishing* is thoroughly infused with knowledge about the traditions and tropes of alchemy. For instance, the egg is arguably the most persistent symbol in alchemical thought. Specifically, the floating eggs of Saskia's dream evoke Bosch. The wheels of the bicycles attached to the car link to a whole iconography of circularity: the *ouroboros* (serpent biting its tail); the *vas*; the ball, as in Dürer's *Melancholia* and so on. Saskia and Rex bury coins next to a tree. Note the alchemical book and the "whitening" store beneath the boy's apartment. And so on. It would be possible to read the entire film with an alchemical key, and we might find analogues in early modern iconography to almost every detail.

But what makes the film potentially interesting for the present discussion are those elements that do not announce themselves as immediately alchemical. Ambivalence emerges between the young man and woman who are just starting their life together, revealing itself, unexpectedly, in awkward silences and nervous giggles in the parking lot of a typical roadside service station, for instance. In essence, we might say that we find alchemy there where it does not present itself in symbols, but as an ambivalent style of language, a doubling back that surrounds the structure of the couple. A departure from the tradition is the fact that they are buried separately, but from the point of view of the evil (al)chemist, this hardly matters. He has achieved the Great Work, something that helps him transcend the tedium of his picture-perfect, bourgeois, provincial life. And just as with the vodka ad in the introduction to this book, a viewer would not have to know about the traditions of alchemy to experience an uncanny feeling in the final shot: the effect is highly claustrophobic, almost as if the camera is alone in the coffin with Rex, having been abandoned by the cinematic *équipe*. It is entirely possible to successfully "read" the film without articulating the signifier "alchemy." But in a more extended reading, we acknowledge that this couple never does reproduce. Their relationship is cut off before they can grow into marriage and parenthood, although it seems clear this is where they are headed. (In fact, the viewer may feel a certain sense of relief when the plot turns from their petty negotiations to something more mysterious and disturbing.) It is almost as if the professor enacts the structure of alchemy without any of the spiritual dimensions (except insofar as such dimensions are reduced to a mere psychopathological mania). It is alchemy in the modern world, without the "aura," fully achieved in the American version of the film that evacuates all of the alchemical referents. In the Hollywood *Vanishing*, an ordinary man and woman die as a result of curiosity, their ingenuous openness to the world, and their stubbornly naïve belief in the uniqueness of their developing relationship.

At the start of Goethe's *Elective Affinities* (1809), Charlotte and Eduard are alone, hermetically sealed, we might say, in a functional but passionless marriage (perhaps functional *because* passionless). Having married late, they are the same age (which is unusual given that, as Charlotte notes, "I, as a woman, had doubtless grown older than you had as a man" [6]). Yet inasmuch as the theoretical "purpose" of marriage is to reproduce, they are, in fact, not too old to fulfill their functions, as we learn later in the narrative when Charlotte actually does give birth to Otto. Nevertheless, this is not their goal. The marriage is based on a clear idea. They have decided to live alone, he to tend to exterior things, she to interior things. They complement each other perfectly—their sameness is not undermined by the slight differences between them. Better, sameness and difference are suspended in a (chemical) solution of ideal equilibrium. Yet Eduard ruptures the seal by seeking to invite into their lives a friend, the Captain. Much of the plot is advanced by the "meddling" of the friend Mittler (a Mercury-like figure). One evening Charlotte overhears a discussion between Eduard and the Captain concerning "relations" (*Verwandtschaften*, or affinities). Thinking they are speaking of *her* relations, she is rather insulted, but soon realizes that the men are employing the term as an analogy for minerals (29). The men are engaged in a scientific conversation that draws on common tropes and rhetorical patterns.

To help place this conversation in perspective, in the late seventeenth century, when Newton was reading and commenting on the ancient alchemical text known as the *Emerald Table*, he was struck by the appearance of dualities that he saw as fundamental to matter itself:

> Inferior and superior, fixed and volatile, sulfur and quicksilver have a similar nature and are one thing, like man and wife. For they differ one from another only by the degree of digestion and maturity. Sulfur is mature quicksilver, and quicksilver is immature sulfur; and on account of this affinity they unite like male and female, and they act on each other, and through that action they are mutually transmuted into each other and procreate a more noble offspring to accomplish the miracles of this one thing. (cited in Dobbs 184)

In some sense this sounds like a confirmation of vitalism (as opposed to mechanism), but Newton was not an orthodox vitalist. Rather, he believed that pairs and generation mimic God's work in nature. So his commentary on one of the foundational texts of alchemy should not be interpreted as a defense of (alchemical) theory (or practice, for that matter).

Instead, he uses his encounter with the *Emerald Table* as an occasion to buttress the ideas that he had been developing on matter in a modern scientific context.

In *Elective Affinities*, the Captain explains that all things in nature tend toward unity and self-enclosure. Some elements have a natural affinity for other elements: "Sometimes they will meet as friends and old acquaintances and come together quickly and be united without either altering the other at all, as wine for example mixes with water." But other elements "remain strangers side by side and will never be united even if mechanically ground and mixed. Thus oil and water shaken together will immediately separate again" (31). Charlotte immediately grasps the use value of the analogy for relationships themselves. In other words, she brings the conversation back to human sociability, while Eduard pulls back simultaneously in the direction of chemistry. He remarks: "Just as these [different social groups] may be joined by custom and law, so in our world of chemistry there are agents which will bind together the things that are holding one another off" (31). Alkaline salt, for instance, helps to join oil and water. Eduard continues: "Affinities are only really interesting when they bring about separations" (32). Charlotte does not like this idea and thinks that to bring together elements is much more worthy. She resists the kind of violence associated with the breakup of a marriage later in the novel. The trio continues their discussion of analogies, each one motivated by his or her own selfish interests. But Goethe makes clear that the introduction of a "third" element—that is, the Captain—is not enough. For in nature, "chemists are much more gallant. They add a fourth party so that 'nobody goes without'" (34). Indeed, the Captain continues, those relations that function "cross-wise" are the most interesting. (Soon, Charlotte's cousin Ottilie will join the group as a fourth member of the party.) The scene is famous, and it makes evident the significance of the applicability of chemistry to social relations. Chemistry provides the scientific matrix within which Goethe can question marriage as a structure for (re)production. As Helmut Müller-Sievers notes:

> Scientific arguments and treatises against preformation [that is, in favor of the theory of epigenesis] contain a clearly legible political subtext: anti-aristocratic sentiments against the high-handedness of parental choice extol the democratic staunchness of the heart. Polemic against arranged marriages is therefore sustained by a discourse on love not as passion, but as legitimate, interior force of self-foundation. Invariably, it espouses the cause of woman's liberation

from the unnatural obligation to the previous generation in favor of her ded-
ication to her new family, from her preformed past as a daughter, that is, to
her epigenetic future as a mother. (12)

What needs to be determined in the chemistry of marriage is, first of
all, whether the father has any particular role to play in reproduction, and
second, whether marriage is necessary or, instead, merely a social ritual
that serves a limited purpose. Where in preformation children are mini-
adults, epigenesis is about marriage based on transferring (male) subjectivity to the next generation. The father oversees education, for instance,
and that is why grafting is an apt analogy to child-rearing. Otto—the biological offspring of Charlotte and Eduard—looks like Ottilie and the
Captain. He symbolizes the "chiastic relationship among the four characters" (Müller-Sievers 158). "This is possible only under hyper-epigenetic
presuppositions. In premodern theories of epigenesis the role of the imagination in the formation of the embryo had served to explain the presence
of birth defects and deformities." Because he does not resemble his parents, Otto "demonstrates the achieved penetration of nature by subjectivity" (160).

The trope of the chemical wedding is common, but not universal, in
traditional alchemical literature. But how are we meant to understand the
wedding trope? In *The Triumphal Chariot of Antimony*, Basil Valentine
writes of being visited in a dream by Mercury, who is about to be married: "There I beheld their marvellous conjugal union and nuptial con-
summation, whence was born the son crowned with the royal diadem"
(Valentine 6). When the dreamer awakens, he still holds the gold ring of
the son, so he knows it was "not . . . a mere dream" (7). What is the position of the "reader" of an alchemical text with regard to the wedding? Is
he a guest, witnessing a performative vow between two individuals? A
voyeur? Or does the reader take a more active role? For that matter, in
what sense is "wedding" simply a coupling or conjoining as opposed to an
actual ritual, the swearing of an oath of fidelity before a religious or secu-
lar officer of the state or sovereign? In other words, is "wedding" a euphe-
mism or alibi for an erotic encounter? Or does the term *wedding* imply
something binding and stately about alchemy?

A group of men meet to discuss the proper relationship to nuptials in
the *Turba philosophorum*, perhaps the earliest Latin alchemical treatise.
One of the philosophers at the assembly, Diomedes, gives his fellows the

following instructions: "Venerate the king and his wife, and do not burn them, since you know not when you may have need of these things, which improve the king and his wife. Cook them, therefore, until they become black, then white, afterwards red, and finally until a tingeing venom is produced." And to combat the accusation that he may have revealed too much, he retorts: "O seekers after this Science, happy are ye, if ye understand, but if not, I have still performed my duty, and that briefly, so that if ye, remain ignorant, it is God who hath concealed the truth from you! Blame not, therefore, the Wise, but yourselves, for if God knew that ye possessed a faithful mind, most certainly he would reveal unto you the truth" (*Turba* 97–98).

Subsequent alchemical literature reveals a series of odd, sometimes disturbing positions in relation to the wedding. In Michael Maier's *Symbola aureae mensae duodecim nationum* (Frankfurt, 1617), twelve famous alchemists from the past, representing different nations, again attend a great banquet at a golden table. The Frenchman Arnold of Villanova (presumed author of the *Rosarium*, and a physician), stands in the foreground of an image and points to a wedding taking place behind him.[4] (See Figure 13.) Indeed, the entire work is composed of text explicating emblems of famous alchemists who "witness," point to, or attend allegorical events. In some sense, the composition of the emblems in the *Symbola* might be compared with images of donors in religious paintings. However, donors tend to occupy separate architectural spaces or niches, or they may be drawn in different scales from the main events, whereas the "real" men of the *Symbola* are not visibly differentiated from the "symbolic" scenes behind them. What are we to make of Arnold's presence? Does he, as philosopher, legitimate the marriage as a *coniunctio oppositorum*? The accompanying text explains that Arnold made real gold in France, like the child from the union of Gabric and Beia (sulfur and mercury). What is the role of this man who oversees the union but does not directly participate in the wedding? Is he a voyeur, a guarantor of the sanctity of the marriage? What is his relationship to the feminine that is so easily elided, dismissed, or forgotten? We can certainly dismiss the emblem as mere metaphor, as if it had no relation to real marriage, real incest, real paternity, or real sovereignty. Yet if we return to Goethe, we recall that (chemical) marriage is always already figurative.

Still, before we plunge into the metaphorical realm, we should acknowledge that it is also possible to study the wedding in the empirical

FIGURE 13. "Arnold of Villanova: The Stone Is Obtained from the Marriage of Gabritius and Beia," from Michael Maier, *Symbola aureae mensae duodecim nationum*, 1617. Research Library, The Getty Research Institute, Los Angeles, CA.

context of the social history of alchemy: some scholarly work of a socio-historical nature views alchemy as the practice of a married couple (perhaps done by poor or corrupt families in their huts), similar to artisanal enterprises like shoemaking or metalwork.[5] In Maier's *Atalanta fugiens*—and this is just one example among many—epigram 3 represents a woman washing in a tub. The poem reads:

> You see a woman, washing stains from sheets,
> As usual, by pouring on hot water?
> Take after her, lest you frustrate your art,
> For water washes the black body's dirt.

Although undone by the language of the poem, the engraving might be studied for details about the practice of washing, as a document of "effects of the real," to borrow a term from Roland Barthes. Yet for much of the alchemical tradition, a wife, no matter how helpful or well-intentioned, is patently antithetical to the highly spiritual concerns of transmutation. When she is represented, as in the Gallé etching, she usually signals the vanity of attempting the Great Work without the proper preparation. So when we arrive at modernism, French philosopher of science and poetics, Gaston Bachelard, in concert with Duchamp, will affirm that alchemy is the work of men—bachelors working with other bachelors (Calvesi 1975, 18). Women must perforce be excluded for the perfection of the opus. The inextricability and ambivalence of theory and practice around the couple makes it difficult to view alchemical emblems as historical documents of women's activities. Yet inasmuch as the everyday does figure in the tradition of alchemical imagery, it is essential to think about such detail as bound up with the metaphysical, not overlaid upon it.

The history of alchemy boasts one exemplary figure of "the good wife" who helps to complete the Great Work: her name is Perrenelle and she became something of a folk heroine in France.[6] Along with her husband, Nicholas Flamel, she has been mythologized, even by modernists like André Breton and Marcel Duchamp. Flamel and Perrenelle represent "good alchemists" who do achieve the Great Work, but, having no heirs, they donate all of their profits to help the poor. Flamel decorates an archway of the Hospital of the Innocents with hieroglyphics. He explicates the figure of his wife: She represents the philosopher's stone, the *prima materia* of the Great Work. The stone is, then, female, but when joined with Mercury (here, male), it will undergo multiplication in order to yield alchemical gold:

> This [Perrenelle] is the *Stone*, which in this operation demandeth two things, of the *Mercury of the Sunne*, of the *Philosophers'* (painted under the forme of a man) that is to say *Multiplication*, and a more rich *Accoustrement*; which at this time it is needfull for her to obtaine, and therefore the man so laying his hand upon her shoulder accords & grants it unto her. But why I made to bee painted a *woman*? I could as well have made to bee painted a *man*, as a *woman*, or an *Angell* rather, . . . But I have rather chosen to cause paint a *woman*, to the end that thou mayest judge, that shee demands rather this, than any other thing, because these are the most naturell and proper desires of a woman. To shew further unto thee, that shee demandeth *Multiplication*, I have made paint the man unto whom she addresseth her prayers in the forme of *Saint Peter*, holding a *key*, having power to open and to shut, to binde and to loose; because the

envious *Philosophers* have never spoken of *Multiplication*, but under these common termes of Art, APERI, CLAUDE, SOLVE, LIGA, that is, *Open, Shut, binde, loose; opening and loosing*, they have called making of the Body (which is always *hard* and *fixt*) *soft fluid*, and running like water; to *shut* and to *bind*, is with them afterwards by a more strong decoction to *coagulate* it, and to bring it backe againe into the forme of a *body.*

It behoved mee then, in this place to represent a *man* with a *key*, to teach thee that thou must now *open* and *shut*, that is to say, *Multiply* the budding and encreasing natures; . . . (going up to infinity), as I have done three times, praised be God . . . for this reason therefore have I made to bee painted a Key in the hand of the man, which is in the forme of Saint Peter, to signifie that the stone desireth to be opened and shut for multiplication. (Flamel 129–31)

The figure of Flamel moves, precisely, in and out of the effects of the real. His bride is a figure for substances to which the gender of female has been assigned. Simultaneously, she is a real woman whom Flamel loves "as him selfe." He considers himself quite lucky to have a discreet and modest bride who assisted him in the Great Work and states flatly: "I have made it three times, with the help of Perrenelle, who understood it as well as myself, because she assisted me in my operations: And without doubt, if she would have indeed done it alone, she would have brought the work to the same or full as great perfection as I had done" (Flamel 29–30). Nevertheless, there is something inherently dangerous in revealing so much information to a woman:

I was afraid a long time, that Perrenelle could not hide the extreme joy of her felicitie, which I measured by mine owne, and lest shee should let fall some word amongst her kindred, of the great treasures which wee possessed: for extreme joy takes away the understanding, as well as great heavinesse; but the goodnesse of the most great God, had not onely filled mee with this blessing, to give mee a wife chaste and sage, for she was moreover, not onely capeable of reason, but also to doe all that was reasonable, and more discreet and secret, than ordinarily other women are. Above all, shee was exceeding devout, and therefore seeing her selfe without hope of children, and now well stricken in yeeres, shee began as I did, to thinke of God, and to give or selves to the workes of mercy. (Flamel 30–32)

So goes the myth. And according to one account, many years after Flamel's (apparent) death, a Turk met a man who claimed to be Flamel.

"And do you really believe this—No, no, my friend, Flamel is living still;—neither he nor his wife are dead; It is not above three years since I left both the one and the other in the Indies; he is one of my best friends! They have been living in various countries long after they had their own coffins buried" (Barrett 43). Long-lived and wealthy, Flamel and Perrenelle make an exemplary, functional, childless chemical couple.

The wife who helps her husband might be read as a figure of resistance to primitive accumulation, inasmuch as this means the dissolution of the family into community and the assignment of workers to wage-earning positions in factories. However, let us keep in mind that not all thinkers see "domestic economy" as a form of resistance to capitalist exploitation or the ruthless forces of primitive accumulation. For instance, Engels believed that the cultivation of a home garden, or the inability to give up the handloom, could keep the poor even more impoverished because they would fail to enter the market in the most favorable conditions for exchanging their labor, and they would defer the (inevitable) move into the factory for a dream of self-sufficiency that would never be realized.[7] For those alchemists who, in reality, were gentlemen at the service of the courts of Europe, for instance, this is not in question. They never did enter the market, and there is no female helper, except perhaps as part of some elaborate fantasy scheme. But inasmuch as alchemy can be tied to sociohistorical practices undertaken by real individuals, and inasmuch as it could be thought of as an atavistic form of labor, it is not necessarily positive, but rather, perhaps, retrograde and repressive. Engels reminds us of the inherent danger of reading into complex symbolic texts something akin to a social history of the family.

In an early modern treatise on alchemy, Philippe Rouillac compares the alchemical oven to a king's room with only one door. Only one valet can enter and tend to the fire. Rouillac explains that women possess an instinct that pushes them to attract men, take care of the home, and keep the pot boiling (*de fere boulir le pot*) (Calvet 143). He notes: "It is in the nature of the female of any species to attract the male, and not that of the male to attract the female; and this is why nature made females inclined to seductive motions (*esmouvoir cupidement*) toward the generation of the species, for the purpose of multiplying and perpetuating itself" (153, translation mine). In Rouillac's narrative, the king is cut up, mixed with mercury, and placed at the edge of the fountain: "It is said that he sits on the edge of a fountain into which we say that he dives and immerses himself when one combines him with his mercury, just like goldsmiths when they want to gild some object they have made" (153). Rouillac follows this statement with a recipe, calling for a mixture of an ounce of powdered gold and four ounces of mercury. This mixture should be put into a vessel, a clear and diaphanous chamber, or the fountain where the king has bathed, or the bed where he lay with his queen. But at this point in the narrative, the queen disappears. The king now resides in a chamber, and only one man can enter to take care of the fire. What happened to (the) woman? Where did she go during the interval of the cooking of the king? She later comes back to tend the fire, replacing the valet, but she returns as a housewife rather than as a noblewoman. Her presence is required, because in the end, "practice is women's work" (*la pratique est euvre des femmes*). And to clarify: "By this the philosophers mean that the practice and fashioning of the philosopher's stone is women's work, in which one of the first things is to keep the fire burning and the pot boiling in their homes, and this is more difficult than to keep our fire burning at the right degree of heat" (154). The narrative moves in and out of the domestic space, and it is not clear if the woman tending the fire is the same as the queen, who seems to have evaporated when the king is cut up with mercury. To focus solely on the female figure as a real female, and on alchemical texts or pictures as documents of real, social interactions, is to fail to see the twisted figurative relation in a treatise like Rouillac's. In fact, the female figure is central (even in its disappearance) to alchemy. It is not a *mere* symptom of the growing activity of real women in the sphere of labor, for instance.

Finally, the chemical wedding cannot be reduced to a social-bonding or monogamous liturgical ritual. It is a marriage of opposites before it is a marriage of a man and woman who will reproduce and form a stable pillar of society. That is why it is commonly depicted as an incestuous union of brother and sister or mother and son. In their opposition, the bride and groom are also predominantly the same.[8] The alchemical *coniunctio* is often interpreted as the philosophical uniting of form and matter. The soul must be separated from the body first so that it can transcend the gravitational pull of the material, or so that the subject can gain new knowledge. What matters most is the drawing of boundaries rather than the actual content—that which is being separated on one or the other side of the divide. To speak in such terms is to use the very language of philosophy, to bring alchemy into the realm of philosophy, to raise its tone.

Clavis Universalis

As a trope, the chemical marriage has been read into one lineage of onieric, or what some authors term steganographic, texts, from the *Romance of the Rose* through *The Hypnerotomachia Poliphili* of 1499; and in turn, through the French Renaissance "alchemical" readers Jacques Gohory (in his *Commentaire du Livre de la Fontaine Périlleuse* of 1572) and former goldsmith/engraver Béroalde de Verville (in his "transcription" of Colonna's text, the *Tableau des riches inventions* [1600], as well as in his *Voyage des princes fortunés* [1610]).[9] The French authors later had a significant influence on Johann Valentin Andreae's *Chemical Wedding of Christian Rosenkreutz*, as well as on a series of other related narratives.[10] The texts in question generally do not refer explicitly to the production of gold, confirming the earlier hypothesis that gold cannot be the single common denominator of the alchemical. The illustrations of these texts generally do not depict laboratories or the various instruments of transmutation. What they share in common is that they deploy readings or have themselves been read in an *alchemical key*.[11] In this sense, the footless man who stands before a garden closed off by multiple locks requiring multiple keys is a perfect emblem of the tradition (see Figure 2).

The Hypnerotomachia is divided into two parts. First, Poliphilo falls asleep in a wood and dreams that he is pursuing his beloved Polia through a series of exemplary, antique places, including the three doors associated with three metals. In the second part, the lovers are joined after a great deal of difficulty, anguish, and dismemberment. Polia is granted a voice and narrates her own version of the quest. Finally, Poliphilo wakes up and finds Polia has vanished. From one point of view, nothing is produced by the text—there is no fulfillment of the Great Work, no production of a golden son. It was all a complex antiquarian dream. Yet most readers (whether early modern or modern) have tended to ignore the narrative structure of the work and focus on particular images or passages. For Béroalde de Verville and his cohort, there is an alchemical feeling to this text, a kind of overarching tone that corresponds with what they know to be alchemy. As the first French translator, Jean Martin, wrote in his preface to the work, "You can imagine, gentlemen, that underneath the cover of this fiction lay many hidden things, which it is forbidden to reveal" (cited in Blunt 123; translation mine). Béroalde defines steganography as "the art of naively representing convenient concepts which, however, underneath their apparent meanings, hide other subjects."[12] During the seventeenth century some readers believed that the recipe for the philosopher's stone was concealed in the hieroglyphs of the text. The alchemical reading, then, is not on the surface of the text, but requires a certain will to interpret alchemically. While we tend to use the phrase "to be read in an alchemical key" in a commonplace sense, the key is actually a *key* element in the creation of the materiality of the text itself and deserves interrogation as such.[13]

The French alchemical readings emphasize the trope of the chemical marriage, and inasmuch as Colonna's text could be read as culminating at this point, we can begin to understand its peculiar reception. Béroalde's transcription, for instance, begins with a group of men on a quest for Xyrile (an anagram of the word elixir). However, by the end of the trials, only one of the men will become an adept, in search of the One True Woman. The focus on an arduous quest for a woman climaxing in a ritual marriage positions *The Hypnerotomachia Poliphili* in a lineage between *The Romance of the Rose* and the seventeenth-century Rosicrucian chemical romances.[14] The *Voyage des princes fortunés* explicitly superimposes the amorous and alchemical quests. The flame of the athanor (alchemical furnace) is the flame of love (Marquet 164). This line of logic has dominated the reception of Colonna's text as one that demands to be read in an alchemical key by modern figures including Jung and his disciples.

The Chemical Wedding of Christian Rosenkreutz

Turning, then, to the seventeenth-century variants of the bride and groom, we find the central influence of Rosicrucianism, and in particular, Johann Valentin Andreae, the principal subject of Frances Yates's book, *The Rosicrucian Enlightenment*. There is debate about whether or not Andreae is the author of the *Fama* (1614) and *Confessio* (1615), brief, nonnarrative accounts of outward changes in society. More widely accepted is his authorship of *The Chemical Wedding of Christian Rosenkreutz* (possibly written before the two treatises and then revised), a narrative of the inner transformation of the men belonging to a secret order (Dickson 30). Christian Rosenkreutz is supposed to have been a real person who lived in the fifteenth century. He made a pilgrimage to Jerusalem and learned many secrets along the way that he passed down to his followers. The brotherhood also acknowledged Paracelsus as an important influence.

According to the treatises, those tapped for membership would essentially be told, "Don't call us, we'll call you."

Yates reads the alchemical wedding against a few moments in history, specifically as a response to the strategic marriage of Frederick V of Württemberg to Princess Elizabeth, daughter of James I, in 1613; the much-hoped-for induction of Frederick into the English Order of the Garter; and the foundation of the Palatinate in Heidelberg before the outbreak of the Thirty Years War. For Yates, the (alchemical) marriage is related to an actual political-strategic union, making the treatises a kind of epithalamium. Yates's reading, while learned and lucid, does not address the older, more embedded and fundamental or material terms of the feminine presence in alchemy. Indeed, *The Rosicrucian Enlightenment* reflects the kind of commitments signaled by Ernest Gombrich in his book of laudatory essays, *Tributes*, where he characterizes Yates as a historian of hopes and reconciliation whose primary contribution was one of reconstructing lost alliances, friendships, and attempts at establishing peace in early modern Europe. Rosicrucianism, which Yates believes is a philosophical project but not an actual society of men, arises from just such a peaceful period. It is a movement, for her, of reform and tolerance. But her history of the movement also fails to account for broader issues of exchange, gender, and the status of gold or money in the economies under consideration. In essence, then, Yates's vision is an ideal one: marriage without economics.[15]

The Chemical Wedding is particularly interesting because it is organized as a narrative of day-by-day events.[16] Yet nothing could be further from a depiction of everyday life: the seven days are purely symbolic increments. Moreover, the narrator vacillates between his absolute control of the material and sequence of events, and his submission to them, as in a dream. Of course, the onieric trope is a common one in alchemy, as in texts such as *The Romance of the Rose* and *The Hypnerotomachia Poliphili*, to say nothing of the writings of Zosimos.[17] But in the case of Andreae's wedding, this function is not explicitly written into a frame for the story, and the anxieties are of a different order. Whether or not the text is a fiction or joke (*ludibrium*), as Andreae hinted, the "two core ideas—the idea of a world reformation and the brotherhood of the learned—were certainly rooted in contemporary Lutheranism" (Dickson 11). Andreae seems to have invented the name of Christian Rosenkreutz, derived from the family coat of arms (in turn derived from Luther) of the rose cross.

The narrative begins on Maundy Thursday, as the narrator receives a visit from a Virgin (an evangelist) bearing an invitation to attend a royal wedding. Soon after receiving the invitation, Rosenkreutz falls asleep and dreams that he is a "captive wretch": "I, together with a numberless multitude of men lay fettered with great chains in a dark dungeon, where in without the least glimpse of Light, we swarmed like Bees over one another, and thus rendred each others affliction more grievous" (Andreae 9). Information is revealed sparingly. The author has no control over what happens or when the Virgin will appear to the men. Her presence brings tranquility. The bachelors may not know the place to which they are moving, but they sense that they are being led there as part of a larger plan. The narrative is highly paratactic and repetitive.

Later in the story, after being teased by virgins, the bachelor guests are shown a curtain behind which sit the King and Queen. The episode is quite peculiar, needless to say. Does this mean the royal couple is already married? If so, when did the ceremony take place, and why weren't the men invited to witness the union as they (and we) might have expected? The men are (again) presented to the King, and the Virgin says: "That to honour your Royal Majesties (most gracious King and Queen) these lords here present have adventured hither with peril of Body and Life; your Majesties have reason to rejoyce, especially since the greatest part are qualified for the inlarging of your Majesties Estates and Empire, as you will find the same by a most gratious and particular examination of each of them" (Andreae 101). The curtained chamber where the royals sit may be an alchemical laboratory or an athanor. The men move into another room containing three *symbolic* kings and queens.

Then the bachelors witness a theatrical performance. Various allegorical figures parade across the stage, and during the last (seventh) act, a bridegroom and bride (prince and princess) are dressed finely. All the spectators cry out, "*Vivat sponsus, vivat sponsa.*" "So that by this comedy they did with all congratulate our King and Queen in the most stately manner" (118). In essence, then, it is through their spectatorship of the play that the adepts actually participate in a marriage ceremony (of the "real" King and Queen).

After a series of trials, the men are inducted into a noble order, while the narrator is punished for gazing on Venus and is forced to take over guard duties from a porter. The text ends abruptly, without closure. As some commentators have surmised, it is possible that Andreae does not want to recount a "return home" from a spiritual experience of salvation. In essence, the text cannot end, because the end of the text is unfathomable. An alternative suggestion is that someone else comes along and uncovers Venus, freeing the narrator just as he had freed the porter (487). The chemical wedding repeats itself endlessly.

John Montgomery maps the entire work according to a precise organizational chart. The first three days are grouped together as the "nigredo" and "albedo" phases of the work, comprised of the subheadings Distillation, Calcination, Putrefaction, Solution-Dissolution, Coagulation, Vivification, and Multiplication-Projection. These correspond, in turn, to four different levels of interpretation from the perspective of the character of Christian Rosenkreutz: the microcosmic dream, the macrocosmic pilgrimage, theological meaning, psychological (personal) meaning. For days four through seven, the same stages correspond to the microcosmic drama (that the bachelors witness in the palace), the macrocosmic wedding (the events surrounding the King and Queen), followed by, again, theology, and psychology. Such perfect architecture may, however, distract us from the narrative, from seeing where it falls apart or seems especially illogical.

We may certainly follow the coherent story of a group of men who are invited to undergo a series of trials to determine their faith. We find a tremendous anxiety about the lack of control over external events in the sequence of the narrative, and about the time allotted to narration itself—a fear that the narrative present might be interrupted or the dream dispelled if the narrator allows himself the luxury of further comment. And while this is clearly a form of alibi against the revelation of information, it is a highly significant element of the way the narrative is structured. What is the relation between the allegorical play and the larger action of the narrative? When does the alchemical process begin or end? Alchemy happens to the narrator and his companions. It is not something they willfully engage in. They are led about, and, it is presumed, they will return to civic life, enlightened and faithful. The author disavows all responsibility for the descriptions, sequence of events, images—all the literary details. They are spread before him, and he acts as a passive recorder. Yet such a fiction is hardly sustainable, for the text is so exquisitely specific in its details. We find a fundamental tension between the pretense of passivity and the rhetorical activity of the text itself. This tension cannot easily be resolved simply by lining up the narrative against a symbolic decoding key.

The various texts under consideration within the rubric of "chemical weddings," particularly those affiliated with Rosicrucianism, have as their central narrative event a wedding, which is rarely described as a recognizable or expected ritual. The protagonist of the text may witness a series of actions, but he is rarely an agent of narrative advancement. He may tend a sealed glass vessel in which the wedding takes place. Like an initiate who is tapped for a secret society, he may have some idea of his chosen status, but he is uncertain about what awaits him. He is sworn to secrecy, yet he writes; he reaps riches, but he disavows wealth. His participation in a wedding (even as voyeur) signals passage into a fraternity where (real) women have no place.

Alchemy, or what we might call a least common denominator of the alchemical, is radically structured around the couple, a duality of opposing tendencies. Can we say that capitalism destroys the mystical marriage and replaces it with a more pragmatic form of union? Or is the mystical itself displaced onto narrative in the Rosicrucian tradition? We see this diachronic evacuation most clearly in the film *The Vanishing*, and particularly in its American remake. Gender as such may have little to do with the marriage. In the next chapter of this book, I turn to a portrait of a (chemical) marriage that draws together many of the issues raised up to this point.

Excursus: Mercury

At times *she* is a bride, wearing her ambivalence like a crown (the sign of alchemical mercury appears literally on her head as a diadem). She is the sum of Diana (the crescent moon) plus Venus, in some variants. Yet at the same time, Gold speaks in *his* own golden voice and explains: "Mercury is my brother; he is female and I am male" (*Hermetical Triumph* 13).

Mercury can be a dog or wolf (if emaciated, the dog may be said to represent "old" Mercury, close to death) or as a winged putto on the top of a wheel (young Mercury) (Calvesi 1993, 116–17).

At times *he* is present as the winged messenger of the gods, god of medicine in its healing and destructive senses, the *pharmakon*, and the hermetic. Of all the Greco-Roman gods, Mercury is perhaps the most polyvalent, both in diachronous terms (in his ancient historical development, from the Egyptian Thot to the Greek Hermes—from the message-bearer (*suer* or *sur* [sound, talk] and *rhema* [word]) to Roman Mercury (from *merx* [reward, the mercantile]), and in synchronous terms (at any given moment in mythography, he fulfills multiple functions). Is the sign of (feminine, alchemical) mercury, the slippery metal that is liquid at room temperature, present in the acoustical homonym of Mercury (the god) or vice versa? Or in Mercury the planet, whose ascendancy might be said, in various alchemical texts, to favorably influence the outcome of a given attempt at completion of the Great Work? In some alchemical weddings, Mercury participates as a third party (like Goethe's Captain), as a glue, or as the sperm or seminal fluid. Weddings take place in "mercurial sea waters."

At times, Mercury is king. Michael Maier's *Lusus serius, quo Hermes sive Mercurius Rex Mundanorum Omnium sub homine existentium* (1616)

FIGURE 14. Frontispiece from Michael Maier, *Lusus serius, quo Hermes sive Mercurius Rex Mundanorum Omnium sub homine existentium* (1616). Research Library, The Getty Research Institute, Los Angeles, CA.

establishes the sovereignty of Mercury "over all things." Yet the reader of this text first encounters an engraved frontispiece in which various representatives of the animal kingdom appear before a king on a throne (Figure 14). Given the work's title, one would expect that this king would be identified with Mercury. However, taking in the seven representatives, we realize that Mercury stands in position number seven, at the right-hand side of the image. In other words, we are led to believe that Mercury is king, yet there is a human king, and he is not Mercury. During the course of the treatise, each element is allowed time to tout its own virtues and usefulness to mankind, but when it comes time for Mercury, he announces that he presides over all of the beings that have come before him. Mercury is mother and father. He gives other metals their splendor and makes them useful to humanity. Without Mercury, the other metals would have no (use) value. Perhaps a seat on the throne would restrict him to a fixed position of sovereignty. He reigns, but he must be mobile.

Mercury-Hermaphrodite

Poliphilo comes upon a marvelous fountain of Venus populated by singing nymphs about halfway through the *Hypnerotomachia Poliphili*. Seven ornate columns of precious stones form a circle, and in one is sculpted a hermaphrodite boy ("*uno puerulo hermaphrodito*"). Amor strikes Poliphilo with an arrow, and he burns with desire for Polia, the object of his quest. He describes his condition as follows: "I almost felt as if I had been changed into another physical form. And such a transformation seemed incomprehensible except by comparison to the embrace of Hermaphrodite and Salmacis in the lively and fresh pond, where they found themselves transformed from two sexes into a single form" (Colonna 360). In his fantasy, Poliphilo is joined with Polia in an embrace, so that they dissolve into a *single* form, like Hermaphroditus with Salmacis.

In Greco-Roman mythology, the god Mercury was raised by Vulcan, who taught him the arts of fire. His tryst with Venus, for example, produces not merely the hermaphrodite, but also vitriol, a compound of metals—the philosophical vitriol that turns all metals into gold and dispenses the "sovereign medicine of the human body" (Maillard 122). Mercury is the father of Pan (in some mythographic strains, born from Penelope), the god, like his father, of all things. French Renaissance alchemists figured Pan wearing the twin crowns of the sun and moon. Hermaphroditus, as the son of Mercury and Venus, is also "all" (both) sexes, and in some treatises this is linked with the theme of the supposed bisexuality of God and of Christ. As mercury takes on the characteristics of other elements with which it is mixed, it has no sex of its own (Maillard 119).

In Ovid's *Metamorphoses* (the obvious reference for *The Hypnerotomachia*) Hermaphroditus, the son of Hermes and Aphrodite (Mercury and Venus), is not a being of both sexes, but rather a male offspring who happens to bear traces (in his physique, but also, more significantly, in his name) of both parents. In this sense, his name might be considered a guarantee of the very legitimacy of his divine heritage.

As a boy, Hermaphroditus leaves Mount Ida to seek adventure. He travels to Asia Minor where he encounters Salmacis. She makes advances and is rejected by Hermaphroditus. The cool river waters are a greater temptation for him, as they are for Narcissus and Diana. The gods, to punish Hermaphroditus for his reticence in love, agree to extend the figure of the embrace to its extreme conclusion, binding the pair into one body; in Ovidian terms, "They were no longer two, nor such as to be called, one, woman, and one, man. They seemed neither, and yet both" (*Nec duo sunt et forma duplex, nec femina dici/nec puer ut possit, neutrumque et utrumque videntur*) (Ovid IV, 378–79). In evoking the Ovidian story, Colonna ignores the portion that concerns Salmacis's uncontrolled desire, her lack of interest in hunting, and the frigid rejection of her advances by Hermaphroditus. All that remains is the emblematic embrace in which Salmacis traps the boy.

In fact, the temporal disjunction between the earlier phase of the boy's life and the period after he is punished and bound with Salmacis appears rather unique to Ovid. Ovid's apparent purpose is *not* to discuss sexual difference, but rather to focus on one specific geological problem: "How the fountain of Salmacis came to its ill-repute, how it enervates men who bathe there with its enfeebling waters and renders them soft and weak" (IV, 285–86). The Salmacis to which Ovid refers at this point is not (only) the female figure locked in the hermaphroditic embrace, but (also) a stream in Halicarnassus believed to exercise certain powers of impotency. Ovid repeats several times the notion of "softening" as the key to Hermaphroditus's transformation. This is the punishment that others will face as well: "Whoever comes to this pool as a man will leave a half-man" (IV, 385–86). Any man who bathes in the river will become a half-man (but not half-woman!), and his limbs will soften. Initially, then, the curse relates to the natural powers of this river to render a man impotent, but nothing is said about making a dual-sexed being. Indeed, Ovid uses the word *semimas*, "castrated male" or "eunuch" (the word has the same meaning as *semimasculus*, and in both cases, the feminine "half" of the figure is eliminated— cut out—rather than built up). *Semivir* is used elsewhere in Ovid to refer to a man who has been turned into a half-beast. It does not, then, mean "half man and half woman," even if the dictionary definition of *semimas* is "hermaphrodite." Hermaphroditus in Ovid's tale loses his male voice, but he does not necessarily take on female characteristics, nor does he become a hermaphrodite in the modern biological sense. It is only by reading the tale closely, and ignoring the anatomical definition of the term, that we can realize the evacuation of the feminine from Ovid's tale, which takes place alongside the diminishment of the masculine.

Overall, several elements in the Ovidian line of the myth make it exemplary for alchemy in the context of early modern literature: the presence of Mercury (albeit as a trace, from a previous generation), the tight embrace, the dissolution in water, the death of the male and female as separate entities, the promise of sterility for those who come after. The figure of the hermaphrodite is employed by Francesco Colonna as a trope to describe the tight embrace of the nymph Polia and her beloved Poliphilo; simultaneously it raises a series of questions about generation and presence. For some readers, the myth is primarily about the geography of Greece; for others it is a tale about unrequited desire; for still others, it is about the *coniunctio oppositorum* of the two parents, with little emphasis on the offspring. When we look for the stable element that binds together the variants, we find it in the tight embrace and the excessive fulfillment of sameness.

Mercury's Complaint

In a masque titled "Mercury Vindicated from the Alchemists at Court," Ben Jonson staged a comic invective in which Mercury complains about the many processes and forms to which he is subjected:

> I am their crude and their sublimate, their precipitate and their unctuous, their male and their female, sometimes their hermaphrodite; what they list to style me. It is I that am corroded and exalted and sublimed and reduced and fetched over and filtered and washed and wiped; what between their salts and their sulfurs, their oils and their tartars, their brines and their vinegars, you might take me out now a soused Mercury, now a salted Mercury, now a smoked and dried Mercury, now a powdered and pickled Mercury. (cited in Abraham 1998, 74)

Poor Mercury. He is a floating signifier, impossible to pin down. Philosophy needs Mercury in order to posit the fixed as fixed: the sun or fixed matter that only knows itself in contrast to the volatile. In this sense, the man who presides over the wedding as witness is there as a third term that guarantees the fixedness of matter. He may act as a standard, like gold. The so-called philosophical alchemists distinguish between common mercury (Hg) and "philosophical mercury" composed of a combination of sulfur and *argent vive* (quicksilver, or "first mercury"; that which has the power, initially, to dissolve matter or the feminine). "Our mercury," as the philosophical-alchemical language would have it, stands apart from the vulgar herd. In order to further distinguish "our mercury," the philosophers will speak about its dualistic tendencies rather than ascribing to it a state of unitary or radical purity. Like the *pharmakon* of Derrida's reading of the Platonic text, "our mercury" is simultaneously destructive and creative, a mediator. Yet any attempt to retrace Mercury's genealogy to some originary and absolute term is vexed, primarily because it would involve the removal of a stable, objective, and knowable chemical compound (mercury; Hg) from the multiple narratives of origin, truth, and secrets in which it/he/she is embedded.

§ 3 A Chemical Couple

> Every new aspect of a science involves a revolution in the technical
> terms of that science. This is best shown by Chemistry, where the
> whole of the terminology is radically changed about once in twenty
> years, and where you will hardly find a single organic compound that
> has not gone through a whole series of different names.
>
> —Frederick Engels, preface to the English edition of
> Marx's *Capital*, vol. 1, 4)

The Scene: Portrait of Lavoisier and his Wife (Figure 15)

The year: 1788

The characters: Antoine Lavoisier (and his wife)

The place: Lavoisier's study

The time: Day

The room is suffused with a uniform light by which the chemist writes and
the painter paints. At first glance, the time of day does not bear mention. We
would not give this detail the time of day, so to speak. The light is invisible
as in an artificial or theatrical setting. But on closer inspection, we notice the
crosshatched blot of white paint on the large glass vessel that lies on its side
on the bottom right.[1] Light enters from an unidentified, off-scene source—a
window or series of windows, we presume—at the upper left of the room.
We are quite familiar with this compositional structure. Similarly, we know
that the dollop of paint on the clear *vas* in the corner represents both a reflection of the window (an "effect of the real") and the clarity of the glass itself (a representational convention such that we might find it not only in a
painting, but even in an etching, in order to indicate depth and mass of clear
glass). Such observations can be made prior to any more developed symbolism surrounding the clear vessel or its place in the scene.

The vessel forms a diagonal link with a fold in the rich red velvet of the
tablecloth, leading to Madame de Lavoisier's arm draped over her husband.
Lavoisier's cocked pen is almost parallel to the arm. The couple appears

FIGURE 15.   Jacques-Louis David, *Portrait of Lavoisier and His Wife*, 1788. Oil on canvas, 102 ¼ × 76 ⅝ in. (259.7 × 194.6 cm). Purchase, Mr. and Mrs. Charles Wrightsman Gift, in honor of Everett Fahy, 1977 (1977.1). Art, New York, NY, U.S.A. Photo credit: Image copyright © The Metropolitan Museum of Art / Art Resource, NY (ART322961).

posed, their limbs awkwardly attenuated. Even if they had assumed such a position for David, it is difficult to sustain the idea that they remained this way, day after day, during the completion of this masterful work. So, as with most portraiture, we imagine that the artist spent considerable time rendering their (specific) faces, but filled in their (generic) bodies without them, "on his own time," so to speak. In other words, portraiture of this type is based on the idea of a beheading: the proleptic figure of Lavoisier's own death. Naturally, however, any violence that might be thought to pertain to this portrait, or portraiture as a genre, is elided in the pleasant experience of immediate viewing.[2]

The room itself is rather bare. There is little extraneous decoration besides flat columns on the severe gray wall, or rather, all decoration is supplied by the (necessary) objects of science. Madame looks outward toward the painter / the viewer. Lavoisier looks up at his wife. His left hand appears to be in motion: perhaps he has lifted it to greet her. To the left of the composition, on a chair, sits a sketchbook. The painted surface is matte, particularly when compared with works in the "Dutch manner" (ter Borch's *Consultation* [Figure 3], for example). The most luminous objects in the room are the instruments themselves: the barometer in a leather case that Lavoisier commissioned from a master craftsman; a magnifying glass; a convex mirror; scales; calorimeters, thermometers, aerometers; and so on.[3] Like many other gentlemen of his era, including the scientist Lazzaro Spallanzani, who will reappear in Chapter 5, Lavoisier was a great collector. He relied on his instruments for his work, but he simultaneously displayed them, for himself and for others who might visit his study. These objects are the tools of his trade, but they are also beautiful objects of curiosity such as one might find in a *Wunderkammer*. The portrait is a display of a great man and his attributes, one of which is his wife.

Scientific Subject

Antoine Lavoisier came from wealth, and his approach to maintaining it was eminently practical. Like his German rival, Georg Stahl, Lavoisier observed fermentation processes to learn about chemical transformations. Such experiments had a mercantile application in alcoholic drinks. He analyzed mineral waters, helped develop street lighting for Paris, and tested the quality of state tobacco. Lavoisier advised the government on soil cultivation, chemical fumigation of prisons, water purification, and uniformity of weights and measures. He denounced the occult experiments of Franz Mesmer; he dismissed the use of divining rods and extraction of gold from vine ashes as nonsense. As a pragmatist, then, Lavoisier is not unlike the early modern alchemist retained as a polymath advisor to the king. He supported the Trudaines, Lafayette, Franklin, Du Pont de Nemours, and Turgot, who appointed him controller of munitions in 1775. He was thus associated with the shift in the manufacture of gunpowder from a private monopoly to a government operation. A long history of graft and rumors of corruption surrounded this shift, which came to a head around the time that David completed the portrait.[4] Lavoisier was decapitated by a Revolutionary tribunal three years after the portrait was painted. The sentence was based primarily on his role as a tax farmer. The tax farm was an institution established in the sixteenth century to collect duties for the coffers of monarchy. By the late eighteenth century the general farmers were seen as tyrants and the corporate general farm *(ferme générale)* as an exemplary symbol of inegalitarian society, hence the executions of many of its former members. Ironically, it was precisely the tax income that allowed Lavoisier the freedom to pursue his scientific work. The painter captures the couple at a moment before this turbulence was in the air.

In the portrait, Lavoisier presents himself as a dignified scientist. While the untidy desk of an alchemist (or even that of ter Borch's ambiguous doctor analyzing urine, Ryckaert's parthenogenesist [Figure 16], or Brueghel/Gallé's crank father, [Figure 4]) is typically depicted holding a skull, an hourglass, or a broken vessel, these symbols of transience are, in essence, replaced in the portrait by nonsymbolic (diegetic) objects of science, well disposed. Lavoisier's rationalism is thus figured precisely in contrast to earlier (alchemical) iconology.

The modern idea of the impersonal, nonauthoritative mode of speaking about the natural world derives, obviously, from Descartes. However, it took a long time for Cartesian thought to penetrate to analytic methods. Ironically, the new chemistry was so far-reaching as to potentially negate Lavoisier's authorship of it: this is a primary tension that extends well beyond the temporal and spatial limits of David's canvas. Nevertheless, the viewer of the painting confronts a Cartesian paradox: either nomenclature reflects the genius of one man, or else it is the truth of nature, and then the "author" does not receive credit for it. In some of his works Lavoisier did act as "author," or rhetorician. He was responsible for an epistemological shift rather than just a new theory or method, "and this shift did in fact eliminate

FIGURE 16.   David Ryckaert, *Scholar with Homunculus in Glass Phial,* seventeenth century. Reiss-Engelhorn Museen Mannheim. Photo credit: Jean Christen.

the concept of the scientific author in its then-accepted meaning" (Anderson 150). As Étienne Bonnot de Condillac noted, the "natural" language of modern science maintains its control by its very anonymity: "It is a naturalness that depends on a ruse, in which the author who created the method gives up his authorship in exchange for the institutionalization of his practice" (cited in Anderson 151). The painting attests to the genius of the scientist (pictured with his muse), yet it places a certain authority in the instruments. It does not depict any particular experiment or document any particular discovery. It is a summation of Lavoisier's status: the very fact that he merits such a grand portrait is itself the signified rather than anything specific about the research. He is writing, rather than working with instruments, so already the painting depicts a moment of narration or explication, after something has been proven. Prior to the period of the portrait, Lavoisier's most important published contribution to modern science was, in fact, in the realm of nomenclature and classification. The portrait can be said, then, to respond to an epistemological shift in the very relation between knowledge and writing.[5]

Lavoisier's *Traité elementaire de chimie* is both pedagogical and scientific, and this is the work he was finishing as the portrait was under completion. Like J. J. Becher, Lavoisier acknowledges the importance of teaching his ideas to colleagues and students in a clear and direct style, but his work is also suffused with a rhetoric of originality that we do not find in alchemical writings. In the *Traité*, then, Lavoisier does not discuss the elementary parts of matter. Instead, he writes:

> Everything that can be said about the number and the nature of the elements is limited, from my point of view, to purely metaphysical discussions. . . . I will therefore content myself with saying that if, by the term 'elements,' one means to designate the simple and indivisible molecules that make up the bodies, it is highly likely that we do not know what they are. (cited in Anderson 180 n.203)

Thus, Lavoisier confronts matter, not as a primitive principal or element, but as it can be known through chemical reaction. Combination was his main interest. He includes a preliminary section that cites Condillac and describes how theory works. This is followed by sections on gases, combustion, oxygen (acids), formations of salts, and experimental instruments and procedures. The work ends with a catalog and drawings (by Madame de Lavoisier) of the very instruments that can be used in the work of combination, and that appear in the portrait. Madame's drawings—the "practical side" of the art—resemble the illustrations one often finds in alchemical treatises. But as Lavoisier makes clear in his work, technology is subordinate to philosophy. Even with good instruments, the charlatans will make mistakes. Indeed, many of the chemist's tools—including calorimeter, pyrometer, gazometer, and balances—were made in the 1780s, after his theory was already in wide circulation. His most original contributions were not in the intermediary sections that treat specific chemical theories, but in the outline of a rigorous method.

In the portrait, Lavoisier is perhaps writing his *Traité*, meant for a broad public as well as for the specialized scientific community. The point of his pen is touching the paper, even though Lavoisier has turned his gaze upward toward his wife. We should, perhaps, find this strange, for while the pen may indeed touch the paper, at the moment he stops writing to acknowledge the entrance of his wife, there is another event that is taking place beyond the picture plane—the painting itself. That is, the fiction that he has been immersed in his work and is only interrupted at the moment of Madame's entrance requires us to negate the complex and distracting preparations of the painterly apparatus. For the pen on paper to make sense, we must believe in the fourth wall, dispelling any ideas of an interaction with David.

The pages of the book extend off the table. In genre painting, this sort of gesture—the illusionistic cartouche or text that seems to penetrate into a third dimension—often serves as a demonstration of painterly expertise. One would normally lift up the pen (with the eyes). Did the chemist have his head leaning on his left hand (like the figure of Melancholia, so familiar from alchemical illustrations)? Or was his hand on the paper, stabilizing it as he wrote? The play between the fiction of spontaneity and the long process of making a complex portrait seems to be figured in the paradox of the pen. While pen touches paper, the ink does not run as we might expect. For the writing that we see on the page is even, uniform (pure writing—words that we recognize as words but cannot actually read). A lie materializes: the scientist is in the middle of writing, captured unawares, yet his pen has no ink. It is not a real pen, but a simulation of a pen that could potentially put all of the instrumentation in the room into question. Is it all a staged fiction? Can one actually work at the moment of the muse's entrance, or is this, in fact, the moment when all work is suspended?

Lavoisier's Wife

David's portrait of Lavoisier and his wife was commissioned by Madame de Lavoisier. The pair was married when Marie-Anne-Pierrette Paulze was only thirteen years old (so that she could avoid an arranged marriage to another man). She devoted her life to bolstering her husband's career.[6] In spite of her tender age, she grew up quickly and soon managed to oversee a household and host famous visitors like Benjamin Franklin. The chemical couple is a myth—just like Flamel and Perrenelle, Pierre and Marie Curie—but a myth that is key to the way science is performed, and its relation with sociability of the eighteenth century.[7]

One critic captioned David's portrait as follows: "If it's all the same to you dear, I'd rather give the revolutionary celebrations a miss and stay in and finish my experiments."[8] The characters in Goethe's *Elective Affinities* behave as if the Revolution had never happened—or better, they combine and separate as if inside a hermetically sealed retort. "Nothing gets done for the general good except through the exercise of unrestricted sovereign power," as the Captain says (Goethe 44). In Hawthorne's "The Birthmark," the scientist Alymer "left his laboratory to the care of an assistant, cleared his fine countenance from the furnace smoke, washed the stain of acids from his fingers, and persuaded a beautiful woman to become his wife" (Hawthorne 47). Spiritual affinities are not always compatible with chemical ones, but in Alymer's case, he aspires to intertwine his love of a woman with his love of science.

From a narrative point of view, it seems as if Madame de Lavoisier has just entered her husband's study. A former pupil of David, she illustrated many of her husband's works and took notes on his experiments. Her presence in the study is therefore not unexpected. But does she really interrupt her husband at this point, or has she come in to show support while he is painted? Albert Boime notes that her sketches are "relegated to a subsidiary area of the painting, and she is pictured mainly as a decorative adjunct to the scientific world of her husband" (Boime 414). Does David underappreciate her contributions? Since Madame commissioned the portrait, thus disturbing his routine with the presence of the artist, it seems almost redundant to say that she interrupts her husband's writing. Naturally all of the political turmoil surrounding the chemist cannot be retrospectively read into the painting. The painter Jacques-Louis David was part of a liberal club in 1789 that advocated moderate reform rather than revolution. Both David and Lavoisier discredit sloppy work. They shared the idea that the scientific model could serve as the basis of new society dispensing laws through representative assembly. The painting shimmers with clarity and rationality. Madame looks at David, as if to say, "You may proceed." Her husband looks at her with slight bemusement. Yes, that's right. He'd forgotten they agreed to have the portrait done. He was so absorbed in his work. In contrast to this approach, Mary Vidal argues that Madame's outward gaze serves to cement the bond of science and art. "Marie is also the site as well as the initiator of the two men's perceptions: as an aesthetic being who is studied by the artist and as a beautiful natural being who is intensely beheld by the scientist" (Vidal 620).

In Hawthorne's work, Alymer's wife, Georgiana, only enters the laboratory for the first time after her husband determines to rid her of a birthmark on her otherwise perfect face:

> The first thing that struck her eye was the furnace, that hot and feverish worker, with the intense glow of its fire, which by the quantities of soot clustered above it seemed to have been burning for ages. There was a distilling apparatus in full operation. Around the room were retorts, tubes, cylinders, crucibles, and other apparatus of chemical research. An electrical machine stood ready for immediate

use. The atmosphere felt oppressively close, and was tainted with gaseous odors which had been tormented forth by the processes of science. The severe and homely simplicity of the apartment, with its naked walls and brick pavement, looked strange, accustomed as Georgiana had become to the fantastic elegance of her boudoir. (Hawthorne 63)

Her curiosity, her entrance into the realm of the scientist, also marks the start of her downfall. She drinks Alymer's concoction from a clear vessel. The experiment is a technical success: the birthmark is gone. But having reached a state of utter perfection, Georgiana dies.

Phlogiston and the Glass Vessel

The (scientific) vessel speaks to a series of experiments around the question of phlogiston, or "fire stuff." Is matter inherently capable of motion, or does it have to be pushed? Stahl thought phlogiston was both the matter of fire and the principle of its motion. Because it was impossible to grasp phlogiston, it should be defined based on its principle characteristic—hence *phlogistós* (Greek for "inflammable"). Stahl believed that phlogiston was present in all matter in some degree and could travel through the air. Before Lavoisier, it was believed that calcination or burning of metals, candles, and even animal breathing released phlogiston into the air. Those like Joseph Priestly, who refused to give up the phlogiston theory, had a metaphysical, or rather, a theological, belief that weight was not a fundamental property of matter. In 1772—more than a decade prior to the portrait—Lavoisier burned phosphorus and sulfur in a glass container. He noted that when they were calcified, they increased in weight. Such an observation went against the phlogiston theory, which presupposed that elements should lose weight when fire stuff is released into the air. In order to successfully perform this experiment, Lavoisier heated the glass vessel to the highest temperature possible in order to achieve complete combustion. Lavoisier's axiom is that nothing is created in nature. In the context of an experiment, an equal quantity of matter exists both before and after; the quality and quantity of the elements remain precisely the same. This provided a rational basis for accounting and measuring matter in all fields making use of chemical operations.

For historical perspective, this scientific, technical and economic appraisal of the principle of conservation of matter needs to be supplemented by the more general consideration of the eighteenth-century issue regarding nature's way to operate independently, without Divine intervention. The principle of conservation of matter gave powerful support to those who sought to comprehend nature as eternal self-moving matter. Epitomizing the materialist conception of nature in the sense that there is nothing prior to matter in motion, it represents one of the intellectual landmarks of the Age of Enlightenment. (Teich 363–80)

In what was perhaps his most significant experiment, Lavoisier brought hydrogen and oxygen together in a glass balloon like the one that lies on the floor in the portrait. To this he added a spark, and the mix gave rise to water. Lavoisier is thus held responsible for naming oxygen and recognizing it as an element, but he also found a way to measure the quantities of hydrogen and oxygen present in water, paving the way for the theory of conservation of matter, which he stated after the completion of the portrait, in 1789.[9]

Lavoisier believed in caloric, not as something real like oxygen and hydrogen, but not unreal like phlogiston. Its effects could be measured. Caloric was real for Lavoisier in the way gravity was real for Newton. It was a "mentally accomplished materialization" of a measurable entity (Anderson 141). Lavoisier did not care if caloric was materially real or not. He measured the relative quantity of caloric present in a given substance based on temperature. And temperature itself is related not to weight but to indirect measures of volume. Caloric combines in a particular quantity with each particular substance in the world. Like "affinity" (the term that Goethe drew upon in his discussion of chemical marriages), caloric is a fictional entity that allows one to read meaning in a series of experiments. Lavoisier, who preferred analysis performed "in the wet way" (*par voie humide*), believed that weightless caloric caused state changes, not chemical changes. In spite of the fact that we now know this idea to be incorrect, Lavoisier's positivist rhetoric surrounding caloric is closer to modern scientific knowledge than Pierre Joseph Macquer's.[10] Macquer thought that the phlogiston theory was a general theory of science. It is possible, then, to read the glass vessel in the portrait as a challenge to this theory. Simultaneously, by reflecting the light of a window off to the side, it is a sign of the painter's mastery of illusion.[11]

Ter Borch's *Consultation* (Figure 3) may help us think about David's portrait. In ter Borch's work, the desk is also filled with the objects of the trade (which also potentially double as *vanitas* symbols). A container lies on the floor in the lower right corner, but it is broken. In Dutch art with a strong symbolic presence, as any student of an introductory art history course knows, the overturned (and broken) vessel stands for the vanity of human endeavors. In the iconography of melancholy, the alchemical *vas* may be figured as the skull or occiput, the very head of the maker himself. Portraits of the melancholic holding a skull (for instance, Domenico Fetti's 1620 *Malinconia*) are thus typically read as portraits of individuals holding the alchemical *vas*. But the *vas* is also like a uterus, and the uterus was depicted as a round bottle with a narrow neck in various works. (Let us keep in mind, then, that Madame de Lavoisier bore no children.)

The refraction and corpuscularity of light were, of course, topics of considerable scientific debate in the period prior to the portrait. The principle of least action supposed that light would travel along the path of least time and distance. Descartes, Leibniz, and Newton all discussed these issues. In the idea of least action, each corpuscle of light knows where it will end up, and then it calculates its trajectory. In this sense, the light on the globe is a sign of God's design.[12]

The glass vessel in the portrait is a summa of these various registers.

The Portrait in the Public Eye

In its cost (7,000 livres) and size (259.7 × 194.6 cm) the portrait rivaled history paintings of the period. David originally intended it for inclusion in the Salon of 1789, but this coincided with the period of the gunpowder scandal, and the portrait was deemed too controversial.[13] Instead, David substituted his *Paris and Helen*, which bears a certain compositional similarity to the Lavoisier portrait. The substituted work also depicts the relationship between a seated male and a female who leans over him. As in the Lavoisier portrait, so in *Paris and Helen* the background information is limited, and the room is punctuated by vertical columns. There is an unseen light source from the upper left-hand corner of the work, yet the room looks entirely sealed, like a tomb. Historical figures—frozen in a mausoleum—displace and mitigate any possible anxiety about politics in this portrait of an intimate relationship.[14] The unmade bed, the lyre, and the languid pose might even be said to represent the libidinous "underside" of the chemical portrait. It seems as if Helen is leaning on Paris to hold her up as she is spent from love. He stares into her eyes. Although they are centered, they are not aware of the painter. He is from another era, peering onto a stage.

If painting, especially as signified in Diderot's writings of the 1750s and 1760s, sought to negate the possibility that someone was standing before the canvas, in the Lavoisier canvas it is difficult to forget that the beholder is David, not just anyone. By their very nature, majestic portraits of this type seem to embody theatricality rather than absorption, in Michael Fried's famous distinction. He writes:

> More nakedly and as it were categorically than the conventions of any other genre, those of the portrait call for exhibiting a subject, the sitter, to the public gaze; put another way, the basic action depicted in a portrait is the sitter's presentation of himself or herself to be beheld. It follows that the portrait as a genre was singularly ill equipped to comply with the demand that a painting negate or neutralize the presence of the beholder, a demand that I have tried to show became a matter of urgent, if for the most part less than fully conscious, concern for French art critics during these years. (Fried 110)

Diderot even criticized a portrait of himself by Louis-Michel (exhibited at the Salon of 1767) in which he is shown holding a pen to paper looking up from his work. Diderot felt he looked more like a diplomat than a philosopher, since he is not captured deep in thought, but rather, in an artificial way (112). It would have been better if the painter left his subject alone, "abandoned to his reveries" (113).

Compositional Doubles

Paris and Helen is certainly not unique in its compositional analogy to David's portrait. A female figure leans over a male figure at work in the frontispiece to Gerard de Lairesse's 1707 treatise on painting, *Het groot schilderboek* (Figure 5). Unlike Van Mander, the major Dutch theorist before him (whose treatise dates from 1604), Lairesse believed that painting was not so much about inborn talent as it was about diligence and the application of mathematical rules. A strict generic hierarchy—with history painting at the pinnacle—would elevate Dutch art above its current predilection for the picturesque and for undiluted imitations of reality. David may well have known Lairesse's treatise, which exalts history painting while accepting the market for genre works in Holland as an unfortunate inevitability. Although the frontispiece may have had no direct influence on David, a comparison of the works stages how the muse (painting/Clio) and the model (the wife/painting) are one and the same—or rather, the feminine both leans on the male (artist/chemist) like the muse, and serves as the object of the painterly gaze. Only by linking the portrait with the complex iconography of Historia and Pictura can we fully appreciate the inextricability of the feminine, scientific work, and painting on display here.[15]

The Flemish painter David Ryckaert's portrait of an alchemist (Figure 16) combines the untidy desk littered with *vanitas* symbols, the vase (here containing not urine, but the coming-to-form of a homunculus), and the wife. Like Madame de Lavoisier, the wife peers over the shoulder of her seated husband.[16] In Ryckaert's work, the alchemist wears an expression of horror. The glass contains a little man, or perhaps the devil. The wife raises her hand in dismay. Meanwhile, in the corner, a child blows a pig's bladder, a common symbol of futility.

These examples help us to think of the composition of the Lavoisier portrait, if not as a type, then at least as a general model that is found elsewhere. The pose allows for the simultaneous display of attributes and of a relationship between man and woman based around mutual visual curiosity or interest in science.

If we wish to extend the alchemical metaphor to the realm of chemistry, we would say that Lavoisier and his wife collaborated on a series of important projects, transforming the base elements of nature into noble inventions and technological advancements. They worked through different methods, including "the wet way," to use an alchemical term. But can we read here a doubling back characteristic of ambivalence? The Lavoisiers represent a kind of idealized collaboration in production, one that will be curtailed by fate. Too busy transforming, or better, sublimating, to go to the revolution (or to have children), the Lavoisiers represent a figure close to the (sterile) hermaphrodite. But there is one element that seems to exceed this sort of narrative explication: the excess of Madame's skirts.[17] Her crinoline bustle—certainly a demonstration of material wealth—is the largest single object in the painting, and it occupies center stage.

As we know, throughout the period in question, scientists took sides in a wide-ranging debate about reproduction. The preformation-epigenesis debate, as well as its application in narrative fiction, can be said to subtend the portrait inasmuch as the couple, a product of an arranged marriage, functions extremely well as a unit. Yet like those exemplary French alchemists Flamel and Perrenelle, they will not reproduce. Ambivalence emerges from a reading of the image that focuses on Madame's body, whose mass extends backward (in the skirt) rather than forward, as in a pregnant womb, an affirmation of Ovism. In early modern painting, the glass vessel may signify the coming to be of the son and the simultaneous purity of the woman. Naturally, we cannot go too far in imposing the long-standing iconological tradition of the *vas* as symbol on this vessel whose presence in this painting is surely motivated by its centrality to Lavoisier's empirical, experimental work. This portrait, we might say, represents an epigenesist couple, one that works together to develop not a son, but a line of scientific thought.

§ 4 Rumpelstiltskin

"There was a miller who was poor" (*Die ware ein muller die arm war*). These are the opening words of the Grimm brothers' tale of "Rumpelstiltskin" (in German, *Rumpelstilzchen*).[1] The story first appeared in the collection of *Kinder-und Hausmärchen* in 1812 (approximately fifty years before the publication of the first volume of Marx's *Capital*), although it is based on an earlier oral anonymous tale.[2] The tale thus reflects a period prior to the mass-production of textiles, when the industry was moving from hand-weaving to industrial machinery.[3] The tale contains traces of atavistic cultures or activities, including milling, spinning, smithying, hoarding, limping, guessing, or riddling; and characters such as kings, dwarves, wives, and firstborn sons.

The story is familiar, but its rhetoric and narrative logic less so. To begin, the miller's trade is not rendering as well as it might. Business isn't what it used to be. There has been some rupture in the cycle of production, perhaps due to external conditions; perhaps due to competition from larger or more efficient mills that have developed in the area. But the miller has one commodity for exchange that is potentially of great value: a beautiful daughter.[4] In spite of being poor, the miller somehow has immediate access to the king ("*Nun traf es sich, dass er mit dem König zu sprechen kam*"). Of course, the miller already knows that the offer of the beautiful daughter will not suffice, as she has no dowry or royal lineage. This is a common problem in fairy tales, and it should not surprise us in the least. Just as immediately as he comes to speak with the king, the miller announces that his beautiful daughter can spin straw (or flax) into gold. The king speaks back to the miller (the tale insists on direct verbal exchange to such a degree that it appears speaking is in some way the equivalent of exchange in general) and declares such spinning to be an art (*eine Kunst*).[5] It seems significant that such rarified spinning is not termed a science or an economy. The term *Kunst* suggests something both specialized and aesthetic. We should keep in mind that in alchemy, "art" is deployed specifically in opposition to "nature" (rather than, say, science). The king imagines that his future bride will mimic nature—that is, the spider—in her ability to transform matter. He is old-fashioned, as he pins his hopes on "art" rather than on the developing science of industrial production.

The king locks the daughter in a room in the castle, provides her with the proper instruments and *raw materials* (that is, she is not asked to grow or reap her own flax—it is provided for her), and announces that if she cannot spin the straw into gold by the morning, she must die. The daughter *does not understand* (*sie verstand gar nichts davon, wie man Stroh zu Gold spinnen konnte*) how to spin straw into gold. It is interesting that the tale does *not* say that she does not understand why she must die if she cannot complete the task. Yet this rule seems entirely incomprehensible. Is her death a punishment for her father's vain boasting? Must she die because she now knows the dirty little secret that the king needs gold? Or does she, like the base metals of alchemy or the alchemical bride, have to die in order for the Great Work to be achieved?

In an earlier version of the tale (1810), the girl is simply asked to spin flax in order to make it usable. By a magical intervention, everything she spins happens to turn into golden thread. This early version is like the story of King Midas who overdoses on gold, his overproduction causing a disruption in the general economy. The miller's daughter is depressed by her failure until a dwarf comes along and offers to help her. She is released from spinning gold thread, which, after all, is not particularly useful (Bottingheimer 149). Two years later, Wilhelm Grimm changes the entire tale.

Now spinning is a matter of life and death. And it is not enough to spin flax, which might indeed be a useful commodity for the community at large. The girl must follow through on her father's promise to produce gold specifically for the king. The daughter is desperate until the arrival of the "little man," Rumpelstiltskin.[6] Each day, for three days, he agrees to spin the gold, as he clearly understands how to do so. The first day, the daughter gives the little man her necklace. The next day, the king arrives and finds the gold, but he grows gold-greedier (*goldgieriger*). On the second day, the miller's daughter promises the little man the ring off her finger.

Why does he accept, since he clearly can make all the gold one might need? Perhaps it is because what he lacks is the (human) fiduciary promise indicated by the ring. (Ironically, while the ring may be a pledge from the king, his greed causes the ring to lose immediate value, or rather, to break or defer the promise.)[7] Or perhaps it is because while he can have all the gold he needs, he is incapable of forming or minting gold into symbols (ingots, seals, rings). The little man accepts the token.

Still, the king is not satisfied. This time, he promises that he will definitely marry the miller's daughter (he will finally honor the promise of the ring that she has already given away!) if she can just spin one more roomful of straw into gold, for "he could not find a more honest bride in all the land than a miller's daughter." The irony here, of course, is that the daughter *is* relatively honest: it is her father whose disproportionate lie has caused trouble. This time, she has nothing left to give the little man. He makes a demand so great—the firstborn son of the king and the miller's daughter—that she cannot accept the offer.[8] Yet she must accept, or she will die. The choice is no choice. She is caught in an aporia from which the only escape must come from a supernatural intervention. The next morning the king finds everything he had wished for ("*alles fand, wie er gewünscht hatte*"), and he marries the girl.

Within a year, as promised, the little man returns to the queen and asks for what she has promised him / spoken about ("*nun gib mir, was du versprochen hast*"). But again, he makes a pact with her. He will leave her the child as long as she can learn his name within three days. The pact, like the rest of the tale, seems inexplicable. What is the value of his name in relation to a son? Without a son, his name will have no value; with a son, his name will have value, and he will guard it for himself. Rumpelstiltskin, like Silas Marner, the protagonist of George Eliot's novel, could have all the gold he wants, but he has realized that gold means nothing to him without a son. In essence, then, he has leveraged his ability to produce gold against a future, so why withdraw the offer?

On the first day, the miller's daughter tries every single name she has ever heard, but without success. On the second day, she manages to arrive at a new list of names, thanks to an emissary who scours the country on her behalf. But again, none of the names are correct. On the third day, the emissary is unable to come up with any more names, but he tells the queen that he traveled to a high mountain in the woods, where he saw a little house, in front of which was a little man, hopping on one leg and reciting a gleeful poem about his name. On the final day, the queen does not reveal her cards right away. She begins by guessing a few other names, none of which are correct. Finally the queen asks the little man, "Is your name by any chance Rumpelstiltskin?" The little man, screaming that the devil must have told her (*"Das hat der Teufel gesagt"*), stomps so hard with his right foot that he drives himself into the ground up to his belly, and then grabs his left foot with both hands and breaks himself in two. And the miller's daughter lives happily ever after with the king, his coffers full (enough) of gold.

Some Questions

Why can't the king find a bride among the nobility? A good marriage would certainly seem an easier way of gaining some gold. Yet the nobility has become sterile, or at least none of the women are honest women (this is a recurring theme in the Grimm brothers' tales). Simultaneously, the king is cash poor. The king is not even imaginative enough to think up the spinning plan. It is the miller who does so. But he may not be as clever as he thinks, since spinning, while it may lead to riches in the short term, is also linked with the long-term diminishment of the woman's value, as in the Grimms' tale of the "Three Spinners." Moreover, by its mere association with poverty, spinning cannot be the fate or attribute of a queen (Schneider 177). Thus, the very fact that the miller's daughter's value derives, at least as far as the king is concerned, from her skill as a spinner, is problematic from the very beginning. Although in the end she is released from her spinning activity, one might say that she is forever tainted by her past (brief though it was) as a spinner. Moreover, many of the spinning fairy tales studied by folklorists associate spinning with demons or spirits. There is always a price to pay for spinning; it entails bargains of the sort that we find in "Rumpelstiltskin." For anthropologist Jane Schneider, the link between evil spirits and flax, above all materials, is due to the massive increase in linen manufacturing in this period, an increase that is symptomatized by ambivalence on a broad cultural level. Cotton cannot be grown in Europe, and the history of its trade intertwines with that of gold; and conversely, linen, a European product, was often exported to countries rich in precious metals. "In their juxtaposition of fabulous marriage opportunities with impossible spinning tasks, they [the spinning tales] warned of risk to the daughters of the poor who overcommitted their labor to marry up, or had it overcommitted by their parents" (Schneider 196). Schneider focuses on the disturbance or ambivalence of these tales, even with their happy endings. There is ambivalence, generally, about reproduction, about excess children who might marry and climb the social ladder, but who might also land the family in the poorhouse. There are severe environmental consequences to flax-growing. It exhausts the soil and causes pollution. Textile manufacturing is also a heavy burden on laborers. It is perhaps for these reasons that earth demons are especially resentful of it.

As should already be clear, the tale of "Rumpelstiltskin" contains various elements of the alchemical. Gold is produced from a common, cheap, base material (straw, or flax). It is produced in secret and at night. A queen and a king join to produce a son (and presumably many more to follow, as we have no reason to doubt that the miller's daughter is quite fertile). The tale is based on triadic numeric patterns (three days to spin, three days to guess the name, and so on). Moreover, the dwarf, who stomps into the ground on one foot, could be linked with the figure of Hephaestus, or Vulcan, who appears often in alchemical imagery.[9] Vulcan limps, or at times has a wooden leg, having been cast down by an invidious Zeus toward the earth. In this sense, Vulcan is linked to Prometheus, the civilizer, stealer of fire, and benefactor of man in defiance of the gods; and to Saturn, who also limps on a false leg. In another variant, Vulcan was rejected by his mother, Hera, because of his congenital infirmity, and like the limping Oedipus, he is expelled from his home, destined to a childhood of wandering, during which he learns the craft of forging. In any case, the etiology of Vulcan's craftiness is normally linked in some way with his gimpyness.[10] In many variants of his mythology, Vulcan is a dwarf, like Rumpelstiltskin and the Egyptian god Ptah. Early gold miners were pygmies, who had easy access to cramped mines. The gold miner makes magical talismans; he works metals with fire, the most dangerous of elements, so he is both sacred and maligned, or apotropaic. His cult may involve a hobbling dance, like that of a cock. All of these elements suggest that Vulcan could be seen as an ancestor of Rumpelstiltskin.

The king in "Rumpelstiltskin" has something in common with those historical kings who sought out alchemy as a possible way of increasing cultural capital / cash for their reserves.[11] In the tale, the miller suggests that his daughter spin, which is not unimportant given that cloth-making was one of the only forms of labor available to women. So the girl (who remains unnamed throughout the story) goes into the locked room. She is only able to transform the worthless straw into valuable *Geld* with the help of the dwarf, but she has to promise him her firstborn child in order to obtain his help. Through the pact, the king manages to shore up his reserves to the point that he is no longer in danger, at least not in the short term. Perhaps that is why he doesn't demand that his bride continue to spin beyond the three-day period. Moving forward, she will continue to (re)produce, but not alchemically. At the end of "Rumpelstiltskin," the queen and king do not die, although we might say that by coming together to reproduce, they already inscribe their own deaths in the continuation of the royal line.

Telluric Demons, Smiths, and Dwarves

In the broadest possible terms, a smith is a *faber* who has contact with metals. Hence a goldsmith can be a banker who deals in—and touches, at times—gold. By this logic, Rumpelstiltskin is also a goldsmith, as in Northern European narrative traditions, smiths and dwarves can be interchangeable.[12] Both may live underground or in mines in the feet of mountains.[13] Dwarves do not like sunlight. Indeed, research suggests that the *Sig* prefix means "sun," and the Scandinavian-German mythological heroic line of Sigurd-Siegfried may be associated with sun gods who have no place taking the treasure that belongs to the realm of the darkness (Magee 144). In his early prose text, *The Wibelungen*, Wagner "argues that the myth of the Nibelung's Hoard is a German version of the primordial myth of the sun god. In this version, the sun god who captures the cornucopian sun for men, is replaced by a hero who captures the Nibelung's Hoard—the source of immeasurable power (*unermessliche Macht*), the cynosure (*Inbegriff*) of all earthly rule" (Shell 37). In *The Ring*, Wagner moves the emphasis away from this general register of solar imagery.

Dieterle convincingly discusses a structure common to smithying tales in which the affirmation of sexuality or sexual production always means the denial of metals and vice versa. Hence dwarves are almost always asexual. Inasmuch as smelting represents a form of separation of ore from its maternal matrix, metallurgy is antithetical to copulation or joining. The earth-dwelling, gold-grabbing, deformed, demonic, asexual figure slips rather easily, we note, into the representational space traditionally reserved for the Jew.[14] In Wagner's *Ring*, the dwarf (Alberich), who has also been read as a caricature of a Jew (Sonnenfeld 89), takes the treatise to Nibelheim and hoards it. He reigns there like a despot, increasing the hoard. Alberich wants to keep the gold in order to have power and social standing; to become assimilated, in other words. Although Alberich and Mime are not labeled Jews, it is clear why they have been interpreted as such, given their apparent materialism and greed for gold (Sonnenfeld 90). The "modern" commercial world of the Jew must be rejected to enable a return to a golden age of harmony, exemplified in the tale of "Rumpelstiltskin" by the nostalgic king.

Spinning, Milling, and Weaving

For the period of three days, the Miller's daughter (over)produces. She is left all alone with her raw materials and her tools, just like Silas Marner in front of his domestic hearth. The antisocial Marner hoards his gold and does not emerge from his house until Eppie brings him redemption that leads him to church, to God, and to sociability. She reconnects him to his community, and this seems a positive step in his humanization. But we might ask provocatively: Is it all good? The miller's daughter and Silas Marner are not (yet) part of a social class defined by its wage labor, because they exist in a state of autonomy, producing at home in an enclosed space. As Lee Edelman has written, the child who appears at Marner's door effects his "release from the 'ever-repeated circle,'" the compulsion to repeat, that Eliot's novel identifies quite explicitly as machinery. Having turned his back on humankind, the weaver, through years of solitude, has become an extension of his loom itself" (Edelman 55). The loom is, for Edelman, "a machine for producing [sexual] sameness," which is finally broken by Eppie—the child as futurity. Both the miller's daughter and Marner could be said to correspond to Marx's description of pre-capitalism: "Each individual household contains an entire economy, forming as it does an independent center of production," more ideal than real (cited in Perelman). This self-sufficiency is threatened by the move to wage labor: "The spindles and looms, formerly scattered over the face of the countryside, are now crowded together in a few great labour-barracks, together with the workers and the raw material. And spindles, looms and raw material are now transformed from means for independent existence of the spinners and weavers into the means for commanding them and extracting unpaid labour from them" (Perelman 75). Just as speaking in the tale could be said to stand in for all exchange, so milling may be said to stand in for the difficult transitions faced by production in general.[15]

In the Grimms' tale of "Three Spinners," a poor mother cannot get her lazy daughter to spin, but when the queen pays a visit, the mother lies and says the problem is one of "under-production"—that is, she claims that she cannot provide enough flax for the girl. The queen offers to take the girl to the palace where she has flax in abundance. Again, the girl is promised to the prince if she can spin all of the flax in the palace. She deceives the queen by subcontracting the work to three elderly women, and she wins the prince's hand in marriage. Upon seeing how the three women are disfigured by spinning, the prince declares that his bride no longer has to spin. The girl's deception, the number three, and the imbalance between the raw materials and the girl's productivity, which is the source of some anxiety, are all elements that place this tale in relation to "Rumpelstiltskin" and with the larger issues of this book.

Silas Marner opens, "In the days when the spinning-wheels hummed busily in the farmhouses—and even great ladies, clothed in silk and Thread-lace, had their toy spinning-wheels of polished oak—there might be seen, in districts far away among the lanes, or deep in the bosom of the hills, certain pallid undersized men, who, by the side of the brawny country-folk, looked like the remnants of a disinherited race" (Eliot 5). And later in the paragraph, "The shepherd himself, though he had good reason to believe that the bag held nothing but flaxen thread, or else the long rolls of strong linen spun from that thread, was not quite sure that this trade of weaving, indispensable though it was, could be carried on entirely without the help of the Evil One." Suspicion surrounds many people in the English countryside, especially when one doesn't know the names of the mother and father of someone. Weavers who tended to move from the towns into the countryside were especially regarded as aliens, and there are also deeply rooted mythological fears associated with weaving (Wiesenfarth 226). Silas Marner weaves and hoards—nothing else. He keeps the gold and only spends silver for his daily wants. He fondles the gold coins every night, and during the day he weaves steadily and without ceasing. He is hypnotized by the monotony of the loom. On New Year's Eve, Silas Marner sits at his fire, when suddenly he sees gold on his hearth. "Gold!—his own gold—brought back to him as mysteriously as it had been taken away! . . . The heap of gold seemed to glow and get larger beneath his agitated gaze. He leaned forward at last, and stretched forth his hand; but instead of the hard coin with the familiar resisting outline, his fingers encountered soft warm curls." The curls belong, as readers will recall, to the first and only child born to the wealthy landowner. Silas "steals" the baby girl, although she is clearly best off with him; thus the novel opens up a kind of social rationality—justice for the good of all. As Northrop Frye noted, the coming of the girl on the Twelfth Night is associated with fertility as the real source of wealth, not gold. Yet for Eliot, this was a realistic novel, not a fairy tale.

Moreover, the novel describes a real period of surplus of thread before the arrival of weaving machines. So Marner, like other hand-weavers of his era, can actually "overproduce" to productive ends. Yet this kind of unbridled production will not be possible a few decades later, suggesting that one should read the novel in a precise realist manner, intimately tied to the land. For instance, the fact that Marner lives next to stone pits is both symbolic and realistic. The dwarf lives in a furnace (volcano, like Vulcan), or hollow stone. But the very doorway to this abode is also the opening to the furnace. "Since the furnace is built over the ore pit, the metal, and therefore the dwarf, is often said to live *under* a stone" (Dieterle 5). There is a primary relation between stones and metals that goes back very far in time, prior to industrialization. This antiquity is evoked in alchemical thought.

Like spinning, milling is an activity that undergoes change with the development of industrial production. Although the miller in "Rumpelstiltskin"—who serves the function of "initiator," according to Ruth Bottigheimer—fades quickly into the background, it seems important to note that the mill, like the spinning wheel, is a common symbol in alchemical literature. The idea of a circular stone that turns in order to transform a base material into something of value is tied, for instance, to the common metaphors of circularity in alchemy, and in particular to the stage of the *separatio* (Calvesi 1993, 36). In this sense, the miller might be seen as a failed alchemist. Perhaps he has no son to whom he can pass down his knowledge. Perhaps he is a poor man with an excess of children. In any case, his daughter must resort to demoniacal powers in order to achieve the Great Work.

Can You Guess My Name?

The dwarf commonly wishes to win the love of a woman so that she will bear a child to continue his name and inherit his wealth. While Rumpelstiltskin does not attempt to win the love of the miller's daughter, the guessing game is consistent with the overall theme of namesakes in folk literature (Gilmour 17). The miller's daughter makes a verbal pact with Rumpelstiltskin. In a sense, she will become the queen and *he* will become the child. His downfall is actually his humane compassion. He should have taken his part of the pact immediately if he truly wished the child more than anything else in the world, as he states. In any case, the reader certainly has the sense that the guessing game fits within ritualistic cultural patterns like cabala, or more generally, the kind of *aenigma* or riddle that develops into early forms of lyric poetry (Tiffany 72–74; 78–82). In such a riddle, an object may pose a challenge such as "Say who I am" or "Say what I am called." The (rhetorical) question calls out for a (performative) response. That is, based on a series of clues, a listener might indeed say what the object is, and by naming it, he or she "forms" lyric in the way that the miller's daughter "performs" the demise of the dwarf.

Rumpelstiltskin tells the queen that she must have heard his name from the devil; but as she heard it (albeit indirectly) from him, logically he must be the devil (Gilmour 20). The devil is a robber of souls, and this is how some have interpreted the desire for the firstborn.

Threes

The number three, common in fairy tales, is often associated with the figure of the fool or dwarf who tells his lord three truths or pays him three compliments (Tietze-Conrat 13). Moreover, the tale could be linked with the three fates, or three spinners, that Freud discusses in his essay "The Theme of the Three Caskets." Freud notes that the choice between three ineluctably ends with the third element—death; lead (the third casket of *The Merchant of Venice*), or here, Rumpelstiltskin's name; or the girl's spinning. *Silas Marner* is also organized around threes.[16] I have already invoked Kofman's compelling discussion of the apparent "choice" in Shakespeare's comedy as masking the fact that metals are, materially, ambivalent—that is, they are all subject to potential reverse transformation.

If we were to fit this tale around the model of alchemy as ambivalent, we might expect to find one narrative/thematic pattern in particular: greed and the subsequent covering up of greed. The greed is the greed of the king. The alibi for his greed is the test to which he submits the miller's daughter. At the end of the test he finds her honest (and his greed is satiated). The girl's base origins are compensated for by the gold in the coffers. This is by no means the first time that a king must look for an honest bride among the plebs and then subject her to a series of tests to prove her worth (other examples include the princess and the pea, Cinderella, the Scandinavian tale of Frida and the prince in the castle "east of the sun and west of the moon," and so on). In each of these tales and many others of this type, the common female exchanges her poverty for nobility, but always at a cost of other kinship relationships or of her former self. She is transmuted into an entirely new state. (Perhaps traces of her past as a spinner and a miller's daughter persist in the future, but we will never know.) Spinning transmutes the motion of the laborer into "an object without motion" or "the thing produced" (Marx 1867, 189). The tale of "Rumpelstiltskin" provides us with a model of reading, alchemically, an economic relation between the feminine and the production of gold through a transformation of base materials. Appearing when it does, it also suggests that the anxious narratives of alchemy are very much alive and not suppressed in favor of more "rational" models of production, even in the early nineteenth century.

§ 5 "The Sandman"

What can be gained from reading, yet again, E.T.A. Hoffmann's 1815 tale "The Sandman"?[1] Over the course of innumerable rereadings, this text, published under the rubric of *Nachtstück* (Nightpiece, a term that Hoffmann could have adapted from a genre of macabre musical pieces), has become for the modern critic inextricable from Freud's essay "*Das Unheimliche*" ("The Uncanny") of 1919. Separated by a century, both texts were written with an eye, or rather, with eyes, toward the second part of the tale, the explosive trauma caused to Nathanael by Olympia, the automaton, and by the evil barometer seller Coppola. Yet given Freud's interest—especially during the period in question—in repression, it would seem particularly important to concentrate on the protagonist's early life as it emerges in the tale and in Freud's analysis.

Freud's notion of the uncanny emerges from the various pathologies of vision and sexuality in the story. Of course, Freud rightly understood that there is never any doubt in the reader's mind of Olympia's status as an automaton. Hoffmann is not trying to fool the reader, nor does he expect the reader to undergo a moment of insight, at least in regard to the passage from animate to inanimate. Instead, Freud focuses on the relation between the childhood experience of the threat of eye removal by the Sandman (factually given in the narrative) and the centrality of the threat of castration to the psyche that Freud was trying to bolster at this point in his career; he thus concentrates on the passage from absorption in the narrative as such to the *meaning* of the narrative, the key to which lies, for him, in castration.

Early in the essay, Freud makes an interesting move from the first-person "I," which he has used heretofore, to a third-person reference to "the writer of the present contribution." Such displacement mirrors the disconcerting changes of address in the letters themselves. Of "this writer"—that is, himself—Freud notes, "It is long since he has experienced or heard of anything which has given him an uncanny impression, and he must start by translating himself into that state of feeling, by awakening in himself the possibility of experiencing it" (220). Freud is not easily scared, in other words. But is this, in general, a quality of intellectuals, such as Clara is becoming in her own way in Hoffmann's tale? *Heimlich* is an odd word that means at once something familiar and agreeable, but also concealed and out of sight. According to the passage from Schelling famously cited by Freud, "everything is *unheimlich* that ought to have remained secret and hidden but has come to light" (225). One connotation of the word is "homelike," something belonging to the house, withdrawn from the eyes of strangers. But the most startling sense of the word is its circular structure. As Freud writes: "*Heimlich* is a word the meaning of which develops in the direction of ambivalence, until it finally coincides with its opposite, *unheimlich*. *Unheimlich* is in some way or other a sub-species of *heimlich*" (226). We should also note that in his list of dictionary definitions of the word—a list that, as he makes clear even before he writes it down, can teach us nothing new, "perhaps only because we ourselves speak a language that is foreign"—Freud does not bother to give an Italian (or Portuguese) equivalent. The reason for his omission is that "both languages seem to content themselves with words which we should describe as circumlocutions" (221). This is an interesting way of avoiding the issue, especially since the equivalents of *heimlich* in Spanish, for instance—*sospechoso, de mal agüero, lúgubre, siniestro*—have their own quite similar equivalents in Italian (not to mention Portuguese). In any case, Freud attributes to Italian, the mother (father?) tongue of the two scientists in the story, the very structure that the uncanny takes in his essay—that is, a circum-locution, a word that "leads back to what is known of old and long familiar" (220).

Freud's goal, more than anything else, is to deconstruct the integrity of the uncanny as a mere phenomenon of "intellectual certainty." Samuel Weber writes on the question:

> In his reading of this text ["The Sandman"], Freud insists that "intellectual Uncertainty"—the term introduced by Jentsch, his predecessor in the study of the uncanny—is not what counts. It is not, he insists, uncertainty or delusion

concerning Olympia that is uncanny in this story, but rather the (castration) anxiety associated with the figure of the Sandman, and hence with the fear of losing one's eyes. And yet, despite the fact that Freud presents this with great conviction and force, "intellectual uncertainty" returns throughout this essay to haunt its main thesis, and in fact to help to dismember it. (Weber 15–16)

The haunting return of the rational cannot help but recall ambivalence. It would seem at first glance that, like ambivalence, *the uncanny* is a term that might wish to be *other*, something deeply structuring in the psyche but that persists in returning to the real, to the realm of the intellect. We shall have to see, then, by what force it achieves this return and what sort of resistance is mounted by Freud (or by the text itself) in the process.

We can begin by focusing on the factually given experiences of the child, as (if) they occurred first, in isolation, and uncontaminated by what occurs later in the story. Indeed, this would be the case if this were a "true story," or better, a true child analysis, a life in which events unfold before and outside of reading itself, without Freud's *Nachträglichkeit* (deferred action) prior to any notion of retrospectivity, or *Zuruckphantasieren*.[2] What is interesting, moreover, is that post-Freudian readings of this story—at least all of those with which I am familiar—understand repetition as occurring between a single early experience (the child's encounter with the Sandman, or Coppelius) and a late experience (the traumatic viewing of Coppola from the tower). However economical such readings may be with regard to the aim of focusing on the vicissitudes of repetition and *Nachträglichkeit*, they also conflate what are clearly two separate incidents in Nathanael's early life: a frightening encounter with the Sandman, who threatens to steal the boy's eyes, and, subsequently, the death of Nathanael's father.

As recounted in the letters that open the tale, on one particular evening, the Sandman visits and Nathanael cannot contain his curiosity. He spies on the Sandman, who then threatens to tear out the child's eyes. After this, Nathanael is assured that the Sandman won't be coming back. However, the adult promise is broken, and the Sandman does, in fact, come back once more. During the Sandman's final visit, Nathanael's father is killed by an explosion. Again, from a certain perspective, it hardly matters that the threat to tear out the boy's eyes and the explosion are actually two events separated by time. Yet it would seem significant from the perspective of the boy, and before the imposition of a longer narrativized structure, that these two, perhaps equally traumatic events occur separated by a shorter period during which the boy is promised that the Sandman will not return.

In the letter to his friend Lothar that begins the tale, Nathanael describes a series of events in his childhood—the periodic visits to his home of a figure called the Sandman—that grant particular significance to an event later in his life, namely the appearance at his student residence of the barometer seller Coppola. But before he can describe the events, or rather, justify his reactions, Nathanael must set the stage for Lothar "in distinct and luminous images." First he offers Lothar a general overview of his childhood. During the day, he recounts, his father was absent, at work. (Nathanael does not inform Lothar of his father's profession, a potentially significant omission.)[3] After dinner, Nathanael and his siblings were allowed to enter his father's study, a dark and disorderly room that was always filled with smoke, like the den of an alchemist in early modern visual iconography. Sometimes, his father would tell tales. Other times, he would sit quietly. The children were always overwhelmed by his pipe.

On nights when his father suffered from melancholy, Nathanael's mother would usher the children off to bed at nine o'clock, threatening a visit from the Sandman. Yet early in Nathanael's development, his mother explained that the Sandman is a mere figure ("There is no such person as the Sandman . . . When I say the Sandman is coming, that just means that you are sleepy, and can't keep your eyes open, as though someone had thrown sand in them") (86). She explicitly and openly speaks figuratively, and the figure bears no connection to the actual arrival at the house of a real man whom the children do not meet. But because of the repetition of the figure and its coincidence with the arrival of a man, of course, the mother appears deluded. She is the one who is "deceived" by the parapraxis or coincidence of the events. She is the one whose unconscious is thus causing the trauma, although she is not consciously aware of this fact. Thus, on certain nights, the threat is posed but immediately withdrawn at the same time that the children hear heavy thuds on the stairs. While he hears his mother's words, the child Nathanael remains convinced that his mother is denying (after having posited) the Sandman's existence to calm his fears. What we have, then, is a case of negation and a chain of reversals that would seem to bear many parallels with the structure of fetishism itself. The logic of the little boy must work something like this: "I know the Sandman exists since my mother has told me he is coming. I hear steps. Therefore, they must be the steps of the Sandman. I am afraid that the Sandman will come and take my eyes. My mother tells me the Sandman does not exist. Clearly she is only pretending that he doesn't exist in order to calm my fears. Therefore, he not only exists but he is worthy of fear."

Finally, in order to clarify the existence of the Sandman, the young Nathanael speaks to an old nurse, and as in the case of Freud's Wolfman, her folkloric or "low" discourse is brought into the boy's already developed chain of logic and made to have its place there. According to the nurse, there is indeed a Sandman, and he is even worse than the boy might have imagined.[4]

As Nathanael explains, the very system of constatives and negations put into action by his mother, his nurse, and his own logic ensures that the threat of the Sandman remains as a specter long after the boy has reasoned that the story of a sandman—who supposedly has a nest under the crescent moon and takes the eyes of sleepless children to feed his own beaked offspring—simply cannot be true. It is at this point in his narration that Nathanael uses the word *unheimlich*, referring to an "*unheimlichen Spuk*"—an "uncanny ghost"—translated by Ritchie Robertson as "fearsome spectre." Why does the translator choose not to use the word *uncanny* when he knows perfectly well that Freud's essay dominates our readings of the tale? Perhaps he wants to shift attention away from Freud—and, hence, away from castration as subtending the story—and toward a more "neutral" sense of the Sandman as a scary man who haunts the boy's imagination. Yet the refusal to engage with Freud at this particular moment—the moment at which Nathanael is working through his responses to the Sandman—seems itself a gesture that is both defensive and uncanny in its detour away from the dominant mode of reception of the narrative.

At the moment that Nathanael rationally admits that the story of the Sandman cannot be true, he continues to refer to the periodic visitor as the Sandman. In other words, Nathanael continues to grant the name Sandman to a man whose physical presence in the house cannot be denied, and whom he knows cannot reasonably be that figure of the monstrous robber of eyes about which he has heard horrific tales. Nathanael engages in a complex form of figuration, giving a symbolic name to a real body, but a symbolic name that is linked with atavistic fears and infantile beliefs. Moreover, he readily admits a true fear of the Sandman, whereas he is fascinated by "horrific" tales of goblins, witches, and midgets (*Kobolten, Hexen, Däumlingen*), and he continues to draw pictures of the Sandman on tables, cupboards, and walls (*auf Tische, Schränke und Wände*). The repetition of the number three expresses a ritualistic quality to his relation to this "fearful spectre," this figure that he both names and represents. Of course, for Freud the continued repetition of the ritualistic representation is a means of defensive disavowal. Yet how can the boy defy his fear through representation when he is not certain of the reality of "the Sandman," whom he has he never seen?

For years, the man called the Sandman comes to the house with varying frequency. Although Nathanael is extremely curious about the Sandman, he cannot summon the courage to ask his father about him. Nathanael's intuition that something is going on between adults, his curiosity and fear of asking, would seem to lend support to the idea that the relation of the two men is a primal scene that will soon be viewed by the boy, a proposition supported by many readings of the tale in the wake of Freud's essay. In other words, their relation has all of the structural elements (from Nathanael's perspective) of a sexual one that he is not supposed to witness. As Samuel Weber writes: "In which sense is this nightmarish scene an Urszene? To be sure, it does not directly depict the parental coitus that Freud usually associates with the concept of 'primal scene.' But what it does show is no less passionate, and less erotic: two men undressing before the eyes of the transfixed child, who is medusized, as it were, before the unexpected spectacle that unfolds before him" (Weber 13).

After this, Nathanael grows up. He is allowed to leave the nursery and move into a room in the same corridor as his father's smoke-filled study. Yet on the nights when the Sandman comes, Nathanael, along with his brothers and sisters, is obliged to go to bed at nine o'clock. So, because of the Sandman, he is forced into a form of regression to an earlier state, a motif that is again consistent with an interpretation of the men's encounter as a sexual one. Each visit from the Sandman is accompanied by a strange-smelling vapor. Although the tale does not offer any more information about this sensory effect, we know that smell is often a sexual marker. One night the abject Sandman comes to visit and Nathanael summons up the courage to sneak into the study and hide behind a curtain, paralyzed with fear. Nathanael learns then that the Sandman is none other than Coppelius, a repellant advocate who occasionally comes to lunch at the house and who wields an inexplicable power over his father.

Thus, through his illicit or unsanctioned viewing, Nathanael's "figure" of the Sandman is collapsed with his actual knowledge of a person, a professional man whom he has met "during the day" (in the light) on a number of occasions.

In the English translation of the text by Ritchie Robertson, the description of the crucial (primal) scene is rendered as follows:

> I was rooted to the spot. Despite the risk of being discovered and, as I was well aware, of being severely punished, I stayed there, listening, and poking my head between the curtains. My father welcomed Coppelius with much formality.
>
> "Come on, let's get to work!" cried Coppelius in a hoarse, croaking voice, throwing off his coat.
>
> My father, silent and frowning, took off his dressing-gown, and the two of them donned long black smocks. I did not notice where these came from. My father opened the folding doors of a cupboard; but I saw that what I had so long taken for a cupboard was instead a dark recess [*schwarze Höhlung*] containing a small fireplace. Coppelius walked over to it, and a blue flame crackled up from the hearth. All manner of strange instruments [*Geräte*] were standing around. Merciful heavens! As my old father bent down to the fire, he looked quite different. A horrible, agonizing convulsion seemed to have contorted his gentle, honest face into the hideous, repulsive mask of a fiend. He looked like Coppelius. The latter, brandishing a pair of red-hot tongs, was lifting gleaming lumps from the thick smoke and then hammering at them industriously. It seemed to me that human faces were visible on all sides, but without eyes, and with ghastly, deep, black cavities instead. (Hoffmann 91)

As Samuel Weber has stressed, in order to see the (primal) scene, and in order to identify the Sandman as Coppelius, Nathanael must poke his head out of a curtain that separates the space of action like a theater. The "wall closet" that Nathanael had thought familiar turns out to be an oven (perhaps something like an athanor, more precisely).[5] Sparks fly, mimicking the act of eyes being separated from their sockets, and thus coinciding with Nathanael's negated belief in the existence of the Sandman. His father no longer appears as the boy remembered, but is transfigured, made to be like Coppelius. Weber writes:

> In the hopes of putting an end to the specter of the Sandman by discovering who he is, whom he resembles, he discovers that the Sandman names the violence of a certain dissemblage, which provokes fear and loathing, to be sure, but which also invokes fascination and desire. For what is most noteworthy

about this scene—and the point where it ceases to be mere story and spectacle and becomes a theatrical scenario instead—occurs when Nathanael, haunted and tempted by those eyes without bodies, leaps out of his hiding place and throws himself at the Sandman's feet. (14)

For Weber, the key to the passage is the dynamic of seeing, and it is precisely this gesture that will be repeated at the end of the tale when Nathanael peers through the spyglass. Moreover, by throwing himself onto the scene, Nathanael loses a narcissistic sense of his body as unified, and is instead either split or made double (ambivalent). While the text does not anywhere signal that the scene may indeed be a hallucination, we should keep in mind that for Freud's reading, it is not essential that it be real. Freud writes:

> As regards the rest of the scene, Hoffmann already leaves us in doubt whether what we are witnessing is the first delirium of the panic-stricken boy, or a succession of events which are to be regarded in the story as being real. His father and the guest are at work at a brazier with glowing flames. . . . Those who decide in favor of the rationalistic interpretation of the Sand-man will not fail to recognize in the child's phantasy the persisting influence of his nurse's story. (1919, 228)

Freud does not state, then, what the men are actually doing, since for him it is completely indifferent. The only thing that matters is Nathanael's perception of events and the psychic linkage he makes between the work of the men over the flames and the tale of the Sandman as a burner of eyes. If Freud were to linger at all on the question of what the two men are doing, he would be engaging in a gesture of establishing something akin to intellectual certainty and would then be indulging the definition of the *Unheimlich* of Jentsch that he precisely wishes to refute.

After the first traumatic viewing of the scene, Nathanael is reassured by his mother, and he believes that Coppelius has left town. However, a year passes and the advocate returns. Lifelessly, the father promises this is the final visit. Once again, the children are ushered off to bed at nine o'clock. Although the children are a year older, they are still infantalized, forced to regress to an earlier stage of their emotional development.

At about midnight, an explosion is heard.[6] Nathanael's father lies burnt and dead on the floor of his study. The incident is the subject of a police investigation, but Coppelius is nowhere to be found, and the case remains unresolved.

If we are to read a "late" text like "The Sandman" in an alchemical key, it seems essential to approach it with the understanding that we will not find alchemy precisely as a literal transformation of baser metals into gold, but as a narrative of memory, universality, bearing some relation to a tradition that is handed down from father to son. Here, of course, the son has been excluded from the circuit, or, if we like, he has been short-circuited. Freud argues in an often-cited footnote to his essay on the uncanny that Nathanael suffers precisely from ambivalence that he resolves by splitting his father into good and bad imagoes.[7] The "good" father, his real father, is a victim of the Sandman and is killed. The "bad" father, Coppelius, wields power throughout the story. In the second part of "The Sandman," this split will yield two Italian fathers, Spalanzani (Olympia's father) and Coppola (Coppelius, the barometer seller).

There is no definite account in Hoffmann's tale as to what causes the explosion, or what the men were doing together year after year. In part, this is because the events are narrated by Nathanael, so we only learn what he himself has witnessed with his own eyes. Some critics simply ignore the question or treat it as transparent and thus unworthy of commentary. Others have deduced that the men were making an automaton.[8] Thus, when Coppola appears later in the guise of a barometer seller, it is because he and Professor Spalanzani have managed to perfect their work and even arrange for a fire that forces Nathanael to move across the hall from Olympia. It is inevitable, then, that he will fall in love with the doll. But does this necessarily mean that earlier in the tale, Nathanael's father, in league with Coppelius, even if reluctantly, was also hoping to make an automaton so that his son would be duped? In his introduction to *The Golden Pot and Other Tales of Hoffmann*, Ritchie Robertson writes that the fight between Spalanzani and Coppola over Olympia—overheard but not seen by Nathanael—is clearly a "repetition of the earlier one in Nathanael's father's study" (xvii). The basis for this statement surely lies with Freud, who writes in his long footnote on the good and bad father-imagoes:

> This pair of fathers is represented later, in his [Nathanael's] student days, by Professor Spalanzani and Coppola the optician. The Professor is in himself a member of the father-series, and Coppola is recognized as identical with Coppelius the lawyer. *Just as they used before to work together over the secret brazier, so now they have jointly created the doll Olympia*; the Professor is even called the father of Olympia. This double occurrence of activity in common betrays

them as divisions of the father-imago: both the mechanician and the optician were the father of Nathaniel (and of Olympia as well). *In the frightening scene in childhood, Coppelius, after sparing Nathaniel's eyes, had screwed off his arms and legs as an experiment; that is, he had worked on him as a mechanician would on a doll.* This singular feature, which seems quite outside the picture of the Sand-Man, introduces a new castration equivalent. (232; emphasis mine)

Structurally, the parallels between the earlier and later events in the tale are undeniable, but a reading that posits the forging of an automaton to dupe Nathanael reduces the (earlier) scene to a mere interaction (and an aggressive one at that) between two men or father figures. For this dominant line of interpretation, certain evocative, sensorial details of the scene—especially the odors, the smoke, the tools, and the fire—are suppressed in favor of structural narrative repetition. In his commentary, Ritchie Robertson continues: "The two [scenes] are linked by the fact that Coppelius then treated Nathanael like a doll, dislocating his limbs and replacing them in their sockets, while now Olympia, Nathanael's sweetheart, is revealed to be a doll" (xvii). Concurring with Freud, then, this critic sees a definite link between Nathanael and Olympia. Both are dolls, at least emotionally. Of course, Hoffmann's only authorial intervention in the scene is to recount it as "a dim reflection in a dull mirror." So, for Robertson: "From the materials provided, we can construct a narrative in which Coppelius and Nathanael's father together try to make an automaton; after the explosion and the death of his collaborator, Coppelius flees the town, to reappear much later disguised as a Piedmontese barometer-seller and in league with the physicist Spalanzani; after twenty years they have now devised the perfect automaton and are trying it out on Nathanael" (xix). Following Freud, Robertson emphasizes the double-ness of the figures and the plot, crystallized around the image of the forging of a doll. But what are the "materials" cited by Robertson to support the idea of a collaboration to make an automaton, other than the fact that the earlier relationship of Nathanael's father and Coppelius conveniently mirrors the later collaboration of two father figures?

Italian Fathers

The names Hoffmann chose for his father figures are certainly significant. Lazzaro Spallanzani was a prominent (Lombard) eighteenth-century naturalist. It is probable that in Hoffmann's time his name was associated with opposition to theories of epigenesis. He was famous for his experiments centered around questions of reproduction. Although he was allied with the (preformation) ovists, Spallanzani also understood that sperm had to come into contact with an egg for generation to take place. He experimented with parthenogenesis, and although this failed, he did manage to artificially impregnate silkworms, and later, a spaniel bitch, using the appropriate semen from the male species in each case. He was interested in the overall "logic of the living"—mechanisms regulating the course of vitalistic phenomena—and in definitions of the boundary between life and death.

Moreover, Spallanzani was notable for his courage in undertaking a dangerous and long voyage to Constantinople, a privilege that apparently roused much envy and bitterness among other scientists. During the voyage, Giovanni Antonio Scopoli accused Spallanzani of stealing valuable items from the public museum for his personal collection. This became a cause celebre among scientists and philosophers of the late eighteenth century. Spallanzani's honor was posited primarily in opposition to his rivals, whom he derided as mere Linnaean nomenclaturists. In fact, Spallanzani's lectures stressed the function of natural processes rather than taxonomy. In the end, Spallanzani was vindicated and his honor restored, to the detriment of one of his main detractors, Alessandro Volta. In short, his reputation as a polemicist and as a would-be parthenogenesist makes him an interesting referent for the father-physicist in the tale.

The name Coppelius is linked, as others have noted, with the Italian word for eye socket (*coppa*), but also with the verb *coppellare*, signifying the purification of precious metals (a *coppella* is a crucible for melting). Moreover, the Latin *copulare* means "to bind or link together, to couple," and it too is a familiar term from alchemy, returning us to the realm of the chemical wedding (Hoffmann 239). As with Spalanzani, Coppelius loses a secondary or pleonastic *l* from his name when it is translated into German. Hoffmann undertakes a haplography, or omission of sounds that are duplicated. For Sebastiano Timpanaro, such a "slip," when it occurs in everyday speech, does not necessarily signify (Freudian) repression, just a normal "tendency to dispense with the superfluous" (Timpanaro 142). Throughout his "materialist" account of the lapsus, Timpanaro focuses his attention on a number of different paleographic "slips." In essence, then, we can see the haplographic omission of the *l* as an example of what Timpanaro calls a "banalization," a reforming of a word to conform to the everyday life of the writer. Perhaps we can also see it as a German correction of Italian excess.

Conspiracy (Theory)

Freud does not really remark on the paranoid nature of the theory of conspiracy that drives Nathanael to his death, but it is more than a theory of his own mind, if we follow the line of reasoning cited above. Moreover, Freud also neglects the element of the primal scene that Samuel Weber has referenced in his focus on the theatrical. This aspect of the text is supposed to be bolstered by the fact that Coppelius is leaning over Nathanael's father, who is dressed in a "feminized" garment, a robe. If the two men are indeed trying to make an automaton (a child), such a reading appears all the more significant.

But suppose the two men are actually engaged in alchemical transformation? Alchemy—or, more generally, a bourgeois vogue for the occult—is something that Freud leaves out of his analysis. We may be no more justified in stressing alchemy than are those critics who imagine that the two men are forging an automaton, especially as Nathanael himself never uses the term *alchemy*. Clearly certain material or narrative elements suggest alchemy could be at work in this early part of the tale. First, the name of the Sandman is repeated in such a way as to suggest a chant or ritual naming ("*Der Sandmann steht . . . Der Sandmann, der fürchterliche Sandmann*"). We have already noted the links between alchemy and the name of the advocate, Coppelius, who comes frequently to the house over a long period of time. In alchemical writing, the Great Work is something that must be pursued over a long period, and it requires great patience; hence many practitioners are said to be prone to melancholy, as is Nathanael's father. The fact that two *men* undertake the process of *copulare* in Hoffmann's "late" version of alchemical experimentation does not negate the possibility of reading the text alchemically. On the contrary, the notion of the encounter between the two men or fathers as a perverted primal scene is only strengthened by the link with the alchemical tradition. The two men work with tongs, forging like Hephaestus (Vulcan). Nathanael's father refers to Coppelius as Master. Finally, the element of a fire (perhaps out of control) is common in alchemical imagery. Indeed, it is often the adept—the practical warrior or second-caste citizen in traditional societies—who undergoes a trial by fire with the master or Brahmin, who is dedicated to metaphysics, looking on. In Dutch painting, the laboratory explosion is an allegory of arrogance, failure to adequately prepare oneself for the Great Work, a sign of hubris (see Figure 11, for instance). In most variants of alchemy, the practitioners (or the metals themselves, depending on the degree of allegory in a given text) undergo a burning, or *nigredo*, that is part of their purification. They will be spiritually reborn, but in "The Sandman," this redemptive element is tragically absent.

When Coppelius discovers Nathanael spying, he focuses on the child's limbs as if he were a mechanical toy. Later in the story it is the rational Clara who uses the term *alchemy* for the first time. She writes: "As for his [Coppelius's] uncanny nocturnal goings-on with your father, I expect the two of them were simply conducting secret alchemical experiments, which could hardly please your mother, since a lot of money must have been squandered and moreover, as is said always to happen to such inquirers, your father became obsessed with the delusive longing for higher wisdom and was estranged from his family" (94).

In order to verify her suspicion or to clarify what the men were doing (in much the way that we, as readers, are now attempting), Clara turns to her neighbor, a chemist, who confirms that an explosion such as the one that killed Nathanael's father could indeed be consistent with the careless work of alchemists. Moreover, the neighbor offers Clara "a characteristically long-winded account" of what might have taken place, "mentioning so many strange-sounding names that I couldn't remember any of them" (94). This is consonant with the discourse of alchemy that uses covernames and deliberately confuses those who are outside. To see the work of the two men as alchemical, then, is to take the side of Clara, she who sees clearly. In their own accounts, neither Freud nor Robertson privileges Clara's *clarification* of what the two men are doing.

Finally, Clara must apologize to Nathanael, for her investigations place his father in a *dark* light and suggest that he was killed by his excessive greed or ambition. She imagines Nathanael chastising her for her ingenuous attachment to the surface of events, her reluctance to accept a profound or mystical explanation for the goings-on. She imagines that he may say she is like a child who takes pleasure in the world and refuses to see the poison/gift concealed in the golden fruit. He will think: "Her cold temperament cannot accept the mystery that often enfolds man in invisible arms; she perceives only the varied surface of the world and takes pleasure in it as a childish infant does in a glittering fruit which has deadly poison concealed within in it [*Wie das kindische Kind über die goldgleissende Frucht, in deren Innerm tödliches Gift verborgen*]" (94). This paragraph of the letter is followed by a repetition of the "signal" phrase "my most dearly beloved Nathanael" [*mein herzgeliebter Nathanael*]" (95). Clara again worries that Nathanael will find her sunny disposition and "rational" explanation to be a form of dismissal of a darker power. He may find her too simple. He may say that she lacks the right words to express herself. Why should she apologize for this, and why does it worry her so? In his response to Lothar, Nathanael admits that Clara did indeed produce a profoundly philosophical document, but she must have developed this "university"-style rhetoric from her discussions with Lothar. "Leave her alone!" Nathanael begs his friend ("*Lass das blieben!*"). Indeed, although the fault lies entirely with Nathanael, who misaddressed his letter in the first place, he is irritated with Clara, and for one reason only: because her letter was so undeniably sensible. And because of this very irritation, he declares that he will not write to her, but instead hopes to see her in person so that her cheeriness (and apparent natural simplicity) will dispel his lingering bad mood. This declaration comes at the end of a letter in which Nathanael mentions that he has peered into Spalanzani's study and seen a remarkably beautiful girl whom he surmises must be "feeble minded." In short, Nathanael's letter chastises Lothar and Clara for allowing his beloved to develop a "higher form" of knowledge that trumps Nathanael's; the letter also suggests that Olympia, locked inside the study, is the real object of his affection, in that her physical beauty coincides with a lack of intellectual substance in what is clearly a confirmation of Nathanael's conscious position and perhaps his unconscious desires. Throughout the story, the threat that Clara poses to Nathanael is one of the superiority of her practical knowledge over his superstitions and false beliefs, a binary that mimics the threat of castration as it is played out in the history of the reception of Freudian psychoanalysis. Clara, through the clarity of her thought, has overcome her anxiety.

Clara's point of view, bolstered by evidence from a scientist (her neighbor), is that the two men were undertaking a form of alchemical experimentation, perhaps out of pure greed, rather than forging an automaton that might in some way directly threaten Nathanael. In a sense, Clara means that they were practicing necromancy or dark arts rather than alchemy in a more rigorous sense. Of course, we don't need Clara to point out the alchemical elements of the tale, or that transmutation and the homunculus are thoroughly intertwined. The second variant implies that the Sandman's threats to Nathanael can be taken both literally and figuratively. The first variant resides in a kind of logic that in some sense engages with the social history of the bourgeoisie, given that men of this class did, during this period, undertake secret experiments, or at least indulged a vogue for occultism. Behind this occult variant we might discern a reference to practices of fraternal groups such as Freemasons or Rosicrucians, societies of men (hence Nathanael's mother must usher the children off to bed quickly and disappear herself; women were not supposed to be in the laboratory, and if they did enter, they were undone, like Georgiana in Hawthorne's "The Birthmark"). In this context, Nathanael's father offers a place to work and takes on the role of the adept, a crucial element in the functioning of the alchemical experiment. If nothing else, the adept dialectically defines the master as such.

If we grant Clara her due, the work of the men could be considered simultaneously as alchemical and as the fashioning of an automaton. And as we have already seen, such a combination is clearly supported by alchemical literature. We might take any of the modern authors on alchemy as exemplary: "The Great Work is, above all things, the creation of man by himself" (Eliphas Levi cited in Klossowski de Rola 8). Whatever else this might mean, alchemy understands itself as the creation of (a) man. Often in alchemical illustrations and treatises, including the writings of Paracelsus, who exercised a significant influence on later German authors, we will find a homunculus (Mercury), either a hermaphrodite or a boy who is born of the conjunction of opposites. This creation, whatever form or idea it may take, stands in alchemical discourse as a figure of True Alchemy or Philosophical Alchemy as opposed to base greed (the mere transmutation of base metals into gold for personal enrichment). Of course, this idealism is also parodied in a work like David Ryckaert's portrait of a scholar/alchemist with an invitro creation (Figure 16), perhaps familiar to Goethe himself. This particular painting, with its odd family drama (the gigantic shadow of the old woman haunting the moment of conception), both evokes and satirizes the dream of alchemical clarity.

Hoffmann's tale thus leads us back to the older debate on preformation and epigenesis that is also evoked by the name of Spa(l)lanzani. As we know, Aristotle believed that organisms generate themselves successively under the guidance of a formative drive. Kant translated this into an idea that logical categories contain the possibility of all experience in general, as if in a seed. "Epigenesis is thus the condition of the possibility of any claim to absoluteness, be this a philosophical or literary absolute. . . . This means that the discourses of epigenesis have a tendency to close themselves off against specific criticism and 'objective' presentation. 'Organic' indeed became the ultimate praise in philosophical and aesthetic judgment in the period of the epigenetic turn, a status the word has not lost since" (Müller-Sievers 4). Eventually, epigenesis "defeats" preformation, and with it, the ovism of thinkers like the chemist Spallanzani. For Hoffmann, he probably stood for the rather mechanical position that all human beings are encapsulated, one generation in its predecessor, in Eve's ovaries. In preformation, since children are already in the ovaries, the father is practically irrelevant. Inasmuch as "The Sandman" is about fathers generating a mechanical child without the help of women, the story could be said to ironically enact a reversal or vendetta against the antiquated idea of preformation, represented by Spallanzani. When Clara eventually has children with her husband, she makes progress. Yet the very circularity of the story would seem to call for caution: we cannot assume that Hoffmann is writing about the teleological triumph of rational science over mystical Paracelsianism.

There is also a powerful literary precedent for the conjunction of alchemy and the homunculus—namely the golem, or God's homunculus, Adam, in the Talmud.[9] In biblical Hebrew, *gimel-lamed-mem* (g-l-m) is an unformed mass. The man formed from clay is linked with the magic of invoking God's name, hence bringing our focus back to the key, the *clavis universalis*. As Gershom Scholem stresses, the golem is marked as dangerous precisely because of his tellurian ancestry, manifest in the brute materials that make up his body.[10] Moreover, he is created through a mystical experience that involves the repetition of certain names or words. In the Talmud, Rava creates a being (a golem), perhaps through just such a recitation of the Sefer Yezirah, the combination of the divine letters, but the being itself is unable to speak. Only God has the capacity to create a speaking man (Adam). Speech is key in the creation of the golem, but it is not a gift that can be passed on from the creator to his creation, and this seems to be a central motif in golem-lore that is absolutely essential for the present discussion.

In one of the most prominent variants of the tradition, Rabbi Loew of Prague—the alchemical city par excellence—is supposed to have forged the golem from clay based on mystical instructions. It was not able to speak and it was incapable of judgment, but it had a human form and undertook various tasks in an automatic mode. In a particular variant of the story, Rabbi Loew discovered that while the golem was unfit for manual labor or daily chores, he was able to spy on other residents and expose the falsity of accusations of ritual infanticide that were levied against the Jews. Once these accusations had ceased, the golem was no longer necessary, and the Rabbi destroyed him by reversing the very process he had undertaken in the creation. In yet another variant prevalent in German romanticism, Polish Jews developed golems to perform work on the Sabbath. These golems, whose foreheads were inscribed with the Hebrew characters meaning "truth" or "God" ("Emeth") grew successively bigger and threatened to rebel. To squash them, the Polish Jews had to pull off the final character. The two remaining characters— Meth—signify death.[11]

The homunculus figure (this time formed not from clay but from urine, sperm, and blood) is central to the *De rerum natura* attributed to Paracelsus. Like Faust, the real Paracelsus (b. 1493) learned medicine from his father before he took to wandering around Europe. Here is an example of the typical alchemical prose of the *De rerum natura*:

> The nature encompassing the Universe is One, and its origin has to be the eternal unity. It is a vast organism in which the natural things harmonize and sympathize in reciprocal form. Such is the Macrocosm. All things are the product of a single effort of universal creation. The macrocosm and the microcosm are one. They form one constellation, one breath, one influence, one harmony, one time, one metal, one fruit. (cited in Pinto-Correia 33)

Much earlier, the writings of Zosimos included a vision of a vessel with man conceived inside.[12] In various texts from early antiquity, a root or mandragola grows to become a man inside a retort or vial. Psychoanalytically, this figure is clearly linked with male fantasy of parturition and/or onanism, especially as sperm often appears as the *materia prima*. In other variants the little man is made from blood, as in the parthenogenesis described by Robert Flood. Flood's man should be understood as an imitation of God. Indeed, in the more explicitly alchemical versions of this fantasy, the philosophical stone is equated to Christ. So the many variants of golem texts form a nexus in which alchemy, the automaton, and mystical, cabalistic language are linked inextricably.

Faustian Pacts

In a speech to Wagner (lines 1021–1055), Faust admits that neither he nor his father deserve any praise for their medical skills. His father brewed "secret recipes" in "the Black Kitchen," or alchemical laboratory. He and his adepts blended "contrariness of every sort," marrying a "Scarlet Lion" (mercury) to a Lily (hydrochloric acid). But in the end, "the patients went on dying." Wagner consoles Faust, saying that both father and son did their best, and a father will always pass his knowledge down to his son.

Goethe studied the alchemists and was influenced by Pietist thought, especially the work of Jacob Boehme.[13] It is probable that he engaged in some forms of alchemical experimentation, but proving or disproving this is of no importance for the present discussion. At the start of part 2, Mephistopheles and Faust are at the court of the emperor, where there is a serious money shortage. Moreover, the realm is in a state of disarray. So, like the historical court alchemists, Mephistopheles helpfully points out that the court possesses much gold—minted and unminted—if only a worthy spirit could summon it forth from the earth:

> Who in this world has not some lack or need?
> One this, one that—here it is cash. Indeed,
> There is no gathering of it off the pavement;
> Yet wisdom taps its most profound encavement
> In lodes and masonwork, where gold unstinted
> Waits underground, both minted and unminted;
> And who can raise it to the light of day?
> Man's gifts of Nature and Mind, I say.
> (4889–4896)

To this the chancellor responds with a doubtful rhetoric, calling the demonic offspring of Spirit and Nature (that is, the alchemical product—or potential gold) an impossible, misshapen hermaphrodite, an "in-between being":

> Nature is sin, the Mind is Satan,
> Doubt they engender in their mating,
> Their epicene misshapen child. [*Ihr mißgestaltet Zwitterkind*].
> (4900–4903)

The palace scene—featuring debates over the worth of gold—leads up to the second scene in which a homunculus will come into being. In Goethe's draft of his intermezzo "Helena," published in 1826, Mephistopheles takes Faust to visit Wagner in his laboratory on their way to Classical Hades. Wagner is constructing a chemical man (*chemisch Menschlein*—not yet called a homunculus). The creature, a dwarf or a gnome (*Zwerglein*), is conceived in a luminous glass (*leuchtenden Glaskobeln*). But he soon bursts out, demonstrating his considerable abilities. For instance, he "embodies a universal historical world calendar" (Goethe 2001, 525). The dwarf, Faust, Mephistopheles, and Wagner all decide to travel south together. "Despite their haste, Wagner does not forget to take along a clean phial, to collect here and there, if he can, the necessary elements for making a little chemical woman" (526). Meanwhile, the dwarf sits in one of Wagner's breast pockets. Having arrived in Greece, the chemical man "crawling along on the earth, gleans from the humus a great many phosphorescent atoms, some radiating a blue, others a purple fire. He conscientiously assigns them to Wagner's phial, though he doubts the possibility of creating a little chemical woman from them" (527). Followers of Caesar and Pompey attempt to appropriate the bits of glowing matter, but the four winds blow them away.

In *Faust* II (2, 6829–7006) Mephistopheles asks Wagner what loving pair he has placed into a vessel in order to create his homunculus.[14] But Wagner calls such methods of procreation old-fashioned. Instead, he is making the man all by himself, a method that is much more pure. It is a little man, but also a hermaphrodite, protected by the glass that surrounds it. Better, he is part of that glass, crystallized, although he aspires to be something more—more spiritually advanced, more human.[15] Following a long-standing tradition, Goethe refers to the alchemical homunculus, generated from water as *prima materia*.[16] It is a being without a body, but it has a watery origin and end. Goethe developed his ideas from Paracelsus, who described the genesis of the alchemical being in the following way:

> Let the Sperm of a man by it selfe be putrefied in a gourd glasse, sealed up, with the highest degree of putrefaction in Horse dung, for the space of forty days, or so long until it begin to bee alive, move, and stir, which can easily be seen. After this time it will be something like a Man, yet transparent, and without a body. Now after this, if it bee every day, and prudently nourished and fed with the Arcanum of Mans blood, and bee for the space of forty

weeks kept in a constant, equall heat of Horse-dung, it will become a true, an living infant, having all the members of an infant, which is born of a woman, but it will bee far lesse. This we call Homunculus, or Artificiall. And this is afterwards to be brought up with as great care, and diligence as any other infant, until it come to riper years of understanding. (cited in Gray 205–6)

Not merely content, then, to take on a human body, he aspires to operate the marriage of opposites—water and fire, matter and spirit, female and male. The imagery of luminous glass suggests a kind of anti-discourse to the difficult earthy materiality of the golem or the mandrake root, but also to real gold mining and the dark matter(s) of the alchemical laboratory / scholar's study.[17] To show what he can do, the homunculus describes Faust's dream (concerning Leda, Helen's mother, and the swan). The homunculus refuses to answer Wagner's questions, but instead wishes to act. There is some debate among critics as to whether or not Wagner would have or could have succeeded in creating him without help from Mephistopheles. When the homunculus speaks, he addresses Wagner as Vätterken (Fatherkin) and the devil as Herr Vetter (Cousin). This might seem to support the claim that he is the product of Wagner's work but that he has some distant affinity with the devil. Wagner carries the little man around in his vessel, taking him to the sleeping Faust. Moreover, Mephistopheles asks what is going on, implying that he was not privy to the preparations for the making of the man. The primary purpose of the homunculus seems to be to lead Faust to ancient Greece to meet Helen. Mephistopheles does not feel comfortable there, and he cannot appear before the symbol of beauty. It is only by mentioning Thessalian witches that the bossy homunculus tempts Mephistopheles to travel to the South, and he informs Wagner that a scholar must remain in his laboratory. Wagner is sad because he realizes he may never see his "son" again, but he has no choice but to obey. The act ends abruptly, and we find ourselves transported in space and time to ancient Sparta, where Faust has an opportunity to meet Helen.

The homunculus sees through Faust, who is transparent like a glass or like Hoffmann's Clara. Indeed, the homunculus sees more clearly than Mephistopheles, and the two of them can be considered cousins because neither is a true man. As in the case of the golem, then, the Faustian homunculus threatens to triumph over man. In any case, Goethe seems to have insisted on the active principle of this being. The homunculus makes fun of Mephistopheles for his "Northern" nature. Other scholars have argued that the homunculus serves another purpose in the narrative—that is, to revivify Helen. In any case, the Faustian paradigm of the man in a glass retort is one that surfaces with significant frequency. The purpose of the homunculus seems to be to bring Faust southward, but he has little self-determination (just as, we may say, Olympia apparently only serves the purpose of duping Nathanael, and then she may die). Clearly, Goethe's narrative—in "Helena," as in *Faust*—is key for Hoffmann.

But we must avoid the specter of some quasi-Jungian attempt to retrieve a universal archetype, as the construction of a "chemical man" might risk taking on this cast. An alchemical reading of Hoffmann's tale does *not* reduce the narrative to a single "hidden" literary or visual topos, however. If Hoffmann wanted us to know for certain what the two men were doing as they worked over the fire, he would have told us. The withholding of information is not merely meant to leave us with "intellectual uncertainty"—it reflects the fact that the little boy does not know what the men are doing. The structure of the trauma is based on witnessing something he was not supposed to see; something undertaken between two men; something shameful, violent, and without a successful end or procreation. From this point of view, it hardly matters whether the collaboration between the men is a form of alchemy, a form of experimentation with the creation of an automaton, or both. On the other hand, the clear vision (Clara's) of the trauma indicates a botched experiment in alchemy, one that failed to achieve a spiritual dimension—that is, it failed to create a man.

To read "The Sandman" alchemically is also to read a certain ambivalence, not only in the text itself, but in that most powerful reading that sticks to the tale like a verso of a page sticks to a recto. If the encounter between the two men in "The Sandman" is both a primal scene—sexually charged for the child Nathanael—and a scene of alchemy, what emerges is an unfulfilled dream of male parthenogenesis, a dream that persists throughout the long history of the West and refuses to die. It is an extremely familiar dream that is apparently worth dreaming, in spite of the risks it entails; a dream of the triumph of the male figure in the couple that would have made gold—that is, synthesized a third element, a son—but without recourse to the mercurial, lunar, or watery feminine that is a counter to the sulfuric, solar, and fiery male in traditional alchemical imagery. Since the feminine in alchemy signals the death of the male, a successful encounter between two men would have represented a triumph over death. Alchemy—that is, the creation of a man—was something worth pursuing, a risk worth taking, even though in "The Sandman" the result is a concatenation of symptoms or pathologies that lead to the undoing of the male, while the feminine, embodied in the clarity of fecund Clara, is salubrious and free of darkness. This dream is what is gained, perhaps, from yet another reading of this (perhaps over-read) tale.

Excursus: Counterfeiting

In Canto XXIX of Dante's *Inferno*, Virgil guides Dante to a circle where the pilgrim hears screams of pain and smells festering limbs (*marcite membre*). Virgil urges Dante to speak to a pair of mutual scab-pickers. First, Griffolino of Arezzo explains that he was burned at the stake for one crime (he claimed to be able to fly and exploited the credulity of a ruler's son), but he is in hell for the crime of alchemy (*alchimia*). The second leper, Capocchio, an ape of nature, also counterfeited metals by alchemy (*falsai li metalli con alchimia*). The canto abruptly ends here. Dante seems less interested in the precise nature of alchemy than in the overall effect it has on society. Even farther down, in Malebolge (Canto XXX), is Maestro Adamo, who minted false florins—symbols of Florence's greatness—and stamped them with the head of John the Baptist. He was burned in 1281 for this crime. Perhaps the alchemists are placed with the fraudulent because they "tried to create gold out of base metals thus attempting to falsify the naturally produced standard of monetary value whereas the money-counterfeiter Maestro Adamo committed the same social crime in reverse debasing the gold with three carats of dross from which he struck the florins" (Armour 18). The falsifiers undermine truth, which is of paramount importance for universal social bonds. "Fraud in general, for Dante, is a sin which breaks *'pur lo vinco d'amor che fa natura,'* solely the natural bond of love which should hold society together" (Ibid.). Dante seems to have viewed alchemy as a process whereby (real) gold might or might not be produced (unnaturally) in such a way as to undermine the economy. These particular sinners aped nature or God's work (which is certainly to be condemned in itself), but the reason they are punished is for throwing a wrench into social harmony.

The contemporary counterfeiter generally prefers to work with the highest denominator of paper money available and does not bother with coins. He uses all available technology to study the current forms of money production. If he manages to pass off his work as true, he may purchase property, disappear from public life, move "offshore"—but he will not necessarily continue to put his false bills in circulation, unless his aim is to undermine a national economy through an act of terror. In fictive narratives the counterfeiter is unable to resist a return to society. He can't leave well enough alone (like a director compelled to make a sequel for a popular film). Although counterfeiting has high costs and forces mints to upgrade their security systems, it cannot be said to radically disrupt the economy— or better, it is built into the system as an assumption, already discounted.

In the field of counterfeiting, it is the very idea, not just the product, that threatens society. Money artists like John Haberle (who painted bills starting in the late 1880s) and, more recently, J.S.G. Boggs, are the targets of extensive government probes. It is illegal to put a bill into a photocopier in the United States, even if the resulting image is so far from the original that there would be no chance of fooling someone. However, when Boggs was accused by the Bank of England of reproducing pound notes, his lawyer argued on center stage in the Old Bailey that his client's notes were original works of art, not "reproductions," which are illegal under British law (Weschler 52). The work of the counterfeiter threatens the very fabric of what society is based on, in the most instinctual or visceral way. After his acquittal in Britain, Boggs devised a project in Pittsburgh that involved a million dollars in "Boggs money" that he hoped would be kept in circulation rather than exchanged by the artist with a single merchant. A panel of judges in the United States debated the status of Boggs's bills. His lawyer argued that the works were like pornography and Boggs should be allowed the right to free expression. However, as Boggs explained, "the government was countering that [my] bills were more like hard-core drugs, contraband and evil in and of themselves, and hence subject to seizure without recourse" (cited in Weschler 143). In his final decision, the Pittsburgh judge determined that the money drawings were most analogous to *child* pornography, "so manifestly evil and obviously self-evident when you came upon it, that you didn't need a jury to make any further determination" (ibid.).

Working in Japan, the money artist Akasegawa also explored the relationship between capitalism and state authority. His notes were not counterfeit, but simulacra, and as such they put into question the validity of all money by "mocking" the yen. Like Boggs, Akasegawa was also severely prosecuted.

In any act of counterfeiting paper money, the feel of the paper is key to the legitimacy of the bill, and this may be even more important than what is on the face. Although the precise formula for the greenback paper is a secret, we know that raw cotton is cooked for two hours in a caustic bath. It is cleaned, bleached, and further refined. Then red and blue fibers are added to the bath. Finally, the green coloring is made from a secret mixture of pigments and binding agents, the *solve et coagula*. In other words, it passes through various stages of alchemical transformation.

Compared with paper money, gold is very difficult to counterfeit because it has a specific atomic weight. Generally speaking, the alchemist would use secret technology to produce gold that would hold up to any comparison. The alchemist makes real gold, not a simulation of gold—but he does so through methods that simulate the long process of Nature's ripening of gold in "her womb." On the other hand, some forms of alchemy might be likened to "sophistication" or adulteration. The gold produced might appear real to the unknowing, but in its core, it may contain baser elements. However, this form of falsification is rare in the alchemical tradition. "Sophisticated" gold would represent a failure for the "philosophical" alchemist. It could only be said to be a triumph for the capitalist alchemist who uses it to squeeze out just a "little more" capital. So we could imagine, in theory, a kind of seizure of alchemy by capitalism comparable to the seizure of any other industry—say, bread-making, for instance. Marx reminds us that capital "is at first indifferent as to the technical character of the labour-process; it begins by taking it just as it finds it" (Marx 1867, 248). Adulterated bread, including "a certain quantity of human perspiration mixed with the discharge of abscesses, cobwebs, dead black-beetles, and putrid German yeast, without counting alum, sand, and other agreeable mineral ingredients" represents a type of sophistry that "knows better than Protagoras how to make white black, and black white, and better than the Eleatics how to demonstrate *ad oculos* that everything is only appearance" (249). Even the sacramental host may be adulterated in such a manner, says Marx! Perhaps a comparison between the bread of the capitalists and the gold of the alchemists is not out of order, at least in one variant of alchemy.

But where the adulteration of bread develops parallel to the development of a class of capitalist bakers and the extension of the working day and night, the same cannot be said of alchemy.

The counterfeiter-sophist-alchemist does not divulge his method. If he succeeds, he may disappear from public life like the counterfeiter, but he might also continue his work (in secret) or teach the art to a select few adepts or to his sons. He does not generally use the gold in exchange for subsistence goods, let alone for property or luxury goods. He may indeed be indebted to a prince who has sponsored his labors, so he may not even be in possession of his own gold. It does not enter into circulation, perhaps because the amount produced is so small. And because alchemy is so difficult and is practiced on such a minute scale—if indeed one accepts that it is practiced at all—it does not disrupt in any significant way the national economy.

§ 6 *Reading* Capital I *Alchemically*

This chapter represents a modest attempt to think about alchemy as the production of gold in the context of a larger discourse on "real" production, "real" money, and "real" consumption, and through Marx, in particular. Naturally, this is a hypothetical exercise, one that begs a rather large line of credit from the reader. The practice of alchemy has never resulted in the production of gold in quantities large enough to affect a discourse on production in any serious way, pace Becher and other early modern courtiers. Alchemy could be said to stand apart from capitalism, for although it can take the form of a bourgeois activity, it is not primarily about the exploitation of labor for the creation of surplus value. Marx wrote little that was explicitly about alchemy, and for the most part he did so in a purely illustrative or analogical way. For Marx, alchemy could be said to represent a quaint and antiquated form of mysticism, not a foundational paradigm for industrial capitalism. But to think of alchemy in terms of production seems, nevertheless, an important exercise.

So what would we expect to find, reading alchemy in(to) Marx? On the surface of the text, we might search for *Decknamen*, hidden codes, claims to the most clarity possible under the circumstances, belied by an utter lack of clarity. As we know, the pretense to write on the precipice of excessive disclosure is a typical rhetorical strategy of alchemy. And indeed, some readers have criticized the relative opacity of Marx's language, his excessive use of figures:

The metaphorical style of *Capital* has attracted much sarcasm. It allegedly attests to obvious imposture. It evinces an inability to submit to the rigours of scientific formalization. It displays the indelible stamp of a speculative—or, worse still, literary—nostalgia. A number of readers are discouraged by a lack of univocal, reliable definitions, by so many terminological variations and inconsistencies! Marx's writing does indeed wrestle with the uncertainties of the language. Many misinterpretations can result. (Bensaïd 205)

Analyzing the first two sentences of Marx's text, Thomas Keenan writes: "The matter at issue here is the appearance or self-announcement of something as something else, the rhetorical structure of simile or metaphor (*als, comme*): semblance, shine, simulation or dissimulation. In those societies where the capitalist mode of production prevails, something (economic) shows itself by hiding itself, by announcing itself as something else or in another form" (Keenan 157). Such formulations should be entirely familiar. But the relative difficulty or even the "magic" said to pervade *Capital* is not sufficient to make of this an alchemical text.

On a macro-textual or narrative level, we might expect to find a series of stages, from dissolution or death (of matter?) leading up to a golden renewal (matter rejuvenated by its unification with ideas?). And suppose we did impose this structure onto the first volume of *Capital*? Various critics have addressed the "logical architecture of *Capital*" (Bensaïd 108). The volume begins with the basic unit of capital—the commodity—and then moves to the functioning of surplus value, so the reader might think that Marx is, in fact, narrating a progression. The commodity comes first in his narration as the most basic experience of capitalism, even though it is the result of labor (Hardt and Negri 64). The volume ends with (so-called) primitive accumulation, moving back in time before the full-blown developments of the central part, and ending, in the chapter on colonialism, with the "redemptive" sentence: "The only thing that interests us is the secret discovered in the new world by the Political Economy of the old world, and proclaimed on the house-tops: that the capitalist mode of production and accumulation, and therefore capitalist private property, have for their fundamental condition the annihilation of self-earned private property; in other words, the expropriation of the labourer" (Marx 1867, 774). Marx himself acknowledged that the first chapter was the most difficult one in the volume. The volume continues, didactically explaining the functioning of capital, but without staging a death or rebirth. One would be hard-pressed to find transmutation from something base into something noble. Inasmuch as volume I, at least, is an outline of the total mechanisms of capital (developed in detail in the subsequent volumes), it does not represent "the first stage" of a process. Finally, how can we reconcile Marx's considerable irony with alchemy's self-serious discourse of self-fulfillment or redemption?

The title of this chapter makes reference to Louis Althusser and Etienne Balibar's *Reading Capital*. Philosophers, Althusser notes, may have read all or parts of volume I of Marx's Great Work, but "some day it is essential to read *Capital* to the letter" (Althusser and Balibar 13). *Reading Capital* is as much a study of reading as it is of *Capital*, and in this regard it conditions the question of how to read (*Capital*), alchemically.[1]

With the numeral *I* in my title, I also want to refer to the series of debates around the reading of Dürer's famous engraving *Melancholia* (Figure 7). Many critics have taken up this work, ignoring the numeral *I* that floats after *melencolia* on the banner borne aloft by a bat. Panofsky put forward the idea that this was to be the first in a series—perhaps meant to encompass the four humors—of which the other engravings were simply never realized. Panofsky believed (mistakenly, according to Maurizio Calvesi) that the German artist was influenced by the Neoplatonic idea of the *furor melancholicus* as a prison. In their massive study of the iconography of melancholy, *Saturn and Melancholy*, Klibansky, Panofsky, and Saxl adhered to the Ficinian idea of *acedia* as a negative condition (Agamben 1977, 18). Yet in other contexts, the saturnine character also yields positive outcomes, including salvation. Melancholy, in a sense, is always ambivalence—*tristitia salutifera-tristitia mortifera*—and is not simply "ponderously pessimistic" (Calvesi 1993, xxi). Seen in a broader light, melancholy is not, as Panofsky suggested, simply a sign of the artist's impotence, but rather "the uterus in which is grown his dream of greatness" (ibid.). *Saturn and Melancholy* focuses on how Dürer was influenced by astrological and humoral traditions of the Middle Ages. At first the authors thought that the engraving was supposed to be *I* in a series on the temperaments (Klibansky et al. 349).[2] But they realized that there was no precedent for beginning such a series with melancholy. They later settled on the following explanation: *I* refers to *melancholia imaginativa*, the first in a series that would lead to *melancholia rationalis* (II), and finally to *melancholia mentalis* (III), as in the sequence deriving from Agrippa von Nettesheim, who would have served to introduce Ficino and the Florentine Academy to Dürer (Klibansky et al. 351). In other words, *Saturn and Melancholy* explains the numerical sequence (hypothetical, since the artist never completed any other work in the series) based on a literary source that links the Italian and Northern Renaissances around the figure of saturnine melancholy.

However, later critics have come to identify the *I* in the engraving not with the humors or with the types of melancholy outlined in Agrippa, but with the first stage of the alchemical process, the *nigredo*. Agamben writes, "It is not surprising . . . that melancholy was identified by the alchemists with the *Nigredo*, the first stage of that Great Work that consisted in, according to the old spagyritic maxim, giving the corporeal over to the incorporeal and making the incorporeal corporeal" (Agamben 1977, 33). The subject can be "cured" of the *nigredo*. "Man himself becomes the object of the *opus* of transformation" in an ideal alchemical narrative (Calvesi 1993, xxvi). If alchemy is the artistic process and spiritual fulfillment, the *I* represents merely a stage to be overcome, a necessary dissolution that has to be followed by reintegration of form (Calvesi 1993, xxvi), a holistic and felicitous unification! The reference to the numeral *I* in the Dürer engraving as apparently initiating a chain of progress—arcane as it may be—underscores what is *not* at stake in the present reading of *Capital I*. By invoking this iconographic debate (without taking sides in it) and by linking it to *Capital*, I hope to do nothing more than raise questions about the structure of this work and about how to read a text like this if we perceive it to be part of a series, especially if we think of *Capital III* as the most concrete of the three (and also the one that humanists tend to avoid).

Difficult Beginnings

Marx posits a transition from the commodity in its plain, homely, bodily form—the base material—to exchange-value, and finally, to the development of the general equivalent. This passage could, perhaps, be thought of as analogous to transmutation in alchemy. But the notion of a transition does not appear sufficient to warrant an alchemical reading of *Capital*. We need to seek out what, precisely, is alchemical in the book and read it in the key of alchemy.

Perhaps the most obvious place to begin is Marx's discussion in the *Grundrisse* in which he writes that consumption is always immediately production, "just as in nature the consumption of the elements and chemical substances is the production of the plant. . . . Consumptive production" (Marx 1885, 91). Production and consumption mediate each other. "The product only obtains its 'last finish' in consumption" (ibid.).

In this discussion, Marx refers to commodities of a practical nature, such as a garment, railroad tracks, or a house. Yet the model that he proposes is useful for understanding alchemy, even if the commodity—gold—is not something whose potentiality can immediately be exploited. Put another way, "in the labour-process, therefore, man's activity, with the help of the instruments of labour, effects an alteration, designed from the commencement, in the material worked upon. The process disappears in the product" (Marx 1867, 180). Isn't this precisely what the traditional alchemist struggles against with all of his rhetorical force?

In the genealogy of capitalist production, Marx notes that the spinning wheel and the loom (standing as signs of the alchemical in the present context and central to "Rumpelstiltskin" and *Silas Marner*) were not invented by capitalism, but capitalism appropriated them. Marx ridicules the idea that the capitalist stored up raw materials, necessities, and tools, and then offered them to the worker so that he might produce for the capitalist. Rather, nature, raw materials, and tools develop alongside of capitalism, and in a complex relationship with labor.

There are a number of "golden" ages of production—transitional ages when labor is in the process of becoming emancipated but is not yet alienated as wage labor under the command of the capitalist. An important part of this process is when the capitalist draws the spinner from the cottage into a space owned by the capitalist. This is the origin of large-scale industry or mass-production. Yet as this happens, bourgeois women continue to spin at home. As in the Low Countries in the seventeenth century (the golden age of alchemy), spinning becomes a domestic practice and a sign of feminine virtue. It is only when women still have to spin, or rather, when their labor is potentially significant for society, that a great deal of anxiety around spinning is generated, as discussed in Chapter 4.

Commodities and Money

Marx begins volume I of *Capital* with an (alchemical) analogy. All commodities, he writes, are "ambivalent," or doubled, in that they may be seen from the perspective of both quality and quantity. In explicating the mysteries of value, Marx places linen on the left side of the balance sheet and the coat on the right. Chemistry is called upon at this point to explain:

> Butyric acid is a different substance from propyl formate. Yet both are made up of the same chemical substances, carbon (C), hydrogen (H), and oxygen

(O), and that, too, in like proportions—namely, $C_4H_8O_2$. If now we equate butyric acid to propyl formate, then, in the first place, propyl formate would be, in this relation, merely a form of existence of $C_4H_8O_2$; and in the second place, we should be stating that butyric acid also consists of $C_4H_8O_2$. Therefore, by thus equating the two substances, expression would be given to their chemical composition, while their different physical forms would be neglected. (50)

The equivalency of the coat and linen is really an equation showing that both embody labor. Only through the equation of two different types of commodities can we see what they share in common as their " 'intrinsick vertue' (this is Barbon's special term for value in use) which in all places have the same vertue; as the load-stone to attract iron" (35 n3). That intrinsic quality (analogous to the lodestone's intrinsic property—that is, a property always found in lodestone regardless of size or shape) is, for Marx, abstract human labor. Barbon's "intrinsick vertue," like "intensive property" in chemistry, is exemplified by the lodestone—magnetite—a rather plain, lusterless, iron magnetic ore. Regardless of the particular commodities in question, abstract human labor is the one constant.

The philosopher's stone of alchemy would *like to be* the lodestone and hence, like abstract human labor, a constant. However, in each variant of alchemy we find that the stone is something different. Sometimes it seems akin to the touchstone, basanite, that can be rubbed on noble metals and subjected to an acid test to confirm purity. Sometimes it is the product of transmutation itself—gold, or the son, Christ—a secret material that can be used to effect further transformation. Sometimes it is described as a substance readily at hand; sometimes one must struggle to obtain it. In the *Turba philosophorum*, Pythagoras explains that the philosopher's stone *is* constant like the lodestone. He tells his companions: "Know, also, that the thing which they have described in so many ways follows and attains its companion without fire, even as the magnet follows the iron, to which the said thing is not vainly compared, nor to a seed, nor to a matrix, for it is also like unto these." But he goes on to clarify that while the stone is everywhere, it is not available to all:

And this same thing, which follows its companion without fire, causes many colours to appear when embracing it, for this reason, that the said one thing enters into every regimen, and is found everywhere, being a stone, and also not a stone; common and precious; hidden and concealed, yet known by everyone; of one name and of many names, which is the Spume of the Moon. This stone, therefore, is not a stone, because it is more precious; without it Nature never operates anything; its name is one, yet we have called it by many names on account of the excellence of its nature. (*Turba* 42–43)

In other words, in contrast to the lodestone, whose physical constancy can be verified by a simple experiment, what is constant about the stone of alchemy is its very ineffability. So, to continue in the spirit of Marxian equations: if magnetism is to the lodestone as abstract human labor is to the commodity, then ineffable secrecy is the equivalent of (magnetism and) abstract human labor. In essence, then, Marx's literary style helps to both clarify and problematize the intrinsic property of alchemy, especially in its relation to real production in the real world.

In contrast, use-value has little relation to alchemy since it does not permit the sort of material distinction that transmutation implies. Marx again quotes Barbon: "One sort of wares are as good as another, if the values be equal. There is no difference or distinction of things of equal value. . . . An hundred pounds' worth of lead or iron is of as great value as one hundred pounds' worth of silver and gold" (Marx 1867, 37). This assertion has interesting implications for the type of alchemy that involved an alloy or transmutation of an equal amount of silver into the same amount of gold. Yes, gold is a more valuable metal, but the initial outlay of expense might be great on the part of the alchemist, so the process would already require that he be wealthy or have the backing of a prince, for instance. And the transmutation would be more a prestigious act than a genuine enrichment.

Labor power initially determines value. Early on, Marx may have accepted the Ricardian notion that gold and silver receive their value from supply and demand, but he later "decided that the values of gold and silver conformed to the law of value and were determined by costs of production, or more exactly by the socially necessary labour-time involved in their production" (Nelson 69). So the introduction of industrial machinery to weaving devalues a laborer like Silas Marner, who stays at home and continues to use his handloom. From here, Marx extends the analogy. "If we could succeed at a small expenditure of labour, in converting carbon into diamonds, their value might fall below that of bricks" (Marx 1867, 40). Like alchemy, this hypothetical conversion is simply a natural process, sped up. But whereas in alchemy the successful conversion of "carbon into diamonds" should and would require a great expenditure of labor, in the real world of capital, value would be determined precisely by circumventing or eliding the arduous process.

Abstract human labor as described by Marx is commonly translated as "a mere congelation of homogeneous human labour." But as Keston Sutherland has shown, "congelation" is a rather poor translation for the German *Gallerte*, a gelatinous and disgusting mass of animals that should remind us of the alchemy of sophistication and the toxic admixtures in the Chicago packing plant that Upton Sinclair described. *Gallerte*, Sutherland notes, is neither fish nor fowl nor meat, but additives: a "sophisticated" mishmash of different forms of labor. The term is part of "an allegorical satire on consumption," the object of which is not the poor "processed" laborer but the capitalist who eats *Gallerte*. Sutherland writes: "What ought to be the fluid labor of living human beings is instead a disgusting, paradigmatically unnatural food product for the bourgeois consumer, 'the vampire which sucks out its [the proletariat's] blood and brains and throws them into the alchemist's vessel of capital.'" The latter part of the quotation is from Marx's *Eighteenth Brumaire*. But where we might be tempted to dismiss both the vampire and the alchemical *vas* as two more examples of alchemy reduced to "magical transformation" or as substitutes for the (mistranslated) process of congelation that labor becomes in *Capital*, we must acknowledge, with Sutherland, that Marx knew very well what he was writing. The traditional narrative of alchemy *should* be one in which all impurities die, giving rise to the touchstone, or son—the philosopher's stone, gold, Christ, the pure one. Yet the very certainty of such a narrative is disrupted by Marx's satire. The capitalist/alchemist may (mis)perceive a teleological progression: "Its fetish-character may prevent the bourgeois consumer from seeing in *Gallerte* the brains, muscles, nerves and hands themselves; that is, the substance of the paradigmatic commodity may be undifferentiable back into the aggregate of its living human origins by any act merely of conscientious perception." Sutherland goes on to ask if the bourgeois consumer can choose to beg off the dish. The answer is: "No, he cannot, because the rendering of human minds and bodies into *Gallerte* is not, on the terms of Marx's satire, an abuse of wage labor by the coven of leading unreconstructed vampires but the fundamental law of all wage labor." Perhaps a form of false consciousness or an inability to perceive that which exists as presiding law blocks the bourgeois from understanding what he is consuming: the blood and brains of the laborer. And this is precisely what the alchemical dream helps to cover up—real labor.

Yet we should be clear that in general terms, gold does not become capital in alchemy, nor does the alchemist become a capitalist. The alchemist does not meet in the marketplace with a laborer who freely sells his labor power. The alchemist *is* the laborer himself, or he may take on an adept, who cannot be confused with the laborer in Marx's sense. Alchemy is not self-sustaining, and because the alchemist normally does not take his gold to the market or make his product socially useful, he does not (normally) produce a commodity. He certainly does not produce enough to renew his vital energy. So to a certain degree, any analogy with capitalism must be understood to be limited. On the other hand, considering economies of scale, the production of alchemy would seem to represent, as we have suggested repeatedly, a utopian potential for self-subsistence, as when Marx notes that the materials (those prior to raw materials) of nature are tiny in quantity. In a note, he cites James Steuart: "The earth's spontaneous productions being in small quantity, and quite independent of man, appear, as it were, to be furnished by Nature, in the same way a small sum is given to a young man, in order to put him in a way of industry, and of making his fortune" (from "Principles of Political Economy," cited in Marx 1867, 178 n.1). Again, this refers to the immediate elements of nature prior to some alteration by means of labor, and it seems essential to note this, since we so often take raw materials to mean those materials given forth by nature, like ores that have not (yet) been extracted. In certain industries, such as the chemical industry, the raw materials disappear in the product, so we can no longer distinguish between the principal substance that formed the product and any accessory materials (181). In other words, the product effaces its process. Gold is not gold until it is extracted from its natural state.

So what makes gold different from other commodities? As we know, the labor involved in its extraction is among the most difficult of all forms of labor. A visual confirmation of this labor pain greets the driver along the roads that lead from Johannesburg to Soweto: strange mountains jutting up from the plain, spotting the landscape. These are the mountains of dust that were excavated from the gold mines with cyanide, and they have polluted the air, causing countless people to suffer and die from respiratory diseases. Gold mining is no easy business. There is something particularly resistant about gold that even new technologies have not been able to overcome. We should acknowledge this, even before we attempt a more rigorous investigation of gold as money. In some versions of alchemical discourse, the labor, the telluric struggle, is made explicit (representations of the alchemical process as mining, for instance), but in others it is effaced in favor of a discourse that is light, airy, perhaps even linked with glass and clarity, as we have seen.

Exchange-Value, Use-Value

Marx teaches us that, in general, exchange-value is relative. "An exchange value that is inseparably connected with, inherent in commodities, seems a contradiction in terms"(1867 36). In contrast, we feel intuitively that gold approaches something like a perfect inseparability, inherent-ness, or intrinsic-ness. Nevertheless, in the first volume of *Capital*, gold is portrayed as just another commodity, in the same sentence as—and apparently equal to—blacking, silk, or wheat. Moreover, in discussing the abstract "common something" that determines exchange-values as relative, Marx notes that this "common something" cannot be of a material nature. "An hundred pounds' worth of lead or iron, is of as great value as one hundred pounds' worth of silver or gold" (37).

Use-values of commodities are combinations of two elements: matter and labor. When we subtract labor from the commodity, there is always some material substratum left, a natural remainder, created without and before the intervention of man. In effect, man's labor works like nature does. Man transforms matter. He brings together and separates. Marx's language echoes the *solve et coagula* of alchemy. He says: "We see, then, that labor is not the only source of material wealth, of use-values produced by labor. As William Petty puts it, labor is its [material wealth's] father and the earth its mother" (43).[3] This familial-conjugal metaphor concerns use-value before any discussion of value. It is easy to see, so far, how one might wish to make an analogy with alchemy, which is, after all, a human labor of transformation, in imitation of nature, bringing together the king and the queen, to produce the (golden) offspring (use-value). Moreover, the analogy of the earth and the mother is especially important in the specific instance of the Northern European tradition of mining mythologies. We should simply note the antiquity and prestige of William Petty's analogy for the dual characteristic of use-values. In the traditional alchemical analogy, the earth is the mother, and the father is equated with the seed or sperm that penetrates the earth at different points to produce different kinds of metals.[4] In Marx's case, we could say that his concept of labor has taken over the role that was assigned by the premodern epigenesist thinkers to a mystical fluid or semen.

Marx explains further:

> Commodities come into the world in the shape of use-values, articles or goods, such as iron, linen, corn, etc. This is their plain, homely, bodily form. They are, however, commodities, only because they are something two-fold, both objects of utility, and, at the same time, depositories of value. They manifest themselves therefore as commodities, or have the form of commodities, only in so far as they have two forms, a physical or natural form, and a value-form (51).

All commodities are characterized by this binary structure. They are graspable material entities, and they are also, as value, "impossible to grasp." All commodities have a common value-form that is "impossible to grasp"— their money form (51). Marx never uses the terms *feminine* and *masculine*, or even *mother* and *father*, to correspond to the two binaries. As is well known, a key point that Marx makes in this section is that human labor creates value but has no value in itself. It becomes value only in its fixed state, when embodied in the form of some object. (What the king and queen / bridegroom and bride do is of little importance. What matters is the body in which their "work" is materialized, deposited, and accumulated; that is why they die with little consequence or mourning.) In alchemical terms, "the presence of death at the union of the lovers symbolized not only the extinction of the earlier differentiated state before union, but, most importantly, it conveyed the alacrity with which the triumphant moment of the 'coagula' could be transformed into the lamentation of the 'solve' or death" (Abraham 1991, 302–03). In other words, the two are almost simultaneous. Death personified (Saturn; a skeleton) is often present at the tomb of lovers. Normally, alchemy starts with the old form (metal; body) that is inherently corrupt. This is dissolved into *prima materia* and then coagulated into pure form. The terms *solve* and *coagula* are really the same as *separatio* and *coniunctio*. Both lead to death of the "body."

Transformation into General Equivalents

The first volume of *Capital* includes various equations, organized into two vertical columns. On the left the author lists a series of commodities whose names are accompanied by an unknown variable. On the right is one commodity, chosen to stand as general equivalent, whose name is accompanied by an unknown variable.[5] The only thing that would seem to distinguish the commodities in the left-hand column from those in the right is their structural position in the equation. But in a real situation, the commodity that, in its bodily form, is socially identified as "standing in" as the general equivalent serves the function of money. The one commodity that, in its bodily form, has attained "the foremost place" as serving this function is gold. This does not mean that other commodities could not "stand in" in the place of gold to the right of the equal sign. But in practice, it is gold that has achieved a peculiar status as doing so. In fact, for gold to achieve (through the course of *history*) this peculiar status, it previously must have been a simple commodity like any other (existing on the left-hand side of the equation). But, over time, as gold began to monopolize the position on the right-hand side, not only did its status change vis-à-vis the other commodities, but the nature of the equivalency itself changed from that of "the relation of commodities to a general equivalent" to "the relation of commodities to a universal equivalent," otherwise known as the money form.

According to Marx, the fact that gold (and, to some degree, silver) easily assumes the money-form has led some thinkers to assume that precious metals have a merely imaginary value, that they are illusory (magic). But this is an error. This kind of thinking came from the mistaken idea that because the money-form of an object is not necessarily an inseparable part of that object, that object is merely symbolic. In essence, those pragmatic economists find the very ambivalence of gold in some sense intolerable. Or rather, we might say that the economists go through a logical or rationalizing process whereby they demonize gold because of its ambivalence. But really, Marx is positing the opposite: that all commodities (and not just those which assume, at a given point, the form of money) are symbols with regard to their values inasmuch as they are merely the "material envelope of the human labour spent upon" them (1867 90). Like the other commodities, gold once stood on the left side of the equation. It too is a symbol (on whose "face" is inscribed a value of abstract human labor). Moreover, even as gold *becomes all the more what it is*, it comes into its own golden perfection, and it still may be thought to retain its membership in the general group of commodities in that its value remains relative to the other commodities with which it once had commerce on the left side of the equation. And for all that gold shines, its value is still determined by the labor time necessary for its production. This is not easy to comprehend, though. Marx quotes William Petty:

> If a man can bring to London an ounce of silver out of the Earth in Peru, in the same time that he can produce a bushel of Corn, then the one is the natural price of the other; now, if by reason of new or more easie mines a man can procure two ounces of silver as easily as he formerly did one, the corn will be as cheap at ten shillings the bushel as it was before at five shillings, caeteris paribus. (from "A Treatise of Taxes and Contributions," cited in Marx 1867, 91)

This passage raises a conundrum because Marx does not elaborate on the "new or more easie mines." His formula implies a singular shift rather than a broad-based technological intervention that would change the rate of exchange in general. But in order for alchemy to exist, it must in fact be such a singular and peculiar event and cannot become a general technology available to the public.

Through sleight of hand and an eliding of the steps leading up to this process, it could seem as if gold and silver spring fully grown into their value, from a godlike thigh, without any pain of labor. "These objects, gold and silver, just as they come out of the bowels of the earth, are forthwith the direct incarnation of all human labour" (Marx 1867, 92). This is what Marx calls the "magic" (and I believe we can translate this to mean something close to "false consciousness") of money. We can understand it as magic only by "forgetting" the steps in between, which is how communities came to stamp one particular commodity (for Marx, this is, generally speaking, gold) with the value of money. We forget mining and minting, colonial occupation and transport, and see only the brilliant coin passing from one hand to the next.

Once we reach the "end" of this history, once gold has become the "socially acceptable" and "convenient" way of expressing values as the money-form (perhaps as a steganography, to use the Romance literary term), it is possible to suppress the other variables of the equation, or better, to speak of only one commodity in relation to gold. Marx writes that "the price or money-form of commodities is, like their form of value generally, a form quite distinct from their palpable bodily form; it is, therefore, a purely ideal or mental form" (95). For our purposes, the fact that gold both takes on the form of money (as a [male] ideal) and yet retains its bodily form (female) makes it quite peculiar among objects, with implications for a materialist study of gender. Yes, it is true that different monies bear different names, and these money-names express a value of commodities, and also "aliquot parts of the weight of the metal that is the standard of money" (100–101). Gold, then, is both body and soul. In other words, it is necessary that value be distinguished from the bodily (female) forms of commodities, and yet also bear the material (but unmeaning and purely social-conventional) form of the monies themselves. In order for a commodity to enter into circulation as exchange-value, as Marx writes in an extremely dense passage, "it must quit its bodily shape, must transform itself from mere imaginary in real gold, although to the commodity such transubstantiation may be more difficult than to the Hegelian 'concept,' the transition from 'necessity' to 'freedom,' or to a lobster the casting of his shell, or to Saint Jerome the putting off of old Adam" (103). We could gloss this key passage as follows: In order for a commodity to enter into circulation as exchange-value, it must quit its bodily shape [female], must transform itself from mere imaginary [male] into real gold, although to the commodity such transubstantiation may be extremely arduous. In a footnote, Marx further expands on the third analogy, the putting off of old Adam by Saint Jerome:

> Jerome had to wrestle hard, not only in his youth with the bodily flesh, as is shown by his fight in the desert with the handsome women of his imagination, but also in his old age with the spiritual flesh. "I thought," he says, "I was in the spirit before the Judge of the Universe." "Who art thou?" asked a voice. "I am a Christian." "Thou liest," thundered back the great Judge, "Thou art nought but a Ciceronian." (103 n.1)

Saint Jerome emerges from this text like the lone alchemist in his study, especially in Northern European painting of the seventeenth century. One need only think of Rembrandt's depictions of saints in meditation to recall how important such images are to the canon of painting. Recall that Jerome was the patron of humanists, and Albrecht Dürer claimed that he was a humanist rather than a mere craftsman.[Figure 8]). The claim of the artist to humanism is thus embedded in the etching itself. Dürer's mastery in his *St. Jerome* lies in portraying the different textures of the materials and the light coming in the window. The perspective is also flawlessly masterful. Jerome lived as a hermit, under the sign of Saturn. The etching, like *Melancholia* (I) has been interpreted as a symbolic self-portrait. In *Saturn and Melancholy*, Panofsky et al. remind us that in *Melancholia*—a print that the artist considered half of a pair with his

St. Jerome—the artist/alchemist/humanist is transubstantiated through the alchemical/artistic process. The female is absent from the scene, but her very absence signifies a passage toward the fulfillment of the Great Work, the dissolution of matter.

Hermaphroditic Gold

Marx continues in *Capital* by asserting that while we may look at a piece of iron, acknowledge its material, bodily form as iron, and yet also imagine it in terms of gold, the commodity can never be simultaneously both iron (bodily) and gold (mental, ideal). The image may remind us of the dawning of the aspect in Wittgenstein, where one sees either a duck or a rabbit in the figure, but never both at the same instant. In order to determine the price of a particular commodity, we see the commodity as gold. Thus, for a moment, iron is turned into gold and the Great Work has been accomplished. But if the Great Work were really accomplished (or perfected, as we might say), then the iron-become-gold would serve as the universal general equivalent. Iron is only valuable insofar as it is actually exchanged (for money). It must be realized. Even though gold is "special" because in the process of exchange it has established itself as the money-form, as Marx says, behind gold "lurks the cold hard cash" (1867 103).

We have, in Marx's discussion of money, all of the elements of alchemy-as-ambivalence: transformation, metamorphosis, and ennoblement—but covered up. Or better, it is gold whose glittery shine prevents us from seeing the (base) cold, hard cash, the greed that lurks behind it. Moreover, the individual coins minted by the various nations (as the business of the state) are like uniforms (covers) doffed in the market of the world, indicating the separation between the internal or national spheres of the circulation of commodities, and their "universal sphere" (125). Coins, then, are shapes taken on, but they are ephemeral. The minting of a coin is immediately simultaneous with a loss of value, like a car that loses its value as soon as it is driven off the lot. For the longer the coin is in circulation, the more it is likely to be worn down, losing its weight, even if its face value remains the same. That is why the states prefer (symbolic) paper money. Gold can be both the money-commodity ("present in its own golden person" [130]) and also money, simply put, when it is put into circulation (as itself) or by a representative (such as paper money), where it "congeals" into the sole form of value, as exchange-value rather than use-value (as is the case with all other commodities). Gold is a mercurial hermaphrodite.

In the sex-gender system that underlies *Capital*, there is continual reference to a dichotomy between the bodily forms of commodities and their ideas or mental forms. Although Marx does not state outright that the bodily form is coded as feminine, it is impossible, in the present context, not to think in those terms. Similarly, Jean-Joseph Goux extends gold (the general equivalent of products in Marx) to fit onto the template of three other general equivalents looming large in modern thought: the father (as general equivalent of subjects, or reigning in the realm of subjectivity), language (as general equivalent of signs), and the phallus (as general equivalent of objects). What Goux notices as a structural homology he also understands as the increasingly established institution of circulating general equivalents over time. He terms this homological relation a paterialism. While Goux's argument is compelling, it is extended as far as the possibility of gold's hermaphroditic quality. It understands gold as one thing (but one thing that can be located in various registers): gold the product rather than its production. It is possible, and perhaps even necessary, to think that gold sheds its hermaphroditic quality once it is produced, finished, perfected. This is not a question of emphasis on process as opposed to product, since embedded in the very fabric of alchemical transmutation is a disavowal (ambivalence) of product. The product must be produced for the process to have validity—or rather, for the Great Work to be accomplished—but the product is simultaneously negated by the rhetoric of (spiritual) transformation or philosophical alchemy.

Goux notes that the symbolic mode underpins Western economies and is intrinsic to them. He writes, "In materialism we find *mater*. Can we not then see idealism, which opposes and represses materialism, as a *paterialism?*" (Goux 213) This leads him to the notion that "the difference of the sexes is symbolic of the symbolic," and also that "the primitive correspondence between parental duality and the two poles of the symbolic schism accounts for the sexed meaning of nonsexual oppositions" (223). Goux refers, then, to the symbolic mode tout court that has been the province of scholars in more traditional Renaissance studies. In some sense, then, an "alchemical Marx" functions as a critique of those concordant projects of scholarship so caught up in promoting one or another of the elements of the binary couple—theory or practice—that they fail to realize that what is at play in the alchemical is a doubling back of one mode on the other. This ambivalent doubling back is not *merely* coincidental with the figures of male and female that are often present in alchemy—it is deeply and decidedly imbricated with such figures. Many studies of early modern imagery present the figures of alchemy without contextualizing them in a binary system (such as the steganographic) that *must* bear some relation to gender. So even if *Capital* is not a narrative or the first in a series of steps toward redemption, and it is not a work about gender, gender difference and the ambivalent undoing of a master narrative of death and resurrection do emerge from an alchemical reading of this Great Work.

§ 7 Digital Gold

Alchemy and Modernism

In the 1959 sci-fi film *4D Man*, Tony Nelson (James Congdon) develops a force field that stimulates the molecular structure of matter, enabling objects to be joined and pass through one another. His brother Scott (Tony Lansing) experiments on himself, speeding up the processes of nature. Whereas iron and gold pieces in a museum might fuse together after centuries, he can fuse them right away. His brain receptors are already highly stimulated due to his exposure to radiation from his experiments with Cargonite, an impenetrable material with "military" potential. The film's structure is very strange, and there is no real ending. Scott simply walks through the concrete of a nuclear reactor and a question mark flashes on the movie screen. Not only has he disrupted his love story with a busty scientist (Lee Meriweather), but he disrupts any hope of narrative closure. Nuclear fear—the title of a book by Spencer Weart—is ambivalence. "There really was a man who studied both science and alchemy, found the secret of atomic energy, and exclaimed that it would lead humanity to paradise or doomsday" (Weart 5). Radioactivity involves penetration of the body by rays that are both good and bad, healing and destructive.[1] Having achieved a transformation of the self (through science), Scott simply disappears, like Christian Rosenkreutz at the end of "his" wedding story, melted into a celluloid punctuation mark.

The Alchemist, a book of spiritual advice by Paul Coelho, was an international best seller. Bruce Dickinson of the group Iron Maiden released a solo album titled *My Chemical Wedding* in 1998. My Chemical Romance is a goth-rock band from New Jersey.

Before this explosion of alchemical referents, a circle of individuals associated with surrealism and with the Curies may have engaged in actual alchemical experiments, as they simultaneously took up the themes of alchemy in their aesthetic practices.[2] Various modern art movements have employed the vocabulary or sensibility of alchemy—from Balla and Delauney to Duchamp, Kandinsky, and Pollock—but not all modernists deploying the vocabulary of alchemy necessarily realize the ambivalent relation of (spiritual) process and (material) product as intrinsic to their work. What would it mean to label a modernist a *genuine* alchemist? Can André Breton and Michel Butor be called alchemists since they clearly had profound knowledge of the traditions and incorporated them into fictional work such as *Arcanum 17* and *Portrait of the Artist as a Monkey*? Or would we require proof that they actually engaged in experiments along with individuals like the mysterious "Fulcanelli" and Eugène Canseliet (who were, perhaps, one and the same)? In what sense should Jackson Pollock's 1947 canvas titled *Alchemy* be read as an accretion of myth-historical layers as well as layers of paint?[3]

Such questions are highly vexed. For instance, many have argued for and against Duchamp as alchemist. He certainly made references to the history or iconography of the alchemical tradition as early as 1911.[4] He denied attempting the Great Work, but can he be taken at his word? And wouldn't such a denial itself—that is, in fact, his very word—be proof enough of the haunting presence of the alchemical? In a discussion with a young artist, Duchamp was asked if one could call his approach alchemical. He replied: "We may. It is an alchemical understanding. But don't stop there! If we do, some will think I'm trying to turn lead into gold back in the kitchen. Alchemy is a kind of philosophy, a kind of thinking that leads to a way of understanding. We also may call this perspective 'Tantric' (as Brancusi would say), or (as you like to say) 'perennial'" (cited in Henderson 9). There is no question of practice, then. The effect of seeing the works of Duchamp in the museum—petrified—is very similar to viewing a reconstruction of Lavoisier's laboratory (as Duchamp himself did). Alchemy is pure thought or disposition for Duchamp at this stage. Does this imply that modern art, especially in its more conceptual or dematerialized forms, has somehow managed to transcend the messy practice long allied with the low labor of the adepts and *souffleurs?*

Duchamp's godson, Gordon Matta (he would add the Clark later), was invited to contribute to an exhibit in New York. For the occasion he cooked a series of Polaroid photographs of a Christmas tree together with gold leaf in a pan of grease, and left the mess in the gallery for a hot summer. He then sent around fried photographs of the Christmas tree to various friends, including Robert Smithson. The "photo-fries" clearly do function as gifts (with the addition of gold, "the token of pure exchange value" [Thomas Crow in Diserens, 31]), as a means of networking and self-promotion like other forms of mail art, or at least as a commentary on the idea of self-promotion in the art world. Matta was reading widely in the realm of alchemy, but mostly texts dealing with its spiritual dimension, and with a particular interest in Jung. He understood alchemy conventionally, as a process in which "mastery is attained, not visibly on the outward artisinal [*sic*] plane as in architecture and painting, but only inwardly" (cited in Thomas Crow in Diserens, 27).

His studio, on the Lower East Side of Manhattan, resembled the traditional alchemist's lab (Figure 17). He had a stove that was always working, glass vessels filled with both wet and dry materials—some boiling, some burned—and pans with slowly cooking algae. Some of the pans were themselves exhibited under the title *Incendiary Wafers*. In 1970 he titled a show *Museum*, displaying an array of substances in various states of decomposition, altered by the addition of traditional alchemical ingredients such as mercury, sperm, quicksilver, salt, gold (leaf), but also more "modern" brand-name elements such as Yoo-hoo chocolate drink and V8.[5] The list of ingredients for this experiment was discovered, as Thomas Crow notes, in a copy of *The Raw and the Cooked* (Lévi-Strauss was a family friend of the Mattas). Yet Matta-Clark's work moves beyond structuralist pairs and traditional alchemical dualisms. Inasmuch as the work is awkward, stinks, and has boundaries that are shifting and difficult to trace (for instance, the very lab itself is a work, a transformation of architecture not unlike the artist's later building cuts, so if particular pans of matter may be shown in a gallery, the gallery does not "contain" the work), Matta-Clark's alchemy is not merely a repetition of (binary) terms.

FIGURE 17.   Gordon Matta-Clark, *Agar, 131 Chrystie St.*, 1969, © 2008 Estate of Gordon Matta-Clark / Artist Rights Society (ARS), New York.

Dematerialization

In the late 1960s, Italian art critic Maurizio Calvesi helped to organize an exhibition at the Attico Gallery in Rome with the alchemical title "*Fuoco Immagine Acqua Terra*" ("Fire Image Water Earth").[6] Janis Kounellis made a gas-powered flame that shot out from a flower. Pino Pascali mounted blocks of earth in the gallery walls. Piero Gilardi exhibited "natural rugs" (actually made of polyurethane)—rectangular floor mats representing fallen fruit. And Michelangelo Pistoletto showed his mirror constructions. All four artists would soon be affiliated with the movement known as *arte povera*, in which alchemy is a dominant theme. Germano Celant, the "father" of this movement, began a 1969 essay: "Animals, vegetables and minerals have cropped up in the art world. The artist is attracted by their physical, chemical, and biological possibilities. He is renewing his acquaintance with the process of change in nature, not only as a living being, as a producer of magical, wonderful things, too" (cited in Christov-Bakargiev 199).[7] The artist is likened to an alchemist who searches for essences. In uncovering the natural process of the world, the artist also discovers himself as a force of knowledge; he makes pilgrimages outside of the space of galleries in order to know himself. "He abolishes his role as artist, intellectual, painter and sculptor. He learns again to perceive, to feel, to breathe, to walk, to understand, to use himself as a man" (199). This aleatory experience "tends toward deculturation, regression, the primary and the repressed; toward the prelogical and pre-iconographical state; toward elementary and spontaneous behaviour. It embraces the primitive elements of nature (earth, sea, snow, minerals, heat, animals)" (ibid.). This language echoes the invocations of "alchemy" as "magical transformation" that we have found to be ubiquitous in everyday speech.

Yet beyond such rhetoric around *arte povera* lies a profound ambivalence in relation to materials, which may change while the artist is working on them. They never reach a stable form where they "die" (petrified in the art market), but continue to live after the artist has released them, however reluctantly, as products. The works may be impossible to grasp as objects as they subsume the cyclicality of production and consumption as part of their very essences.

Gilberto Zorio made a series of works using Pyrex vessels. These containers engage the viewer in a dialectic between heaviness and lightness, transparency and the liquidity of the glass, and alcohol that eventually evaporates. For Zorio, although the glass may appear pure like the alchemical *vas*, it is ultimately merely silica, *materia bruta*. Its transparency allows you to see the content, and because the tops are open, smells also escape. In some of his works, he uses copper sulfate, a turquoise blue. Over time, the chemical reagent evaporates, leaving behind crystals or sediment. He is intensely interested in evaporation, because as alcohol evaporates, it enters the space around the crucible, transforming it; yet it does so in a time frame that is too slow for the human senses to perceive. The process of evaporation can only be noticed over a period of weeks, months, even years, so it requires repeated visits to the gallery for its full realization. A similar observation can be made about an early piece by Zorio titled *Tent*. Over time, salt deposits gather on the canvas of a small, umbrella-like tent that the artist placed at the beach. The piece has been exhibited in a number of important expositions, and with each showing, the salt crystals grow or become more encrusted. Like the early modern alchemist, Zorio speeds up changes of materiality.

In recent years Zorio has continued to engage with alchemy. With works like *Crogiuolo (Per purificare le parole)* (*Crucible [To Purify Words]*, 1982), various materials—some traditional, some "chemical"—are mobilized in a two-dimensional image of an alchemical vessel (Figure 18). Like his Pyrex constructions, a series of works each titled *To Purify Words*, and three-dimensional crucibles, this particular "conventional" nonsculptural piece *represents* a moment in alchemical transformation. It might be dismissed as "flat," in spite of the fact that the work superimposes two separate rectangles asymmetrically. Yet by mixing in reagent elements such as phosphorus or copper sulfate, Zorio can be said to do more than *merely* represent alchemy. The dematerialized work of contemporary artists, while entirely fresh, recalls the experience of ter Borch with certain of his works that he painted in the so-called loose style, or "the wet way," as opposed to layering paints on drawings or dried "dead colors."

To grasp the full importance of alchemy in and beyond *arte povera*, we should leave behind, for now, the two-dimensional support and think about the long-standing trope of sculpture as living material. For example, in his *Vita*, Benvenuto Cellini boastfully describes the casting of his Perseus. When his assistants fail to keep the molten metal alive, he recounts:

Then I had someone bring me a lump of pewter, weighing about sixty pounds, which I threw [*lo gittai*] inside the furnace on to the caked metal. By

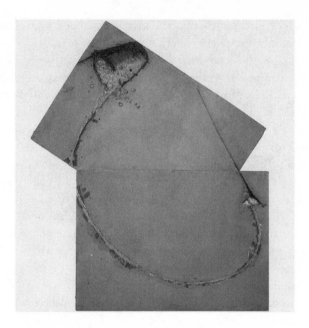

FIGURE 18.   Gilberto Zorio (Andorno Micca, Biella, 1944) *Crucible (To Purify Words)*, 1982, A.D-03974A-L/IS, mixed technique on paper. 130×165 cm, Collezione Intesa Sanpaolo.

this means, and by piling on the fuel and stirring with pokers and iron bars, the metal soon became molten. And when I saw that despite the despair of all my ignorant assistants I had brought a corpse back to life, I was so reinvigorated that I quite forgot the fever that had put the fear of death into me. (Cellini 347)

Cellini reflects a belief common in the sixteenth century that metals in their natural state are watery, not solid. As Aristotle believed, pneuma is present in water, so all liquids have souls. Metals, in other words, are animated. When Cellini pours liquid bronze into the statue, it comes to life and simultaneously cures the sculptor of his own mortal illness. It represents the fulfillment of an impossible alchemical transformation. But how is a modernist to deal with such ideas?

One possible answer to this question comes from Robert Smithson. He upheld the belief that all matter is based on flux and sedimentation. Refusing refinement through "technological miracles" helps artists return to a positive geologic chaos. In a materialist sense, this corresponds to the notion of nomadic artists dispersed all over the geographical spectrum, liberated from the (New York) art market. Yet we should clarify that Smithson is not a mechanist. For instance, he does not like the idea of Duchamp's *The Bride Stripped Bare by Her Bachelors, Even* (or *Large Glass*) as a representation of a mechanization of the sex act:

> Where I tend to agree with [Carl] Andre is when he says that Duchamp is involved in exchange and not use value. In other words, a Readymade doesn't offer any kind of engagement. Once again it is the alienated relic of our modern postindustrial society. But he is using manufactured goods, transforming them into gold and mystifying them. That is where alchemy would come in. But I see no reason to extrapolate that in terms of the arcane language of the cabala. (Smithson 312)

Andre wants to transcend the bourgeois order and sees Duchamp as responsible for the proliferation of multiple commodities. Smithson, for his part, finds the occult boring. Rather, alchemy facilitates a realization of the alienation of the artist from his products. "The artist is supposed to draw from the well of his labor power, but the alchemy that turns it into gold for the dealer leaves him nothing but slag ('coagulated labor-time,' Marx would say)" (De Duve 57).[8] Beginning in the late 1960s, the most expedient way—perhaps the only way—for politicized critics and artists to resist the market was to do away with saleable, easily consumable objects in favor of actions, ideas, or even decomposable works of limited duration. Artists abandoned painting, for instance, as it represented the most easily identifiable form of the commodification of art. *Arte povera* sprang from a generation of practitioners who felt that no object, no matter how well intentioned, nontraditional, or idiosyncratic, could escape becoming a commodity or transcend the conditions of the market. The market is a monstrous machine that incorporates everything into itself, even opposition to it. It is no longer possible to imagine a relative scale of objects, some more commercial than others. In this context, materiality—a movement toward creating a perfect identity of the thing and idea—unambiguous and stripped of excessive reification, serves to authenticate the poverty of art. So "dematerialization" in *arte povera* might best be thought of as a process of ridding oneself of excess objects, of trying to climb out from behind commodities and strip one's work down to a bare distillation, and in this sense it is clear how *alchemy* became a key term.

In response to an essay by art critics Lucy Lippard and John Chandler, the Art-Language Group wrote an (unpublished) letter/essay dated March 23, 1968 (cited in Lippard 43–44). The Group argues that most of the objects to which the critics refer can clearly be recognized as art-objects—perhaps not traditional, but still matter in one of its forms: solid, gas, or liquid. Even *Map Not to Indicate etc.*, a conceptual print that plays with geographical boundaries, by one of the group's members, Terry Atkinson, while quite idiosyncratic, is still a work on paper. In this regard *Map* is, like Zorio's chemical crucible, matter. "The map is just as much a solid-state object (i.e. paper with ink lines upon it) as is any Rubens (stretcher-canvas with paint upon it) and as such comes up for the count of being just as physically-visually perusable as the Rubens" (43). And the Art-Language Group members go on to note:

> Matter is a specialized form of energy; radiant energy is the only form in which energy can exist in the absence of matter. Thus when dematerialization takes place, it means, in terms of physical phenomena, the conversion (I use this word guardedly) of a state of matter into that of radiant energy; this follows that energy can never be created or destroyed. But further, if one were to speak of an art-form that used radiant energy, then one would be committed to the contradiction of speaking of a formless form, and one can imagine the verbal acrobatics that might take place when the romantic metaphor was put to work on questions concerning formless-forms (non-material) and material forms. (43–44)

Today, the word *dematerialization* has come to achieve a potentially powerful place in the environmental sciences and in the global monetary system. The expression refers commonly to the replacement of a material object with electronic signals; electronic money is a prime example. Telecommuting (or, more radically, the creation of global service centers in places like India) to reduce fossil emissions is another. Dematerialization results in reduction of waste or by-products, a lessening of the environmental footprint. Generally, the impetus for dematerialization does not lie in regulatory enforcement, but rather in (neoliberal) market-driven competition. In this sense, dematerialization does not figure as part of a contrarian retreat from hyperproduction or a return to nature, but rather is a predictable part of the capitalist process itself, a flexible strategy that some critics say contributes to an exploitative geopolitics and a breakdown in old-fashioned forms of human interactivity, identity, and community.

While the virtual nature of dematerialization that we are currently facing was not necessarily anticipated by Lucy Lippard, Germano Celant, and other critics who used the term specifically with regard to the art market some thirty years ago, it seems essential to invoke its current usage for its broad political implications and the ambivalence it suggests in any relation with objects, whether art objects or pure commodities.

Dematerialized Gold: E-money and the Infosphere

Let us assume, then, that we have left the modernist age of playful dematerialization and "analog gold" for a new age—the so-called new economy of the "future." *Futurity* is an important term, for while the phrase *new economy* was widely used to describe the economic boom around the dotcom explosion of the late 1990s and the equity markets associated with this boom (indeed, the NASDAQ is sometimes reductively called the market of "new economy stocks"), the new money-forms or radical economic-epistemological breaks implied by some theorists who write about e-money is still to come. In *Multitude*, Hardt and Negri call for a novel form of accounting, "something akin to the way Einstein's theory of relativity transformed our understanding of the regular, metrical spaces of Euclidean geometry" (Hardt and Negri 149). As they note, Marx may be said to have presciently understood such a rethinking when he wrote that wealth is not reducible to money or property. "The real wealth, which is an end in itself, resides in the common; it is the sum of the pleasures, desires, capacities, and needs we all share. The common wealth is the real and proper object of production" (149). Hardt and Negri's optimism acknowledges that such production will necessarily have to take place alongside of and intertwined with the irrepressible developments of the new money-form-to-be. It may be that the prediction is somehow performative: saying that a new money-form will develop makes it so. But for now, the Internet is merely another vehicle for moving money that is easily convertible to any of the world's major currencies and, ultimately, to gold. Of course, gold has lost much of its previous luster, and it scarcely increased in value at all during the boom and its immediate aftermath.[9] During this transitional phase, and at least since the Bretton Woods monetary system began to falter, gold has become a highly specialized form of value, traded in specialized mutual funds but rarely seen or touched in its bullion or ingot form by the average person. Gold is a senior citizen.

In contrast, e-money—a widely accepted general term for all computer-based or digitized fund transfers—is young. Cybercash refers more narrowly to fund transfers enacted over the Internet. Although the two terms are often used interchangeably, many experts believe that we are moving ever closer to the Internet as the sole vehicle for transfers (that is to say, away from convenient electronic vehicles like ATMs; away from telephonic banking; and so on). Economists understand the advent of cybercash as a revolutionary break in the history of money-forms, equivalent to great monetary phase-shifts like the agrarian, metallic, gold standard, paper money, and so on. Yet digital cash is not yet in circulation: it is currently merely a projection into the future. It will entail the installation of software on computers that can make payments and extend credit to users. Eventually cybercash could evolve into a full-fledged independent money-form, qualitatively different from previous forms. In other words, it would not simply involve moving around existing money-forms, but would entail a separate economy based entirely on the Internet, including, for instance, payment for e-work, new credit channels, and new financial contracts to fund online activity of various types. In essence, then, the (alchemical) product that is projected into the digital future will change social relations.

> Circulating on computer networks that span the planet, cybercash transcends physical space and national boundaries. As such it will inevitably become a major force in fostering globalization, allowing individuals to engage in exchange, production and credit relations with actors across the globe. Flowing with the speed of light by means of the latest communication technologies (for example fiber optics or broadband), cybercash also compresses real time to an instance of seconds and thus greatly accelerates the pace at which things get done in the pursuit of economic activity. (Guttmann 15)

This utopian vision is tempered by a system of checks and balances to assure that the power to create these new money-forms will not lie in the hands of the people, but rather, will be under the control of central banks (which profit from the increased dematerialization of money). New money-forms will require a fiduciary relationship, and in the past, this kind of relationship was inherent in the uniqueness of gold or other precious metals and/or the guarantee offered by third parties such as banks. The difference between the undeniable materiality of gold and the dematerialized quality of cybercash seems to be of paramount importance. Yet the two forms share a quality of being supranational. The potential problems that result from cybercash—questions of intellectual property rights, potential for use by terrorists, fraud, and so on—are vast and are outside of the scope of this discussion. Even if, at least initially, e-money is denominated in national currencies, relative prices will have to differ because the transaction costs for e-money are so much lower than for paper money. Or indeed, it may come to be that e-money will end up reinforcing the power of underlying existing nonelectronic currencies such as the dollar or the euro, if, for instance, it turns out that the e-euro is the strongest of the digital currencies. In this sense, it is clear how cybercash and e-money work in concert with prevailing mechanisms and rhetorics of globalization that have a utopian ring about them (the monetary equivalent of esperanto), but end up reinforcing existing national and corporate powers.

It would seem that behind the great optimism fueling the so-called dot-com revolution and behind the promise of new money-forms associated with the Internet, there still lies, as Marx might say, the cold hard cash. That is, the dollar, the yen, the euro, and so on (and in a more shadowy realm, gold) are still the standards that are projected as the units of value behind e-money, or cybercash. Thus, we could say that virtual capitalism is now in a transitional phase, during which the use of prepaid Internet shopping cards, electronic purses, smart cards, e-banks, and so on all function to facilitate Internet transactions, but the fundamental money-form has not changed. All of these transactions must ultimately be calculable in currencies (and for our purposes, in gold). As the technology develops, many experts believe that cybercash will evolve into a new money-form in which credit and loans will be extended through the Internet, outside of the current banking channels; payments for e-work might be made in this new form. An example of this tendency is the payment of workers with stock options rather than salaries or bonuses immediately calculable in dollars. Such options are similar to the kinds of tendencies we have witnessed in history, from an agrarian (barter) money-form to a metallic money-form to a paper money-form. In each case, the transition was slow, and the older forms still continue to function, overlapping with the new forms. Even today there are still pockets of agrarian money-forms that function alongside paper money: a farmer might choose to exchange his goods with workers or other farmers but also participate in money exchange. And, of course, gold and silver linger as specialized

markets behind the money-forms of today, even though they were replaced precisely because their scarcity inhibited growth in a global sense.
So it might be supposed that in the futuristic scenario of the total dematerialization of money, units of currency might still be calculated using
older symbols, and paper money might be available for some particular
forms of transaction for a long time after cybercash has become dominant. Nevertheless, the experts lead us to believe that coins and bills will
become curiosities in the near future.

What happens to gold in the new economy? Will it also become something of the museum, or will it, by its very material scarcity, persist eternally as a form of value? In order for cybercash to be successful, people will
have to trust it. Previously, acceptability came from the money-form
itself—metal—or from third parties (banks) that upheld the fiduciary relationship. U.S. coins are stamped with the words "In God we trust." Now
all we have to trust is technology itself, supporting the invisible transfer of
invisible funds. However, deep-seeded fears about privacy, security, and
forgery have slowed down the advent of e-money. Ultimately, say the experts, these problems will be overcome by technological advances, and the
Internet will lead to new forms of capital: "intangible (productive) capital
in knowledge-based production and fictitious (financial) capital mobilized
through online securities markets" (Guttmann 204).

These questions should not be pondered in some kind of pure economic vacuum, but exist in relation to social and political life.

> Circulating on computer networks that span the planet, cybercash transcends
> physical space and national boundaries. As such it will inevitably become a
> major force in fostering globalization, allowing individuals to engage in ex-
> change, production and credit relations with actors across the globe. Flowing
> with the speed of light by means of the latest communication technologies
> (for example fiber optics or broadband), cybercash also compresses real time
> to an instance of seconds and thus greatly accelerates the pace at which things
> get done in the pursuit of economic activity. (Guttmann 15)

Under these new conditions, gold may not be able to keep pace.

In the present, however, gold is commonly available as a stalwart. The
Monex Corporation, for instance, offers bullion stamped with "Liberty"
and an image of American bald eagles as a hedge in a highly volatile market. In a grave tone of voice, a spokeswoman for the corporation insists
that, now more than ever, we must buy gold (along with the Chinese) to

protect against a brewing storm of deficits and bear markets. But if we were to posit a "master craftsman" at home attempting alchemy, whatever output he might be expected to generate would be nothing in the new economy. He would have nothing to be ashamed of. No world leaders would ask for his help in shoring up their national treasuries. He would be considered quaint, and his workshop might be a point of historical interest for bored schoolchildren on a field trip; or he might be an artist, revered in a small, elite circle of patrons, critics, and intellectuals, but unknown to the world at large. So perhaps in order to find "modern-day" alchemy, we must look elsewhere, beyond gold, to biomedical technology or biofuels, for instance. Following Hardt and Negri, we could understand alchemy as a kind of post-Fordist form of immaterial labor, and alchemy's eccentric temporalities a quasi-autonomist move beyond the working day of the Fordist factory.

At the same time, alchemy remains a common metaphor to describe the transformations of our monetary interregnum. We need only consider the quotation cited in the introduction to this book: "A modern alchemy succeeds where the old failed. The ancients of the Middle Ages were never able to change lead into gold, but the medium of electronics turns magnetized particles (bits) into money-like value. Money seems for a time to be conjured out of nothingness, to be returned to nothingness either quickly or at an indeterminate moment" (Solomon 85). Yet it seems important to stress that the economic theorists use alchemy in a merely metaphorical sense, stripped of the ambivalence that could be said to define it at its base, even if the base of e-money is indeed binary (code). E-money is a clear example of the Internet, not as deterritorialization (as in the work of Italian activist Bifo, for instance) or rhizomatic network, but as a vehicle that potentially— at least for now—strengthens the dominant forces of globalization.

Liquid Gold and Future Fuels

Alchemy has recently been called upon to fulfill yet another metaphoric duty: standing in for production of alternative fuels or energy sources (some of which are being developed in the very places where the dot-coms boomed a decade or so earlier). In this arena, we find, again, something beyond the mere *recycling* of alchemical language. Processes considered as (partial) solutions to global warming by greenhouse gas emissions and the global energy "shortage" are profoundly alchemical—that is, ambivalent.

Carbon is a true *pharmakon*: a poison and a gift, powering the modern world. Carbon released into the atmosphere mere years or decades ago is now being taken up by plants. But fossil carbon taken from the earth accumulated over millions of years. Carbon, then, is a temporal problem, and thus it is intimately linked with the nexus of alchemy and mining.

A research group from Purdue University recently developed a method of producing biofuel that they claim could meet all U.S. transportation needs. It involves adding hydrogen to biomass from a solar or nuclear (or other) energy source during a phase called "gasification." During this phase, raw materials are normally broken down into carbon dioxide, carbon monoxide, and hydrogen. These are then turned into liquid fuel. In the Purdue process, hydrogen is added during gasification, suppressing the formation of carbon dioxide and converting all of the carbon atoms into fuel. According to a federal study, as much as one billion tons of biomass are potentially available in the form of crop waste, animal manure, grains, and other crops. Even human waste might be a suitable *prima materia*. Using an anaerobic thermal conversion machine that looks remarkably like an early modern alchemical athanor, scientists are working on transmuting cellulosic ethanol through anaerobic thermal conversion rather than fermentation or acid hydrolysis. Biomass is heated in an oxygen-free environment to produce carbon monoxide and hydrogen. The carbon monoxide and hydrogen are then reconstituted into various alcohols, such as ethanol, that might be used for fuel. The process is extremely fast—it requires minutes as opposed to days of fermentation.

Green venture capitalist extraordinaire Vinod Khosla, a founder of Sun Microsystems, writes of one particular method for biofuels:

> We learned to formulate corn ethanol way back—it's nothing more than moonshine. What makes the E3 Biofuels facility so novel isn't its spectacular equipment but the way the equipment is fueled. The most important structures here happen also to be the least beautiful: a pair of four-story million-gallon fuel tanks, each filled to the brim with cow manure. Historically, ethanol plants were fired by coal or natural gas. But methane, produced from manure, powers this operation. Not only do no fossil fuels go into the plant, very little pollution comes out. It's a nearly closed energy loop (some corn has to be bought from other farms). (Khosla)

In various cases noted above, a base material is transformed into the liquid gold (fuel), bypassing the traditional methods of petroleum extraction and refinement. At the time of this writing, the,state of the alternative fuel "industry" is, like some alchemy that I have described throughout this book, rather piecemeal and ad hoc. "There is no single silver bullet," the scientists tell us. The various processes that are being attempted all have something in common—they work with the products of nature, but in some kind of hyperefficient or sped-up mode. The dream of future fuels, like recycling, is one in which the *prima materia*—excrement or waste—is turned into gold through the "magic of technology." Like many abuses of "alchemy," this dream distills the word to an essence, effacing process in favor of product. If future fuels can be made from "nothing of value" (even, possibly, air, as French inventor Guy Nègre hopes), they will also produce energy without emissions. Negre's vision is that someday air itself will provide the energy to compress air: a closed loop with no room for ambivalence.

Yet as we have seen, ambivalence continually returns in alchemy. I certainly do not mean to advocate for ambivalence as a critical practice, as some ideal way to keep difference suspended (in a chemical bath?) or as a form of Deleuzian schizoid analysis. Ambivalence should not be confused with multiplicity for its own sake, for in alchemy the Many may simply function to cover up that which wants to be One:

> It is also a stone and not a stone, spirit, soul, and body; it is white, volatile, concave, hairless, cold, and yet no one can apply the tongue with impunity to its surface. If you wish that it should fly, it flies; if you say that it is water, you Speak the truth; if you say that it is not water, you speak falsely. Do not then be deceived by the multiplicity of names, but rest assured that it is one thing, unto which nothing alien is added. Investigate the place thereof, and add nothing that is foreign. Unless the names were multiplied, so that the vulgar might be deceived, many would deride our wisdom. (*Turba*, 207)

Still, inasmuch as it represents "both" (two, but only two) alternatives, ambivalence might also seem a form of mastery: "Ambivalence occludes multiple alternatives, ambiguity, and multiple meanings (polyvalence), forcing a dominating tension of opposites. Ambivalence—pathologized—both shrinks the world into oppositions and prevents (blocks) movement through it" (Garrison 224). Ideally, then, ambivalence should not be diagnosed or resolved, but rather, remain a potentiality. As Mark Garrison notes, while Jung, Bleuler, and Freud were all "in touch with ambivalence," they "failed to remain ambivalent about ambivalence" (230). I posit ambivalence as a key to thinking about alchemy, but do I so with ambivalence.

Notes

Notes to Introduction

1. The clear bottle and window on the left create a crucial link between this advertisement and Dutch painting of the seventeenth century, which is fundamental to my thinking about alchemy in the broadest terms. For the window composition see Cole and Pardo 1.

2. Such alchemical-temporal experimentation is especially characteristic of the Italian art movement known as *arte povera* discussed in more detail in Chapter 7.

3. It has even been suggested that *kimiya* came to Arabic from Chinese, where it signified a liquid extracted from gold (Zinguer 171). Newman follows the historian A. J. Festugière in distinguishing a number of phases in early alchemy: (a) alchemy as a form of technology—gems, stones, dyes, and so on (from Egyptian antiquity to ca. 200 B.C.E.); (b) technical recipes with an interest in "sympathies" and "antipathies" of material elements (ca. 200 B.C.E.–100 C.E.); (c) the joining of philosophy and chemistry, exemplified by the figure of Zosimos (ca. 300 C.E.).

4. Many alchemical texts list the (often seven, but sometimes as few as three or four) stages of the process. Yet there are nearly as many variations in these stages as there are alchemical treatises. For instance, a fairly common list might include: *calcinatio, sublimatio, solutio, putrefactio, distillatio, coagulatio,* and *tinctura* (Calvesi 1993, 136). The *Rosarium Philosophorum* (almost certainly a medieval text, but printed in 1550) instead offers: solution, conjunction/fermentation, conception/putrefaction, mortification, extraction/impregnation, purification/ablution, jubilation/sublimation, regeneration. And so on. The question of which series to accept as dominant is tied, obviously, to the difficult question of an alchemical canon.

5. Although the progressive stages as mentioned above do not constitute oppositions, what Derrida writes in this context is still important to keep in mind. That is, a list is only useful when there is a guiding principle or matrix within which the single elements can be measured. In alchemy, if the stages themselves may vary, what remains invariable is the declaration that the stages must be followed in their particular order (whatever it might be), so that no stage is skipped, and each one is allowed to reach its fulfillment before the alchemist moves on to the next stage. Failure to proceed in this manner interrupts the Great Work and constitutes a "falling back" to the beginning (often represented with an image of the alchemist literally losing his footing, stumbling, or tumbling from a ladder). In other words, the "matrix" of the alchemical list of stages is linear and teleological. Any deviation from the trajectory means failure (or provides a post-factum alibi for failure). See the epigram of the footless alchemist locked out of the garden from Maier's *Atalanta fugiens* (Figure 2) for a visual example of this trope.

6. The prefix *ambi* (or *ambo*) might be thought to signify "both" of any two (and only two) objects, as when we refer to ambidexterity. The question of whether we can extend ambivalence to a situation in which more than two objects are in play is complex, and it certainly has implications for the discussion of the theme of a choice of three (caskets, women). Sarah Kofman notes that while ambiguity may refer to one sense or another, ambivalence is simultaneously two opposing senses: "*Le sens et le non-sens; non pas l'amour ou la mort mais l'amour et la mort*" (28).

7. "An Act to Repeal the Statute Made in the Fifth Year of King Henry the Fourth, Against the Multiplying Gold and Silver," *Anno Regni Gulielmi et Mariae, Regis & Reginae Angliae, Franciae & Hiberniae* (London: Charles Bill and Thomas Newcomb, 1688). For centuries, transmutation had been a felony. Now,

> whereas since the making of the said statute, divers persons have by their study, industry and learning, arrived to great skill and perfection in the art of melting and refining of metals, and otherwise improbing them and their dies (which very much abound within this realm) and extracting Gold and Silver out of same; but dare not exercise their said skill within this realm, for fear of falling under the Penalty of said statute, but exercise the said art in foreign parts, to the great loss and detriment of this realm: Let it be therefore enacted by the King and Queens most excellent majesties, by and with the advice and consent of the Lords Spiritual and Temporal, and Commons in this present parliament assembled, that from henceforth the aforesaid branch, article or sentence contained in the said Act . . . shall be repealed. . . . Provided always, and be it Enacted by the Authority aforesaid, That all the Gold and Silver that shall be Extracted by the aforesaid Art of Melting and Refining of Metals, and otherwise Improving of them and their Dies as before set forth, be from henceforth Employed for no other Use or Uses whatsoever, but for the Increase of Moneys: And that the place hereby appointed for the Disposal thereof, shall be Their Majesties Mint within the

Tower of London; At which place they are to receive the full and true value for their Gold and Silver so extracted from time to time, according to the Assay and Fineness thereof; and so for any greater or lesser weight: And that none of that Metal of Gold and Silver so refined and extracted, be permitted to be used or disposed in any other place or places within Their Majesties Kingdoms and Dominions. Provided also, and be it further Enacted by the Authority aforesaid, That no Mine of Copper, Tin, Iron, or Lead, shall hereafter be adjudged, reputed or taken to be a Royal Mine, although Gold or Silver may be Extracted out of the same. (443–45)

A letter from Newton to Locke dated 1672 credits this repeal to the efforts of no less a personage than Robert Boyle (*Alchemy* 283).

8. For an overview of Jung's intellectual development and engagement with alchemy, see Jaffé.

9. Maurizio Calvesi addresses this conundrum. He was accused of being a Jungian, but he claims that he was simply interested in the visual images he found in Jung's *Psychology and Alchemy* (Calvesi 1993, xxi).

10. Evola, xviii. On Evola and his political ideology, see Cassata and Schnapp. In addition to his writing, Evola also produced a number of Dadaist-type paintings. His *Paesaggio interiore, illuminazione* (1918–20, now in the Kunsthaus of Zurich) includes a number of geometrical blocks. On one of them, the artist wrote "Hg" (the chemical symbol for mercury) in red ink. This is a very interesting gesture, especially as the inscription seems entirely disjoined from the composition itself, as if it had been an afterthought, and a reflection of the troubled relationship between modern chemistry as abstraction and alchemical materiality.

11. Dee's *Monas Hieroglyphica* (1564) was an attempt to retrieve divine language and unify various branches of natural philosophy in a single cipher or universal emblem. The *Monas* contained traditional astrological symbols that could be translated into any language and generate all possible letters. In the preface to the work, Dee defined the word *monas* as "unit"—perhaps the first time this word is found in English: "Note the worde, Unit, to expresse the Greke Monas, & not Unitie; as we have all, commonly, till now, used." He goes on to explain: "And, an Unit, is that thing Mathematicall, Indivisuble, by participation of some likenes of whose property, any thing, which is in deede, or is counted One, may reasonably be called One. We account an Unit, a thing Mathematicall, though it be no Number, and also indivisible because of it, materially, Number doth consist: which, principally, is a thing Mathemeticall" (cited in Josten 91–92). Naturally, I would not exclude Dee from the alchemical realm simply because he was obsessed with this figure of unity. On the contrary, we might see his *Monas* as defending, precisely, against ambivalence.

12. One need only think of the television commercials for the Monex Corporation. A woman, using the grave tone usually reserved for prepaid cemetery

plots, warns viewers that gold is the only stalwart in the present chaotic world. Also see the company's Web site: www.monex.com. Today it is indeed possible to trade in gold through a mutual fund (ticker symbol "GOLD," no less). The investor will have no actual contact with gold ingots. More important, the mutual fund places gold at an ever further degree of removal from material presence since the fund does not directly follow the price of gold, but rather, hedges the "generality" of gold as an idea.

13. As Marc Shell notes, however, hypothesis is inherently bound up with money. To make a hypothesis is to ask for credit that may be called in later, when a conclusion is reached and meaning exhausted. When Plato criticized the sophists, he simultaneously expressed anxiety about coinage—that is, as a division between symbolic and material value: "Was not even Socratic dialectic . . . pervaded by the monetary form of exchange? Was not dialectical division a kind of money changing, and dialectical hypothesizing a kind of hypothecation, or mortgaging?" (Shell 2).

Notes to Chapter One

1. Warburg's method implies a montage of different temporalities: archaic, ancient, and modern. The Mnemosyne project was unfinished at Warburg's death in 1929, but the idea survives in his library, now of the Warburg Institute, in London.

2. "Low" images, including advertisements, are not marginal to Warburg's project, then, but rather, fundamental. They speak to the complex question of transmissibility and tradition that underlies the entire "nameless science" of Aby Warburg.

3. "For him, 'the survival of antiquity' served as a touchstone for the extent to which the conflict between ancient and modern conceptions of faith had penetrated the consciousness of the age." The idea of a formal, intuitive "imprint" on the viewer came from Anton Springer (Foster, introduction to Warburg 6).

4. In a personal correspondence, Arthur Wheelock indicates that he is also puzzled by this figure and is unable to figure out its purpose in the composition. He feels that perhaps the left-hand side of the painting may have darkened since the time it was produced. It is possible, he notes, that this figure is meant to be in dialogue with another hypothetical figure facing the viewer.

5. This pun was later taken up by Jacob Cats (1577–1660) in his book of emblems.

6. Hollander takes the term from Angus Fletcher's masterful book *Allegory: Theory of a Symbolic Form*. It is important to stress allegory here as a spatial and geometrical disposition of images, deriving, in part, from rhetorical and theatrical traditions.

7. Béroalde de Verville, discussed in Chapter 2, also started out as an apprentice goldsmith, moving into etching, emblems, and eventually alchemical narratives. See Zinguer 188.

8. Another link in the etching–alchemy nexus is the fact that in the nineteenth century, the French society of etchers made use of Rembrandt's "old magician in his sorcerer's studio" (Figure 6) for their publicity posters and the cover of their trade magazine. They replaced the mysterious letters in the ball of light with their logo, a move that some members apparently found blasphemous.

9. Dou virtually invented the "niche picture," and he produced many of them. Sometimes a human figure leans out from a window frame or some object is extended outward as an illusion or trompe l'oeil. Hollander writes: "Whether the niche pictures are allegorical self-portraits or kitchen scenes, their essential theme is always painting itself. He exploits the organization of space, along with the properties of trompe l'oeil and the restrictions of the niche format, to explore and celebrate the painter's craft" (50).

10. We will again find the wiping of the baby's bottom in the background scene, or *bywerk*, of Heerschop's painting of an alchemist setting his experiment on fire (Figure 11). Here, what happens in the back room might simply be read as a representation of everyday life, an indicator that the alchemist is attempting the Great Work at home while life goes on around him. Yet when we take together the *vanitas* objects, the explosion, and the emblem of the production of the basest of all materials, we come to appreciate the intricate relationship of narrative and emblematic in Dutch art.

11. Stoichita 76–77. For the influence of Flemish art on Filippo Lippi with regard to the use of light and shadow, see Meiss and Edgerton.

12. In a book on Duchamp as alchemist, Moffitt notes that the word *clarity* (*clarté*) is potentially equivocal. One of Duchamp's primary sources was Pernety's dictionary, which states: "This word stands for the [stage of] whiteness which follows the blackening of the [alchemical] matter in *putrefactio*" (cited on p. 366). But there are approximately eighty cognate terms for *clarity* in alchemy. So Duchamp argued that in order to avoid confusion, one must ignore etymology and focus on the present-day or common use of this term.

13. For William R. Newman, there is an important distinction between the homunculi of Christian Rosenkreutz and that of Paracelsus (to be discussed in greater detail in Chapter 5). In the Rosicrucian text, the "homunculi are symbolic of the regeneration of the soul after passing through the darkness of confusion and unbelief into the clarity of Andreae's Lutheran Christianity—and this they do as a couple." On the other hand, Paracelsus follows in the tradition of the creature made from sperm alone. "With the *De rerum natura* [possibly by Paracelsus] the myth of the homunculus had come full circle: the Western world then had an opportunity to either accept or reject the project of male parthenogenesis. *The*

Chymical Wedding of Christian Rosenkreutz is actually a part of the rejection—rather than an affirmation—of the Paracelsian homunculus, despite its obvious debt to the literary tradition of Paracelsus" (235).

14. It is not surprising that the model for David Ryckaert's alchemist (Figure 16) is recycled by the artist in a number of his tavern scenes.

15. In artists' studios, which serve as a model for many of the interiors, there were generally one or two windows, usually on the north side of the room to keep sunlight from directly hitting the canvas. Some artists used wax paper or curtains to block out light or manipulate where it would fall. See W. Martin; Boschloo.

16. James Elkins underscores the importance of the title of an important book by Hubert Damisch, *The Cadmium Yellow Window*. For while the window is an opening for light into the interior space of a painted room, it is, in actuality, an opaque deposit of minerals on a canvas. This paradox has a significant impact on the matrix of alchemy, painting, clarity, and the composition type of the alchemist in his study. Hollander elaborates on the presence of the window:

> The standard "Dutch interior" was more or less established by the mid-1650s. Brighter colors returned, along with precise details of textures and facial features. Compositions became vertically oriented, with fewer figures, a more analytical treatment of space, and usually a visible light source indicated by a window. In the usual format a room whose back wall is parallel to the picture plane has a window to one side and a doorway into another a room. (Hollander 42)

17. Dürer's *St. Jerome in His Study* of 1514 (Figure 8) is another example of the composition type in consideration here. It is from the same period as his *Knight, Death and the Devil* (1513) and his *Melancholia* (1514) (Figure 7).

18. A long-standing tradition links alchemy with artisanal secrets about colors, including the unusual reds of Chartres' windows, to give one example. It is worth noting here that Goethe developed a theory of colors. He departs from Newton's more physical interpretation of color, based on light striking objects and hitting the eye. Instead, for Goethe, human perception is crucial to the equation. When viewed in this "light," Goethe's choice of Rembrandt's etching for *Faust*, in which the alchemist/scholar perceives a magic spell in a burst of light, seems all the more significant.

19. For some of the solutions to this problematic, see Duits.

20. In this regard, it is interesting to think about the biography of a painter like Parmigianino (1504–40). According to Vasari, as Parmigianino studied alchemy he neglected his painting and failed to deliver on some commissions. Alchemy and painting appear thoroughly contradictory:

> While racking his brain—not with thinking up beautiful devices or working with paintbrushes or paints—he would lose the whole day in dealing with coals, wood, glass

vessels, and other such trinkets, which cost more in one day than he earned working for a week on the church of the Steccata; and not having other means, but needing them in order to live, he consumes himself—bit by bit—with his furnaces. (Vasari, *Le vite* cited in Newman 124)

See Pagden.

21. See Calhoon 1998. Even the making of paper (the support of the photo-graphic image, the support of the symbol of value in the form of money) is a highly alchemical process. Wood fibers are treated in chemical baths, subjected to multiple stages of dissolution, congealing, and bleaching, before the noble product finally emerges.

Notes to Excursus: Ambivalence

1. Inasmuch as (ambi)valence connects with medical alchemy (exemplified by Paracelsianism in the sixteenth century), it stands at odds with philosophical alchemy (anti-Paracelsianism). But of course, "valence" in the sense I am using here is only one of a number of possible registers. In philosophical alchemy (ex-plicitly defined as non-practice), the corresponding term to *valence* might be *virtue*.

2. The poem to accompany epigram 38 from Maier's *Atalanta fugiens* reads:

> The ancients called this twin being REBIS,
> In body male and female, Andrygyne
> 'Twas born upon two mountains, so they say,
> Hermaphrodite, whom Venus born to Hermes.
> Don't spurn the dual sex, for male and female,
> One and the same, will give the king to you.

3. Kofman discusses Freud's interpretation of *The Merchant of Venice* in his es-say "The Theme of the Three Caskets." Whereas the first two suitors in Shake-speare's play allow themselves to be fooled by appearances—that is, they choose the gold and silver caskets—Freud's error is precisely the opposite. He only cares about the casket of lead. Kofman writes:

> If one pays attention to the three caskets, or better, to the three metals that correspond to them, one perceives that all three teach the same lesson since they are actually indis-sociable, all three profoundly ambivalent. This ambivalence, in turn, is the possibility of their 'false appearances,' seducing and deceiving those who fail to recognize [*mé-connaissent*] them for what they are. It is also the condition of their convertibility or transmutability. (41, translation mine)

Ambivalence, then, is something inherent in gold itself ("*l'ambivalence struc-turelle profonde de l'or*" [42]), not a psychological state. All metals share the same (base) origin, yet the glitter of gold blinds us to this truth (*séduisant et dupant tous ceux qui la méconnaissent*).

4. Varchi's *Questione sull'alchimia* probably comes out of his engagement with the Florentine circle of Cosimo I, who is said to have engaged in alchemical experimentation. As is typical of many such treatises, the *Questione* claims to be an account of an actual debate on the subject that took place among a group of gentlemen.

5. "True alchemy (*archimia vera*) transmutes not only the accidents of things, but also their substance, so that the artificial gold produced will be identical to natural gold, even in its medical virtues. Sophistical alchemy (*archimia sofisticata*), on the other hand, transmutes only the accidents of matter, so that the base metals may appear to be gold or silver, but will retain their base substance intact" (Newman 136). False alchemy is necromancy.

6. Grilliat gives the example of a patient who said of a nurse, "Raymond is nice he's garbage" (*Il est gentil Raymond c'est une ordure*) (174). This is uttered without any inflection or affect. It is a phrase without any punctuation or hierarchy between the two ideas.

7. Mark Garrison writes about Bleuler's relationship with the term *ambivalence*, which Bleuler saw as a secondary symptom of schizophrenia rather than a primary one. But, as Garrison notes, "Bleuler's need to identify one symptom as primary belongs not to the nature of schizophrenia itself but instead to the nature of the medical model [linear and monovalent] with which he was working" (216). Garrison's thesis is that ambivalence, rather than being understood as inherent to schizophrenia, should be understood as inherent to language itself (hence it makes its appearance, in schizophrenics, in associative disorders). Bleuler's pioneering article on the concept appeared as "Vortrag über Ambivalenz," *Zentralblatt für Psychoanalyse* 1 (1910).

Notes to Chapter Two

1. The 1998 film *Spoorloos*, directed by George Sluizer, is based on Tim Krabbé's contemporary novel. An American film version by the same director was released in 1993. It starred Keifer Sutherland and Sandra Bullock as the young lovers. Jeff Bridges played the deranged chemistry teacher. Hollywood had to evacuate the story of its particular iconography, turning it into a tale of pure suspense and of the psychological obsession of a man for his missing lover. In other words, the alchemical elements are gone, but the ambivalence of the couple remains as a purely psychological portrait.

2. Rembrandt's wife, Saskia, was the (unnamed) model for many of his paintings, as well as the explicit subject of numerous others. "Saskia," then, certainly can be considered an emblematic name for bringing the seventeenth century into the film (or vice versa).

3. Nicholas Royle repeats Freud's strange remark: "To some people the idea of being buried alive by mistake is the most uncanny thing of all." He then comments: "There is a certain comedy in James Strachey's translation here. The English version might be taken as positing that being buried alive *per se* is not necessarily uncanny; what is really uncanny is when it happens *by mistake*." In the German, this idea is the *Krone*, or crown, of all uncannies. "Finally one gets to be His or Her majesty: a coronation fit for royalty." This is especially fitting for *Rex* Hofman, we might add. "In any case," Royle concludes, "this crowning achievement doesn't really mean anything, except as the 'transformation' of a different fantasy, namely 'intra-uterine existence'"(Royle 143). The links between the uncanny and alchemy will be further explored in Chapter 5.

4. Arnold's presence here is probably due to the fact that he was presumed to be the author of the *Rosarium*, a text that includes a number of chemical weddings. He was also famous in legend for having created a homunculus in a glass vessel that he later smashed before the creature could develop a soul (Newman 7). Perhaps we can read a ghostly reminder of a (failed) act of creation in his presence at the wedding.

5. For an excellent study of this type, see M. E. Warlick, "The Domestic Alchemist: Women as Housewives in Alchemical Emblems," in Adams 25-48.

6. Flamel is supposed to have been a Parisian bookkeeper, born in 1330, who came into possession of a book belonging to one "miserable" "Abraham the Jew." After making a pilgrimage to Spain to consult with a Jew about the *materia prima* required for successful transmutation, Flamel returns to Paris and is able to achieve the Great Work three times with the help of his partner and wife, the good Perrenelle. The couple is unable to conceive a child, but their riches are donated to good works, and they carve the process in hieroglyphs in the church of St. Jacques for others to decipher. The figures include a man and a woman who morph into a hermaphrodite. Whether or not Flamel really existed or did undertake the acts described by his biographers and sculpted in hieroglyphs is of little importance in this context. Instead, it is significant that the Renaissance accepted the narrative as an explanation for the carvings on the Paris church of St. Jacques, as a justification for his wealth, and as a story about the functioning of a childless marriage as partnership. Van Lennep notes the complex connections in Flamel's biography between the presence of Jews, the theme of the blood sacrifice of innocents (part of the ritual described in the mysterious book that Flamel refused to undertake), gold, and the arch at the Innocents Cemetery, which was built in 1183, the year that the Jews were expelled from France for having sacrificed a boy from Pontoise, the town where Flamel may have been born (Van Lennep, 1984, 261). This web of referents begs the question: Is it possible that Flamel himself practiced usury? And is his "sin" covered up in the elaborate

narrative of his life as a devout Christian who stumbled across alchemy and donated all of his riches to the church?

7. As late as the 1930s in the United States, Henry Ford, a "farm boy at heart," required that his employees tend gardens. Spies from his Sociological Department cited those who were remiss in their horticultural responsibilities. "While Ford might want a full-time effort from his workers on the job, he knew that they would experience irregular employment. Gardens would help tie workers to Ford. They would also blunt the criticism of those who would point to the plight of workers during their periodic bursts of unemployment" (Perelman 115). In Zola's *Gérminal*, the miners keep gardens for subsistence crops as they are slaves to the mine. Gardening stands as an open-air, pleasant, self-sufficient activity, but with the strike, all crops are soon exhausted and the miners begin to starve.

8. In this sense, the chemical bride and groom differ from the unequal couple, a common theme in Northern painting beginning around 1500 and the subject of a book by Alison Stewart.

9. Zinguer offers a preliminary list of early modern French chemical novels. Béroalde's best-known work is *Le moyen de parvenir*, a satirical anti-Paracelsian treatise. It was published in 1616, a few years after the *Voyage* and after his "transcription" of the *Hypnerotomachia*. Like Paracelsus, Béroalde held a medical degree. See Giordano for an extensive discussion of *Le moyen*. In essence, the French "re-readings" of the *Hypnerotomachia*, rather than opening up the text, could be said to close it off and make of it a guarded and silent object. Béroalde defined his mode of writing as steganography—covered writing, a binary system, a mode of symbolizing that turns back on itself, first positing, then disavowing meaning and accessibility. This is not the place to develop readings of these rather obscure texts, but I note that they do constitute something like a mini-genre, and they certainly help contribute to a (retrospective) alchemical interpretation of the *Hypnerotomachia Poliphili*. For the influence of Colonna's text on French writing in the seventeenth century, see Blunt.

10. Christian Rosenkreutz is the name of the narrator/protagonist of the *Chymische Hochzeit* by Andreae Valentin. Andreae appears to have invented the name. Rosenkreutz was supposed to have been born in 1378 and to have died in 1483 or 1484. His tomb was supposedly "discovered" in 1604 (Dickson 790). According to the *Fama fraternitatis*, Christian travels to Jerusalem, and when he returns to Germany, he initiates several monks into the secrets of metal transformation and curing the sick. They form a brotherhood based on six rules: they must heal the sick for free; they must not wear any clothes or ornaments that will identify them as R.C. (Rosy Cross) Brothers; they will meet once a year; they will choose a successor before they die; "R.C." will be the token of the fraternity; and they will remain active in silence for 120 years. Indeed, the

brethren state that they are the ancestors of Adam, Moses, and Solomon. Among the important influences on the *Chymische Hochzeit* is the *Theatrum chemicum*, published in six volumes by Zetzner from 1613 to 1661 (appearing first in four volumes in 1602). Andreae probably was familiar with the earlier volumes, since the same publisher reissued them three years before his text. There was a great deal of speculation about Andreae's identity during the seventeenth century and beyond. Some believed he was Francis Bacon. In the early twentieth century Rudolf Steiner gave a series of lectures in which he conflated Rosicrucianism with anthroposophy (Montgomery in Andreae 548). Some scholars argue that the *Chymische Hochzeit* should be understood as a Christianizing corrective to youthful indiscretions, the works that Andreae called *ludibria*. Others believe that Andreae was never an occultist, but always a Lutheran who scoffed at the brothers of the Rose Cross. As should be clear, my own interests lie in closely reading the text, and I leave to others the historical-philological accounts of the author and his intentions.

11. Yet as Polizzi notes, an alchemical "overlay" to these texts can be abusive (265).

12. In *Le voyage des princes fortunez* (1610), Béroalde specifically defines steganography in his *"Avis aux beaux esprits"*: *"les magnificences occultes à l'apparence commune, mais claries et manifestes à l'oeil et à l'entendemente qui a reçu la lumière qui fait pénétrer dans ces discours proprement impénétrables, au non autremente intelligibles"* (13; cited in Giordano 93 n. 27). In the *"Receuil steganographique"* of the *Tableau des riches inventions*, Béroalde explicates the alchemical symbols of the frontispiece to his book. Ultimately, the *"Receuil"* has little to do with Colonna's text. It functions more as a pretext to explain a rhetorical-literary theory.

13. Naturally, the expression "in the key of" immediately evokes the musical guideline for the disposition of notes. This notion is taken up by Michael Maier in his *Atalanta fugiens*, a series of musical pieces. Van Lennep believes that the *Atalanta fugiens* was conceived as a total sensorial work, comprising vision and hearing. The musical score accompanying each emblem is for three voices, representing the three tonalities (deep, middle, light) of alchemy. Maier was in Prague, the musical center of Europe, where he probably met Monteverdi in 1596, and perhaps also Hans Leo Hassler, a great proponent of musical automata. However, Maier probably composed the *Atalanta* in the court of Maurice of Hesse.

14. A nineteenth-century biographical dictionary of alchemists includes Jean de Meun, author of *The Romance of the Rose*. Francis Barrett notes that some have read the work as a tale of love, while others have seen beneath the text "the process for the stone of the philosophers" (29). In particular, verses 16914–16997 are said to contain much veiled information regarding the Great Work.

15. Yates has been sanctified in the academic world, but Vickers (1979) offers scathing critique of her book on Rosicrucianism. Yates upholds the Rosicrucians as philanthropists who denounce false and greedy alchemists. They practice medicine and criticize doctors who accept money for their work. Vickers argues that Yates is off the mark in many ways. Andreae was not really pro-Rosicrucian. Moreover, *The Chemical Wedding* has only slight parallels with the other works (tendentiously) attributed to him. Perhaps, Vickers notes, Andreae was trying to Christianize the myth of the wedding. In any case, for Vickers, Yates's scholarship concerning Rosicrucianism is highly suspect and inconsistent. In her work Yates suggests that Rosicrucian furor died out because of the Thirty Years War, and because the men were the object of a conspiracy. "She is continually polarizing a situation, rendering it as a violent conflict, imputing anger, malice to the participants. She uses metaphors derived from wars to account for—dare one say, create?—an animus against these forces of what she calls enlightenment" (Vickers 299). Yates wants so badly to uphold hermeticism that she tends to identify too much with it, even engaging in a suggestion of the efficacy of magic (305). She exaggerates when she posits a movement or a "Rosicrucian age." Too much importance is given to Rosicrucianism as a precursor to the Royal Society and as a summation of the age.

16. The first edition of the work, *Chymische Hochzeit: Christiani Rosenkreuz, Anno 1459*, was published in 1616 in Strasbourg by Lazarus Zetzner. All of my citations are to the first English translation by Foxcroft (London, 1690), unless otherwise noted.

17. In *On Virtue*, Zosimos recounts a dream in which he sees men being boiled alive in a glass vessel. "They too must undergo a transmutation into pneuma, which requires that they undergo this punishment (*kolasis*). Upon awakening from his dream, Zosimos decides that this is an alchemical allegory" (Newman 30).

Notes to Chapter Three

1. Although entirely "modern," David's portrait of Lavoisier and his wife was influenced by earlier Dutch genre painters like Metsu and Dou, precisely in the sheen on the glass retort.

2. There is something uncanny about this type of portrait that does not fully elude even the casual viewer. I mean something similar to the effect of those cardboard figures that one finds, for instance, at fairs or tourist locales where a subject can insert his or her head into a cutout in order to be photographed with a celebrity or in a historical scenario. Usually such photographic souvenirs fool no one. You can see the edges of the cutout, or there is a problem of scale between the head that is inserted and the scene at large. Nevertheless, such images

are strange and can certainly elicit a double take. I am arguing that all monumental, posed portraiture is subtended by a temporality that may be violent, inasmuch as the viewer senses the absence and presence of the subject from the scene of painting at different moments, and such a perception disrupts any idea of ideological uniformity and evenness that the portrait might wish to convey.

3. Lavoisier's laboratory has been reconstructed in the Paris Conservatoire des Arts et Métiers. Marcel Duchamp was apparently quite influenced by his visits to the museum. His godson, Gordon Matta-Clark, who built an alchemist's lab in the Lower East Side of Manhattan, could be seen as another inheritor of Lavoisier.

4. Jean-Paul Marat, for one, helped bring about the chemist's execution. Marat was also a scientist, and he had been denied admission to the Academy of Science due to Lavoisier's denunciation of his experiments on combustion. It should be noted that Marat's later turn against the chemist and the academy bears elements of a personal vendetta.

5. In contrast, consider J. J. Becher, an avatar of the seventeenth-century court alchemist. To the question "Why write?" he answers, "In order to teach": "My writings will not be obscure but clear; not prolix [let us recall that this work is over a thousand pages long!] but succinct" (Becher 702). Still, he comments, let us recall that old proverb: "The writer should keep some of what he knows to himself" (*Scriptorem semper plus debere scire, quam scriptum suum*).

6. Although arranged marriages were beginning to be outmoded, many people still adhered to them. (Jacques Paulze chose the twenty-seven-year-old Lavoisier for his daughter over a much older man—there was apparently some attraction between the chemist and his daughter.) Of course, the idea that she could only really love Lavoisier is all part of the myth of the happy (chemical) couple that we must take *cum grano salis* (if we are Paracelsians, that is).

7. Marie Curie wrote a thesis in physics at the Sorbonne (the first woman to do so), determining the atomic weight of radium: 225 ± 1. In 1902 she shared the Nobel Prize with her husband and Henri Becquerel. The Curies did not apply for a patent for radium, presumably because they wished to be known as scholars (at least according to a self-created mythology). It is probable that they simply did not know about the potential industrial uses for radium.

8. It is interesting to think about this citation in relation to *Faust* (part II): Wagner stays behind in the laboratory rather than attend the Walpurgisnacht celebrations.

9. Engels compares the overturning of the phlogiston theory with Marx's "discovery" of surplus value. He writes:

Priestley and Schelle had produced oxygen without knowing what they had laid their hands on. They 'remained prisoners of the' phlogistic 'categories as they came down to them. . . .' Lavoisier, by means of this discovery, now analysed the entire phlogistic chemistry and came to the conclusion that this new kind of air was a new chemical element, and that combustion was not a case of the mysterious phlogiston *departing* from the burning body, but of this new element *combining* with that body. Thus he was the first to place all chemistry, which in its phlogistic form had stood on its head, squarely on its feet. And although he did not produce oxygen simultaneously and independently of the other two, as he claimed later on, he nevertheless is the real *discoverer* of oxygen vis-à-vis the others who had only *produced* it without knowing what they had produced. (Engels, preface to Marx, vol. 2, 15–16).

Similarly, the idea of surplus value was certainly known before Marx, but he stood it on its head.

10. Pierre Joseph Macquer (1718–84) was known as a practical chemist (he supervised the royal porcelain factory, for instance). He wrote an influential dictionary (1766; revised in 1778), and he is best known for being a supporter of precisely the phlogiston theory that Lavoisier helped to overturn.

11. It is interesting to note that John Dee spoke with angels using a "scryer." Scrying was an ancient method of divination, looking to a shiny or reflective object to aid in prophecy. See Harkness.

12. Terrall cites Leibniz: "There is no doubt that all things are regulated by a supreme Being who, even as he imprinted on matter the forces that denote his power, destined it to execute effects that mark his wisdom" (179).

13. David's favorite disciple, Eleuthère Irénée du Pont, went to America and founded the Du Pont gunpowder firm, known for explosives, plutonium, and, of course, chemicals (Boime 412).

14. Mary Vidal argues that both *Paris and Helen* and the Lavoisier portrait are depictions of love between a couple where the intimate relation is of a sensual nature, but also creative. She suggests that depicting loving couples was still morally suspect at this time, hence the portraits are somewhat daring (607). Both works represent a merging of sexual, psychological, and intellectual elements in the marital bond. Both reflect relaxed affection and creative harmony. She writes: "Monsieur Lavoisier gazes with admiration at his wife, his more secret desires now expressed in the realm of the symbolic (his extended leg, the flask on the floor)" (608). She also states that Madame de Lavoisier is not entering or exiting the room, but that she clearly belongs there (617).

15. Louis Boilly, another pupil of David, painted *L'Optique* (1793), the composition of which also resembles the Lavoisier portrait. A mother peers over the shoulder of her son as he looks through a device called a zograscope, used to view the popular prints known as *vues d'optiques*. In Boilly's painterly work, the mother holds out her arm, perhaps selecting the next print to be looked at or holding it to avoid curling that might distort the image for later viewers. Her arm forms a beautiful line with the recto of the folio. She looks out at the painter/viewer, while the child continues to look through the plate, but even his head

is turned slightly toward the painter as if he cannot resist some curiosity about what is happening in the space between the pair and the painter.

16. Ryckaert painted a number of more traditional alchemist compositions, such as one (now in Budapest) from 1642. Here the alchemist sits on a tripod in front of a fireplace, studying a book. He holds a glass vial in his right hand. A young boy, probably his assistant, helps with the fire. An owl under the table serves as a symbol of the blindness of the alchemist.

17. The bustle reached the height of fashion in the late nineteenth century. What Madame de Lavoisier wears is a crinoline underskirt. Sander Gilman (259 n.51) notes that this garment gives women a look of primitive eroticism, yet it is also held to be legitimate in good society.

Notes to Chapter Four

1. Bottigheimer notes that the Grimm brothers' spinning tales do *not* tend to begin like "Rumpelstiltskin" (i.e., "There once was a miller," ". . . a soldier," ". . . a farmer," ". . . a king," and so on). "These phrases are only story initiators, however, for the miller does not grind, nor does the soldier bear arms, nor the farmer plough, nor the king rule. Each of these initiators identifies a character in the tale to follow. . . . Yet, among the 200 folk tales, of which approximately thirteen concern spinning directly or indirectly, not a single one begins: 'There was once a spinner'" (142). I mention this because the miller does, in fact, disappear from the story, and because "Rumpelstiltskin" can be (and often is) read in the context of the spinning tales. Bottigheimer believes that the spinning tales do not use spinning as an initiator because spinning was such a common task (usually performed by women) that it would have been pointless to define a character as such. There are no "spinners" by profession or primary identification, only women who spin.

2. Jack Zipes outlines the development from an oral tale in which a girl spins but can only make gold thread, not actual yarn. Her bargain with a little man called Rumpenstünzchen (a nonsense name) guarantees him her firstborn if he will help her correct the productive defect. At the end of the tale he flies out the window on a cooking spoon. This element suggests a possible link with flights to the witches' sabbath, consistent with the dwarf as demonic. The Grimm brothers apparently combined this tale with other written and oral versions. The published tale of "Rumpelstiltskin" is an amalgam of different materials, but the common thread, so to speak, is a girl who fails as a spinner (Zipes 48).

3. Indeed, this very development is captured in a footnote of *Capital* (n.337). Marx offers a modern instance of the combination of different handicrafts under the control of a single capitalist. He cites Blanqui on the silk-spinning and weaving industries of Lyons and Nîmes, where women and children had once been

employed in tasks that did not corrupt them. "Since Blanqui wrote this, the various independent labourers have, to some extent, been united in factories." Engels adds his own note to Marx's note on Blanqui: "And since Marx wrote the above, the power-loom has invaded these factories and is now—1886—rapidly superseding the hand-loom."

4. The Grimm brothers' tale "The Robber Bridegroom" also begins with a miller who has a beautiful daughter. He decides to marry her off, but the wedding fails to take place when the girl learns that the bridegroom-to-be is a murderer.

5. Spinning often bears a negative connotation. It may be associated with the devil / the spider. See Rieken. On the other hand, in Ovidian terms, Arachne is a positive figure who comes to prominence, not because of the place of her birth or the social standing of her family, but through her art. There is an important link, then, with the bride in "Rumpelstiltskin," who spins with art in lieu of a dowry. Of course, Arachne is ultimately punished for outdoing the gods.

6. Various scholars have attempted to analyze the name Rumpelstiltskin, and some have tried to link it with the devil or evil demons. Zipes argues that the name is ultimately meaningless (43–44). Of course the acoustic range of the utterance means something. Its non-sense is replete with meaning. It presents itself as an empty signifier, but this is itself significant. Zipes's essay is aimed at recategorizing the tale, which has normally been read as a "helper tale," hence placing Rumpelstiltskin's character and the guessing of his name on center stage. Instead, Zipes wants to focus on the activity of the female spinner in the sociohistorical context of the eighteenth and nineteenth centuries. Naming is an extension of spinning—a productive act, like spinning yarns or telling narratives, according to Zipes. Perhaps the most convincing evidence for the derivation of the name comes from the Grimms themselves: the *Rumpelgeist*, like the poltergeist, or goblin, is a demonic (evil) spirit that taps or knocks (Grimm 1953, vol. I, 418). All of these spirits belong to the class of *Hausgeister*; people hear them tapping or walking in houses (*poltern oder rumpeln*). These figures are related to the Spanish *trasgo* (from *trasguear*), or the French *sotarai, sotret*. In particular, Rumpelstiltskin echoes with stilts: "*Stilt, stilz das alte stalt.*" He is a "little mountain man" (*bergmännlein*), and his name must be guessed like other figures: "*Eisenhütel or Hopfenhütel, die einem Hut von eisen oder mit hopfenlaud umkräntz tragen.*" Other names for this type of figure include *klopfer, poppele,* and *popanz*—friendly goblins. The little man of this tale is distinguished, then, by the tapping of his leg into the ground; or the tapping that is also associated with mining (tapping a vein), as in Zola's *Germinal*, for instance.

7. In "The Robber Bridegroom," the miller's daughter hides behind a barrel while the band of murderers cut up a young bride. The bride's finger, holding her ring, flies into the lap of the daughter, a sign of the precariousness of the symbolic power of the ring to equal fidelity (or life).

8. Dwarves are not conceived by a union of man and woman, but rather by "decree of the gods" (Motz 91), so they themselves do not possess women and can only give rise to life through their craft.

9. Grimm 1953, vol. II, 822. The Northern European god/giant Loki is similar to Hephaestus/Vulcan.

10. The infirmity and deformity of Vulcan (Hephaestus) have been attributed to different origins. The former is the price he paid to acquire his art. The second is symbolic of his special powers. Of course, the two are not absolutely distinct. Delcourt recounts that Zeus gives Aphrodite in marriage to Hephaestus, the smithy. She presents him with three children—Phobus, Deimus, and Harmonia—but they are actually not his; they were conceived out of her relation with Ares, god of war. When Vulcan realizes the deception, he makes a bronze net to catch the lovers in bed. Then he demands the return of all the wedding gifts he gave to her adoptive father, Zeus. In the end, Aphrodite deceives her husband further, and he is never paid. He is madly in love with his wife and must accept his fate. The narratives, complex as they are, attest to a man who is lame and duped. The medieval concept of a limping devil/Jew has origins in Genesis 32:29. Ginzburg analyzes a whole series of tales of limping that he calls "asymmetrical deambulation" linked with a journey to the world of the dead. Silas Marner also limps. Lévi-Strauss was interested in family patterns of ambulatory disequilibrium. Vernant explains that for Lévi-Strauss, lameness was related to autochthononous men, who, born from the earth, have trouble walking. The son who does not take after his father is lame. Lameness represents a failure of generational legitimacy to extend in a straight line. The Labdacid line, including Oedipus, exemplifies this problem. While the story of Oedipus gives a particular explanation for his lameness (his bound feet), this does not preclude the possibility of reading the narrative of Oedipus in relation to the structures of (inherited) lameness. In *Faust*, Mephistopheles limps on one foot as well. In Icelandic narratives, the dwarf Völundr is lame (Motz 116). Indeed, it is possible that the word *dvergr* (from which we get the English *dwarf*) is traceable to an Indo-European root meaning "damage," and dwarves suffer some physical deformity to mark them as "other" from humans and suggest a price to pay or sacrifice (Motz 118).

11. Becher proposed alchemy to the princes of his day as a "natural" model for production, a way around the depletion of the reserves without having to tax his subjects excessively, and as a benevolent means of upholding noble status. See P. Smith.

12. By the time we arrive at Marx's *Capital*, we find that the dwarf has morphed into the machine: "From being a dwarf implement of the human organism, [the tool] expands and multiplies into the implement of a mechanism created by man" (Marx 1887, 387).

13. In his extensive research on smiths, Eliade did not develop the fact that they often live underground (Motz 3). Motz notes that the majority of the German tales come not from the regions rich in metals and mines, but from Münster and Osnabrück in the northwest. This lack of direct connection between geology and storytelling is interesting. She does relate the tales to a distant origin in potters and craftsmen, who come to be associated with mountain-dwelling dwarves from the Icelandic sagas and who appear as figures of alchemists in various traditions. The craftsmen did not work iron or metal, but clay or stone, materials that are "incomparably more important than metals to the origin and continuation of fruitfulness and life" (7). Motz argues that the potter/stonesmith may be a central figure in communal rituals of a very early period in the region, perhaps involving a priest figure who presided over funerals (hence his connection with monolithic stones). In any case, the Gothic German verb *gasmidan* meant "to cause or effect" and was not strictly linked to metals. Old Icelandic also preserves this generic sense of a maker that had to have a noun attached to it to give it a particular meaning (81). The tools of the smith come from pre-metal or neolithic origins. *Hammer* originally meant "stone," *steinn* in Icelandic means "anvil," and even the Greek *akmon*, or *anvil*, derives from the root for "stone." Many of the mountain- or earth-dwelling figures complete tasks for humans. They may come at night, and if people leave a payment, they will find the work done in the morning—broken tools will be fixed, and so on. The dwarves are also associated with hammering or tapping of the smith. There are other variants in which the people insult the smiths by leaving excrement instead of payment, or by cheating the smith out of his due. As punishment for their bad deeds, smiths often sink into the ground (54–56). These mountain men may be dwarves or giants, and there appears to be much movement from one aspect to another. In *Faust*, Goethe places mining gnomes (a word that was apparently invented by Paracelsus!) in the carnival ceremonies at the start of part 2. They are goblins who live in the earth and guard the hoard, and they are associated with Mephistopheles' plans to unearth the buried treasure beneath the palace.

14. The elements that would allow such a reading also raise key questions about the Nibelungen. In the first scene of Lang's film, we see Siegfried living among the dwarves (smiths), yet he is physically distinct from them. Their dirty faces, atrophied movements, beards, and fits of laughter render them particularly undistinguished. It is well known that Adorno believed Wagner's villains also looked and sounded like Jews. Siegfried Kracauer appears to have noted the same with regard to Lang's depiction of Alberich, king of the Nibelungs (Levin 10). Levin argues that Alberich also embodies a negative conception of Hollywood cinema, given his particular role in the film.

15. So Marx writes: "The whole history of the development of machinery can be traced in the history of the corn mill. The factory in England is still a 'mill.' In German technological works of the first decade of this century, the term 'mühle' is still found in use, not only for all machinery driven by the forces of Nature, but also for all manufactures where apparatus in the nature of machinery is applied" (1887, 348n.).

16. Wiesenfarth 232. In fairy tales, the third time is often the charm. Jacob Grimm writes of fairies from Brittany (*korred* or *corrigan*) who comb their hair next to a river. If they do not find husbands within three days, they must die (Grimm 1953, vol. 1, 370).

Notes to Chapter Five

1. The association of the gritty feeling in the eyes at night with a "sandman" who comes at night was apparently common lore in Hoffmann's time. Nevertheless, all of the scholarship that I have found suggests that the details about stealing children's eyes, eating them, and the crescent moon are Hoffmann's own additions.

2. Whitney Davis diagrams the vicissitudes of *Nachträglichkeit* in his brilliant readings of the interactions between Freud and his patient, the Wolfman.

3. Brantly (325) suggests that the father can be considered a greedy philistine for being both a lawyer and an alchemist.

4. Whitney Davis addresses the role of the nursemaid in the logic of the Wolfman.

5. Bachelard writes of the athanor as an enclosure of volatile desire: "What may at first sight hide its psychological character is the fact that alchemy quickly took on an abstract aspect. The alchemists worked with the *enclosed fire*, the fire confined in a furnace. The images which are created so lavishly by open flames and which lead to a more free and winged kind of reverie, were now reduced and decolorized to the benefit of a more precise and concentrated dream." And he goes onto say that "several of the furnaces and retorts used by the alchemists had undeniable sexual shapes" (Bachelard 51).

6. In alchemy, the risk of explosion is great, especially during the Middle Ages, when it was not known that gases had to escape from a closed vessel. Traditionally, the "dry way" was faster and much more dangerous. The alchemist had to keep constant watch over the athanor, which is why it often helped to have a wife—provided she did not get in the way. It was often the adept who caused the explosion due to his lack of experience (and indeed, the chemical explosion sometimes figures in alchemical literature as a rite of passage). Hence, the fact that the father is destroyed during his own initiation into the secret art

underscores the idea that the story is about an experiment that fails precisely because it short-circuited.

7. In "Doestoevsky and Parricide" (published in 1928 but probably begun in 1926), Freud makes the connection between guilt, fear of castration, and ambivalence even more directly:

> The relation of a boy to his father is, as we say, an "ambivalent" one. In addition to the hate which seeks to get rid of the father as a rival, a measure of tenderness for him is also habitually present. The two attitudes of mind combine to produce identification with the father; the boy wants to be in his father's place because he admires him and wants to be like him, and also because he wants to put him out of the way. . . . At a certain moment the child comes to understand that an attempt to remove his father as a rival would be punished by him with castration. (183)

8. Brantly outlines a number of different positions concerning the men's activities. She notes:

> Critics have not always been clear about what Coppelius and Nathanael's father are actually doing in this hellish scene. For example, in an article written in 1965, S.S. Prawer writes concerning Coppelius, "As a lawyer and secret alchemist he is also the embodiment of greedy Philistinism." In 1977, however, Gunter Hartung dismissed the explanation of alchemy. The homunculus-theory would "account for the faces Nathanael sees in the fire, Coppelius' desire for eyes, and also his interest in the mechanisms of Nathanael's hands and feet. Such an interpretation would also provide a direct link between Coppelius and Giuseppe Coppola, both being craftsman of eyes for automatons." (326)

9. Following Moshe Idel, Newman stresses that the golem is not precisely comparable to the homunculus since the golem is not made from semen or (menstrual) blood (186). "If it were not rash to draw a modern comparison, perhaps one could say that the golem belongs to the realm of 'hard' artificial life, the world of robotics, cybernetics, and artificial intelligence, where ordinary biological processes are obviated or simulated by nonbiological means. The homunculus proper is a child of the 'wet' world of in vitro fertilization, cloning, and genetic engineering, where biology is not circumvented but altered" (187).

10. In this sense, the golem is like Rumpelstiltskin, who also comes from the ground and returns there after his angry fit.

11. This tale is recounted by Jakob Grimm and also forms a key element in Achim von Arnim's complex tale "Isabella of Egypt." In this tale, the princess, Bella, fashions a man from a mandrake root who can find gold that is buried underground. He is a dwarf and very much linked to telluric culture, again, like Rumpelstiltskin or the dwarves of the sagas. Bella rejects the malformed root in favor of the archduke. She wants to marry the archduke because she secretly hopes to bring her people back to Egypt from diaspora. But as in the tale of Rumpelstiltskin, the dwarf is actually quite clever. So the archduke calls upon a

Jew to make a golem version of Bella to dupe the mandrake. The golem Bella has *truth* inscribed on her forehead, but once the first letter is removed, she turns back into clay. In this sense, she is eternally linked with the mandrake, who also has his origins in the clay of the earth.

12. Newman writes that scholars have tended to project the idea of the homunculus in the late Renaissance back onto Zosimos and late antiquity. Zosimos's homunculus reflects his religious idea of purging dark matter in order to make it pneumatic through a process of distillation. Zosimos does write that the priest becomes a "little man or homunculus" and that "this image opened up a major iconographical tradition in alchemy—the Middle Ages saw the creation of numerous illustrations of men, women, and animals in alchemical bottles." Moreover, the theme of the little man in the bottle became fused with the theme of (chemical) marriage. But for Newman such images should not be taken literally, but symbolically. "The *anthroparion* of Zosimos is not an example of artificial human life, but of the rich symbolism of alchemy, which employed every conceivable image to veil the exact nature of the processes being described" (173).

13. He also translated Cellini's *Vita*, which contains analogies of the artistic process to alchemy. See Koenigsberger, who writes that there is "almost an embryonic Faust figure in Cellini" (11). She notes that both men shared a passion for the spiritual transformative nature of art. Goethe was engaged in writing a sequel to Mozart's *Magic Flute*, which has alchemical elements in the purification and rebirth of Pamina and Tamino, reborn after having been buried together, like the couple in *The Vanishing*.

14. There is considerable scholarly debate about Mephistopheles' role in the construction of the homunculus. Some question why he would ask what Wagner is doing if he would be implicated in the process. The response, "We are making a human being," implies that Wagner believes the devil is involved. Moreover, if Mephistopheles is involved, why does he ask Wagner to prove the being's capabilities? Höfler argues that the homunculus in *Faust* II is actually a product of both Wagner and Mephistopheles (two fathers) (25). Newman points out that the

> crystallization [of the homunculus] may have served as a way of making the homunculus less unseemly to a squeamish audience, but it was also a way of poking fun at contemporary naturalists who posited an inorganic origin of life. . . . If we put aside the issue of crystallization rather than production from semen, the Paracelsian provenance of Homunculus becomes evident. Like the homunculus of the *De rerum natura*, he is "spiritual" and practically bodiless. A product of art, Homunculus is intelligent beyond mere mortals and capable of having philosophical discussions upon birth. (Newman 297)

15. He is most certainly not a child. Eckermann wrote (*Conversation*, December 20, 1829): "I talked of the way to render the Homunculus clear on the stage.

'If we do not see the little man himself,' said I, 'we must see the light in the bottle, and his important words must be uttered in a way that would surpass the capacity of a child' " (cited in Goethe 2001, 541).

16. For Goethe there is only one stage in the continual formation of the processes of nature: metamorphosis. Goethe's homunculus is a go-between linking Northern and classical ideas of Walpurgisnacht (Walpurgis Night, an ancient pagan holiday supposed, in some traditions, to be a meeting of witches). Wagner is looking for a chemical bride in an earlier version of *Faust*, but in the final version, Wagner has a smaller role. He helps the homunculus to exist but doesn't make the Southern journey with him. Eckermann sees the relation of Mephistopheles and the homunculus not as father and son, but as demon-crony. Goethe probably knew Paracelsus primarily through the faithful translation of the homunculus recipe in Johannes Praetorius's *Anthropodemus Plutonicus, einer Sammlung von allerley wunderbaren Menschen* (1666–67). See Block for a brilliant reading of the larger issues at stake in the North-South relation.

17. The vessel should be thought of in relation to genre paintings of both the doctor (or quack) examining the urine of a patient, as well as the alchemist in his laboratory.

Notes to Chapter Six

1. The initial plan for *Capital* called for a total of six volumes, including one on the state and one on foreign trade. See Bensaïd 103.

2. Hartlaub also thought that identifying the *I* as the beginning of a temperament series was wrong, but then he

> flies off at a tangent by introducing the freemasonic idea of the grades of apprentice, journeyman and master (the latter two possibly embodied in Dürer's *Knight, Death and the Devil* and *St. Jerome*). But what Hartlaub says is lacking, i.e. "literary evidence for a regular tripartite division of Saturnine development," appears abundantly in the *Occulta Philosophia*, a German source, be it noted, whereas there is no evidence for any connexion with masonic ideas." (Klibansky et al. 350 n.)

3. This observation is followed by one of Marx's many fascinating footnotes in which he cites the Italian political economist Pietro Verri. Marx leaves the text in the original Italian, which I have translated:

> All the phenomena of the universe, whether produced by human hand or by the universal laws of physics, are not actual new creations, but modifications of existing matter. Unification and separation are the only elements that can be found, analyzing the idea of reproduction, and even then it is a reproduction of value (value in use, although Verri in this passage of his controversy with the Physiocrats is not himself quite certain of the kind of value he is speaking of) and wealth, as when water, air and earth transform into fields of grain, or even when by human hand insect glutin is transformed into

velvet or some little pieces of metal organized to form a pistol repeater. (*Meditazioni sulla Economia Politica*, first printed in 1773, cited in Marx 1887, 43)

Putting aside the very interesting question of the status of Marx's footnotes and the editorial decisions about what to translate, the passage itself is very representative of a way of thinking that is alchemical. Verri posits the idea that all human intervention is merely a modification of previous existing matter: *solve et coagula*.

4. The language also echoes alchemical writings. For instance, Sendivogius writes that God throws his *semence* into the center of the earth, and whatever isn't used is spit back out, just as man throws his sperm into the womb of woman and whatever isn't used is expelled. The seed is sublimated in the center of the earth. Metals are brought out by streams and rivers. First the four elements push their seed into earth. Seed of metals is no different from any other seed on earth—that is, it is a humid vapor. "That is why the alchemists seek in vain the reduction of metals to their prime matter, which is nothing other than vapor" (Sendivogius 13, translation mine). If humans want to engender metals, they need not take the whole body (mercury, as a conjoinment) but only the sperm or seed. The male and female should be joined until they form (*imaginent*) a sperm to make an offspring, "because there is no point in anyone trying to make the prime matter" (32). Only God can make the son, the *prima materia*.

5. Mary Poovey writes about one of the epistemological effects of double-entry bookkeeping: "to make the formal precision of the double-entry system, which drew on the rule-bound system of arithmetic, *seem* to guarantee the accuracy of the details it recorded" (30).

Notes to Chapter Seven

1. See Weart for an analysis of nuclear ambivalence.

2. In this regard, the remarks of Nicholas Royle on surrealism and the uncanny are particularly relevant to alchemy and modernity. He writes: "People can always think of [surrealism] as an 'artistic movement' which has 'had its day,' or suppose that (in Jean Baudrillard's words) 'surrealism can only survive as folklore' . . . could we not suppose that surrealism remains a strange 'non-event' that has no proper place, but still *haunts* . . . precisely everywhere and nowhere?" (97–98).

3. Perhaps Pollock's title is arbitrary and can teach us nothing new about alchemy in the modern world:

> Never very articulate himself, but responsive to the articulateness of others, Pollock had—at least since his first one-man show—frequently encouraged the people close to him, those whose sensitivity he trusted, to free-associate verbally around the completed work. From their responses, from key words and phrases, he often, though not always, chose his titles—typically vague, metaphorical, or "poetic." He thought of

each title as a convenience in identifying his work rather than in any sense a verbal equivalent of its subject matter. (Friedman 94)

4. The bibliography on Duchamp is vast. There are also many specific works treating his relationship to alchemy or dematerialization (that is, Duchamp as the first conceptual artist). De Duve and Krauss are particularly helpful in summarizing the primary issues.

5. On the one hand, Matta-Clark's work may seem to embrace structuralist pairs, but "sophistication in the register of social science retrieved his work from the cul-de-sac of incorrigible occultism (without leaving behind its emotional depth and psychological self-examination) to take on a form far more accessible and friendly to the detached, analytical values of the New York art world as he knew it" (Crow in Diserens, 30). Crow concludes that what set Matta-Clark apart from some of his contemporaries was his command of mythography and the play between the dualities of structuralism and the archetypes of Jung. Recall, also, that Matta-Clark's godfather was Marcel Duchamp.

6. Calvesi's essay for the catalog, "Lo spazio degli elementi," appeared in June 1967. See Christov-Bakargiev 220.

7. Interestingly, Celant studied with Eugenio Battisti, a philosopher and critic who wrote on alchemy and hermeticism in the early modern period. In Battisti's seminars, as early as 1963, Celant met Umberto Eco and Pier Paolo Pasolini, as well as art critics Maurizio Calvesi and Giulio Carlo Argan.

8. In an attempt to dupe an art dealer, Joseph Beuys once carved a price—90,000 DM, to be precise—into the side of a clay bathtub. The artist knew that as the clay hardened, it would crack. As it happened, one of the fissures sliced through the price, separating the nine from the zeroes. *Arte povera* artists made similar temporal interventions in their work. There is a certain loss of control—the artist sends his work out into the world with the knowledge that it will evolve and change from the way he released it—yet this is highly pleasurable, or even ludic (as in Beuys's case). It is also, however, melancholic, for it signals the absence of the artist from the long, geological processes of nature.

9. Over the course of the gestation of this book, gold has risen from about $300 to an ounce to over $1,000 and is currently quoted at over $900. Various mutual funds allow investors to have gold-based positions. The ticker symbol "GOLD" is held by Randgold resources, a company whose mission is as follows: "To achieve superior returns for shareholders through the development and management of resource opportunities focusing on GOLD."

Bibliography

Abraham, Lyndy. *A Dictionary of Alchemical Imagery*. Cambridge: Cambridge University Press, 1998.

———. "The Lovers and the Tomb: Alchemical Emblems in Shakespeare, Donne, and Marvell." *Emblematica* 5, no. 2 (Winter 1991): 301–20.

Adams, Alison, and Stanton J. Linden, eds. *Emblems and Alchemy*. Glasgow: Glasgow Emblem Studies, 1998.

Agamben, Giorgio. *Potentialities*. Edited and translated by Daniel Heller-Roazen. Stanford, CA: Stanford University Press, 1999.

———. *Stanze. La parola e il fantasma nella cultura occidentale*. Turin: Einaudi, 1977.

———. *State of Exception*. Translated by Kevin Attell. Chicago: University of Chicago Press, 2005.

Agrippa von Nettesheim, Henry Cornelius. *The Philosophy of Natural Magic*. 1531. Translated by J. Freake, 1651. Reprint, Secaucus, NJ: University Books, 1974.

Alchemy: A Comprehensive Bibliography of the Manly P. Hall Collection. Los Angeles: Philosophical Research Society, 1986.

Althusser, Louis and Etienne Balibar. *Reading Capital*. Translated by Ben Brewster. London and New York: Verso, 1990.

Altus (Jacob Saulat). *Mutus Liber*. La Rochelle, France: Pierre Savouret, 1677.

Amore, Franco, and Gennaro Accursio. "Evoluzione del concetto di ambivalenza nella teoria freudiana." *Giornale storico di psicologia dinamica* 10, no. 20, ns. 0391-2515 (June 1986): 121–42.

Anderson, Wilda. *Between the Library and the Laboratory: The Language of Chemistry in Eighteenth-Century France*. Baltimore, MD: Johns Hopkins University Press, 1984.

Andreae, Johann Valentin. *The Chymische Hochzeit: Christian Rosenkreutz*. Translated by Edward Foxcroft. 1690. Notes and commentary by John Warwick Montgomery. The Hague: M. Nijhoff, 1973.

Anzelewsky, Fedja. *Dürer: His Life and Art.* Translated by Heide Grieve. New York: Alpine Fine Arts, 1980.

Apter, Emily, and William Pietz, eds. *Fetishism as Cultural Discourse.* Ithaca, NY, and London: Cornell University Press, 1993.

Armour, Peter. "Gold, Silver, and True Treasure: Economic Imagery in Dante." *Romance Studies* 23 (Spring 1994): 7–30.

Bachelard, Gaston. *The Psychoanalysis of Fire.* Translated by Alan C.M. Ross. Boston: Beacon Press, 1964 (1938).

Bal, Mieke. *Reading Rembrandt: Beyond the Word-Image Opposition.* Cambridge: Cambridge University Press, 1991.

Barchusen, Johann Conrad. *Elementa chemiae quibus subjuncta est confectura lapidis philosophici imaginibus repraesentata.* Leiden, the Netherlands: Theodorum Haak, 1718.

Barrett, Francis. *The Lives of Alchemystical Philosophers: With a Critical Catalogue of Books in Occult Chemistry and a Selection of the Most Celebrated Treatises on the Theory and Practice of the Hermetic Art.* London: Lackington, Allen and Co., 1815.

Battisti, Eugenio. *L'antirinascimento.* Milan: Feltrinelli, 1962.

Bazzi, Adriana. "Creato embrione con due sessi." *Corriere della sera,* July 4, 2003: 14.

Beccaria, Cesare. *Elementi di economia pubblica.* 1804. Reprint, Milan: P. Custodi, 1822.

Becher, J. J. *Physica subterranean: Profundam subterraneorum genesin e principiis hucusque ignotis, ostendens.* Leipzig, Germany: Gleditschium, 1703.

Bensaïd, Daniel. *Marx for Our Times: Adventures and Misadventures of a Critique.* London and New York: Verso, 2002.

Bertozzi, Marco, ed. *Aby Warburg e le metamorfosi degli antichi dei.* Ferrara, Italy: Franco Cosimo Panini, 2002.

Bleuler, Eugen. "Vortrag über Ambivalenz." *Zentralblatt für Psychoanalyse* 1 (1910).

Block, Richard. *The Spell of Italy: Vacation, Magic and the Attraction of Goethe.* Detroit, MI: Wayne State University Press, 2006.

Blunt, Anthony. "The Hypnerotomachia Poliphili in 17th Century France." *Journal of the Warburg and Countauld Institutes* 1, no. 2 (October 1937): 117–37.

Boime, Albert. *Art in the Age of Revolution 1750–1800.* Chicago: University of Chicago Press, 1987.

Boschloo, A.W.A. "Raam Vertellingen." In *Ontrouw aan Rembrandt en andere verhalen: Een bloemlezing vit kunstschrift met antikelen over de 17de-eeuwse Nederlandse kunst.* Amsterdam: Kunstschrift, SDU / Openbaar Kunstbezit, 1991.

Bottigheimer, Ruth B. "Tale Spinners: Submerged Voices in Grimms' Fairy Tales." *New German Critique* 27 (1981): 141–50.

Brantly, Susan. "A Thermographic Reading of E.T.A. Hoffmann's 'Der Sandmann.'" *The German Quarterly* 55, no. 3 (May 1982): 324–35.

Brinkman, A. "Brueghel's 'Alchemist' and Its Influence, in Particular on Jan Steen." *Janus: Revue internationale de l'histoire des sciences de la medecine* (Amsterdam), July 27, 1976: 233–69.

Calhoon, Kenneth. "Alchemies of Distraction: James's *Portrait of a Lady* and Fontane's *Effi Briest.*" *Arcadia* 34 (1999): 1, 90–113.

———. "Personal Effects: Rilke, Barthes, and the Matter of Photography." *MLN* 113 (1998): 612–34.

Calvesi, Maurizio. *Duchamp L'invisibile.* Rome: Officina, 1975.

———. *La melanconia di Albrecht Dürer.* (Includes the essay "A noir [Melencolia I]," first published in 1969.) Turin, Italy: Einaudi, 1993.

Calvet, Antoine. "Une pratique de l'or portable au XVI siecle: le Traité du Grand Oeuvre de Philippe Rouillac" in Matton, Sylvain, ed. *Documents oubliés sur l'alchimie, la kabbale et Guillaume Postel: Offerts, à l'occasion de son 90 anniversaire, François Secret par ses eleves et amis.* Geneva: Librairie Droz, 2001.

Cassata, Francesco. *A destra del Fascismo: Profilo politico di Julius Evola.* Turin, Italy: Bollati Boringhieri, 2003.

Cellini, Benvenuto. *Autobiography* (*Vita*). Translated by George Bull. London: Penguin, 1956.

Christov-Bakargiev, Carolyn. *Arte Povera.* London: Phaidon, 1999.

Cole, Michael. "Cellini's Blood." *The Art Bulletin* 18, no. 2 (June 1999): 215–35.

Cole, Michael, and Mary Pardo, eds. *Inventions of the Studio, Renaissance to Romanticism.* Chapel Hill and London: University of North Carolina Press, 2005.

Colonna, Francesco. *Hypnerotomachia Poliphili.* 1499. Edited by Giovanni Pozzi and Lucia A. Ciapponi. 2 vols. Padua, Italy: Antenore, 1964.

Conley, Tom. "Mapping Béroalde: Between *Le palais des curieux* and *Le moyen de parvenir.*" In *Studies on Béroalde de Verville*, edited by Michael Giordano. Paris and Seattle: Papers on French Seventeenth Century Literature, 1992.

Crow, Thomas. "Gordon Matta-Clark" in *Gordon Matta-Clark.* Corinne Diserens, editor. London and New York: Phaidon, 2003.

Davis, Whitney. *Drawing the Dream of the Wolves.* Bloomington: Indiana University Press, 1995.

De Duve, Thierry. "Joseph Beuys, or Last of the Proletarians." *October* 45 (Summer 1988): 47–62.

De Duve, Thierry, and Rosalind Krauss. "Echoes of the Readymade: Critique of Pure Modernism." *October* 70 (The Duchamp Effect) (Autumn 1994): 60–97.

De la Garanderie, M.-M., ed. *Mercure à la Renaissance.* Proceedings of conference in Lille, 1984. Paris: Librarie Champion, 1988.

Delcourt, Marie. *Héphaistos ou la légende du magicien.* Paris: Société d'édition "Les Belles Lettres," 1982.

————. *Stérilités mystérieuses et naissances maléfiques dans l'antiquité classique.* Paris: Librairie Droz, 1938.

Denton, Margaret Fields. "A Woman's Place: The Gendering of Genres in Post-Revolutionary French Painting." *Art History* 21, no. 2 (June 1998): 219–46.

Derrida, Jacques. *La dissémination.* Paris: Seuil, 1972. Translated by Barbara Johnson as *Dissemination* (Chicago: University of Chicago Press, 1981).

De Vries, Lyckle. *Gerard de Lairesse: An Artist Between Stage and Studio.* Amsterdam: Amsterdam University Press, 1998.

Dickson, Donald. "Johann Valentin Andreae's Utopian Brotherhoods." *Renaissance Quarterly* 49, no. 4 (Winter 1996): 760–802.

Dieterle, Richard L. "The Metallurgical Code of the 'Volundarkvita and Its Theoretical Import" *History of Religions* 27, no. 1 (August 1987): 1–31.

Dobbs, B.J.T. "Newton's Commentary on the *Emerald Tablet* of Hermes Trismegistus: Its Scientific and Theological Significance." In Merkel and Debus, *Hermeticism and the Renaissance: Intellectual History and the Occult in Early Modern Europe,* 182–91.

Duits, Rembrandt. "Figured Riches: The Value of Gold Brocades in Fifteenth-Century Florentine Painting." *Journal of the Warburg and Courtauld Institutes* 62 (1999): 60–92.

Edelman, Lee. *No Future: Queer Theory and the Death Drive.* Durham, NC: Duke University Press, 2004.

Edgerton, Samuel. *The Heritage of Giotto's Geometry: Art and Science on the Eve of the Scientific Revolution.* Ithaca, NY, and London: Cornell University Press, 1991.

Eliot, George. *Silas Marner.* London: Dent, 1949.

Elkins, James, ed. *What Painting Is: How to Think About Oil Painting Using the Language of Alchemy.* New York and London: Routledge, 1999.

Evola, Julius. *The Hermetic Tradition: Symbols and Teachings of the Royal Art.* Translated by E. E. Rehmus. Rochester, VT: Inner Traditions, 1995.

Flamel, Nicholas. *Nicholas Flammel, His Exposition of the Hieroglyphicall Figures Which He Caused to Bee Painted upon an Arch in St. Innocents Church-yard, in Paris . . . By Eirenaeus Orandus.* London: Thomas Walkley, 1624.

Foster, Hal. "The Art of Fetishism: Notes on Dutch Still Life." In Apter and Pietz, *Fetishism as Cultural Discourse,* 251–65.

Freud, Sigmund. "Doestoevsky and Parricide." In *The Standard Edition of the Complete Psychological Works.* Vol. 21: 175–96. Translated by Alix Strachey. London: Hogarth Press, 1953–1974. Originally published as "Dostojewski und die Vatertötung," 1928.

————. "The Ego and the Id." In *The Standard Edition of the Complete Psychological Works.* Vol. 19: 1–59. Translated by Alix Strachey. London: Hogarth Press, 1953–1974. Originally published as "Das Ich und das Es," 1923.

————. "The Theme of the Three Caskets." In *The Standard Edition of the Complete Psychological Works*. Vol. 12: 291–301. Translated by Alix Strachey. London: Hogarth Press, 1953–1974. Originally published as "Das Motiv der Kästchenwahl," 1913.

————. "The Uncanny." In *The Standard Edition of the Complete Psychological Works*. Vol. 17: 218–53. Translated by Alix Strachey. London: Hogarth Press, 1953–1974. Originally published as "Das Unheimliche," 1919.

Freud, Sigmund, and Josef Breuer. *Studien über Hysterie*. Frankfurt, Germany: Fischer, 1970.

Fried, Michael. *Absorption and Theatricality: Painting and Beholder in the Age of Diderot*. Berkeley: University of California Press, 1980.

Friedman, B. H. *Jackson Pollock: Energy Made Visible*. New York: Da Capo Press, 1995.

Garrison, Mark. "The Poetics of Ambivalence." *Spring* (1982): 213–32.

Gaskell, Ivan. "Gerrit Dou, His Patrons and the Art of Painting." *Oxford Art Journal* 5, no. 1 (1982): 15–23.

Gilman, Sander. *Difference and Pathology: Stereotypes of Sexuality, Race and Madness*. Ithaca, NY: Cornell University Press, 1985.

Gilmour, Simon. "Die Figur des Zwerges in den Kinder- und Hausmärchen der Brüder Grimm." *Fabula* 34, no. 1–2 (1993): 9–23.

Ginzburg, Carlo. *Ecstasies: Deciphering the Witches' Sabbath*. Translated by Raymond Rosenthal. New York: Penguin, 1991.

Giordano, Michael. "Reverse Transmutations: Béroalde de Verville's Parody of Paracelsus in *Le Moyen de parvenir*: An Alchemical Language of Skepticism in the French Baroque." *Renaissance Quarterly* 56 (2003): 88–137.

Goethe, Johann Wolfgang von. *Elective Affinities (Wahlverwandtschaften)*. Translated by David Constantine. Oxford: Oxford University Press, 1994.

————. *Faust*. 2nd ed. Edited by Cyrus Hamlin. Translated by Walter Arndt. New York and London: Norton, 2001 (1809).

Gombrich, Ernest. *Aby Warburg: An Intellectual Biography*. 2nd ed. Oxford: Phaidon, 1986.

————. *Tributes*. London: Phaidon, 1994.

Gordon, Barry. *Economic Analysis Before Adam Smith: Hesiod to Lessius*. New York: Barnes and Noble, 1975.

Goux, Jean-Joseph. *Symbolic Economies After Marx and Freud*. Translated by Jennifer Curtiss Gage. Ithaca, NY: Cornell University Press, 1990.

Goux, Jean-Joseph, and Thomas DiPiero. "Banking on Signs." *Diacritics* 18, no. 2, Pecunia non olet (Summer 1988): 15–25.

Gray, Ronald. *Goethe the Alchemist. A Study of Alchemical Symbolism in Goethe's Literary and Scientific Works*. Cambridge: Cambridge Univ. Press, 1952.

Grilliat, Denis. "L'ambivalence comme paradigme de la différence structurale entre schizophrénie et névrose." *Bulletin de psychologie* 51, no. 2 (March–April 1998): 173–79.

Grimm, Jacob. *Deutsche Mythologie.* 3 vols. Basel: Benno Schwabe, 1953.

———. *Kleinere Schriften.* Hildesheim: Georg Olms, 1965.

Guttmann, Robert. *Cybercash: The Coming Era of Electronic Money.* Houndsmills, UK and New York: Palgrave, 2003.

Hardt, Michael and Antonio Negri. *Multitude. War and Democracy in the Age of Empire.* New York: Penguin, 2004.

Harkness, Deborah. *John Dee's Conversations with Angels: Cabala, Alchemy, and the End of Nature.* Cambridge: Cambridge University Press, 1999.

Hawthorne, Nathaniel. "The Birthmark." In *Mosses from an Old Manse.* Boston and New York: Houghton Mifflin, 1854.

Henderson, Linda. *Duchamp in Context: Science and Technology in the Large Glass and Related Works.* Princeton: Princeton University Press, 1998.

Hermetical Triumph or the Victorious Philosopher's Stone. London: Thomas Harris, 1745(?).

Höfler, Otto. *Homunculus—eine Satire auf A.W. Schlegel. Goethe und die Romantik.* Vienna: Böhlau, 1972.

Hoffmann, E.T.A. *Der Sandmann: Textkritik, Edition, Kommentar.* Edited by Ulrich Hohoff. Berlin and New York: Walter de Gruyter, 1988.

———. *The Golden Pot and Other Tales.* Translated by Ritchie Robertson. Oxford: Oxford University Press, 1992.

Hollander, Martha. *An Entrance for the Eyes: Space and Meaning in Seventeenth-Century Dutch Art.* Berkeley: University of California Press, 2002.

Hutin, Serge. *La vie quotidienne des alchimistes au moyen age.* Paris: Hachette, 1977.

Jaffé, Aniela. "The Influence of Alchemy on the Work of C. G. Jung." In *Alchemy and the Occult: A Catalogue of Books and Manuscripts from the Collection of Paul and Mary Mellon.* Vol. 1. New Haven, CT: Yale University Press, 1968.

Jentsch, Ernst. "On the Psychology of the Uncanny." 1906. Translated by Roy Sellars. *Angelaki* 2, no. 1 (1995): 7–16.

Jong, H.M.E. *Michael Maier's* Atalanta Fugiens*: Sources of an Alchemical Book of Emblems.* Leiden: Brill, 1969.

Kantorowicz, Ernst. *The King's Two Bodies.* Princeton, NJ: Princeton University Press, 1997.

Keenan, Thomas. "The Point Is to (Ex)Change It: Reading *Capital*, Rhetorically." In Apter and Pietz, *Fetishism as Cultural Discourse*, 152–85.

Khosla, Vinod. "My Big Biofuels Bet." http://www.wired.com/wired/archive/14 .10/ethanol_pr.html.

Klein, Melanie. *Love, Guilt and Reparation and Other Works, 1921–1945.* New York: The Free Press, 1975.

————. *The Psychoanalysis of Children.* Translated by H. A. Thorner. New York: The Free Press, 1975.

Klibansky, R., E. Panofsky, and F. Saxl. *Saturn and Melancholy: Studies in the History of Natural Philosophy, Religion, and Art.* New York: Basic Books, 1964.

Klossowski de Rola, Stanislas. *Alchemy: The Secret Art.* 1973. Reprint, New York: Thames and Hudson, 1985.

Koenigsberger, Dorothy. "*Leben des Benvenuto Cellini*: Goethe, Cellini and Transformation." *European History Quarterly* 22 (1992): 7–37.

Kofman, Sarah. *Conversions: Le* Marchand de Venise *sous le signe de Saturne.* Paris: Editions Galilée, 1987.

Krabbé, Tim. *The Vanishing.* Translated by Claire Nicolas White. New York: Random House, 1993.

Kristeva, Julia. *Melanie Klein.* Translated by Ross Guberman. New York: Columbia University Press, 2001.

Levin, David. *Richard Wagner, Fritz Lang and the Nibelungen: The Dramaturgy of Disavowal.* Princeton, NJ: Princeton University Press, 1999.

Lippard, Lucy. *Six Years: The Dematerialization of the Art Object from 1966 to 1972.* Berkeley: University of California Press, 1973.

Long, Pamela. *Openness, Secrecy, Authorship: Technical Arts and the Culture of Knowledge from Antiquity to the Renaissance.* Baltimore, MD: Johns Hopkins University, 2001.

Macy, Michael W. "Value Theory and the 'Golden Eggs': Appropriating the Magic of Accumulation." *Sociological Theory* 6, no. 2 (Autumn 1988): 131–52.

Magee, Elizabeth. *Richard Wagner and the Nibelungs.* Oxford: Clarendon Press, 1990.

Maier, Michael. *Atalanta Fugiens.* Oppenheim, Germany: Theodore de Bry, 1618. Translated by J. Godwin in *Magnum Opus Hermeticum Sourcebooks* 22 (Grand Rapids, MI: Phanes Press, 1989).

————. *Lusus serius, quo Hermes sive Mercurius Rex Mundanorum Omnium sub homine existentium.* Oppenheim: Luca Jennis, 1616.

————. *Silentium post Clamores.* Frankfurt: Luca Jennis, 1617.

————. *Symbola aureae mensae duodecim nationum.* Frankfurt: Luca Jennis, 1617.

Maillard, Jean-François. "Mercure alchimiste dans la tradition mytho-hermétique," in De la Garanderie, *Mercure à la Renaissance*: 117–130.

Marcuzzo, Maria Cristina, and Annalisa Rosselli. *Ricardo and the Gold Standard: The Foundations of the International Monetary Order.* Translated by Joan Hall. Houndsmills, UK: Macmillan Academic and Professional, 1991.

Marotti, William. "Simulacra and Subversion in the Everyday: Akasegawa Genpei's 1000-yen Copy, Critical Art, and the State." *Postcolonial Studies* 4, no. 2 (2001): 211–39.

Marquet, Jean-François. "Béroalde de Verville et le roman alchimique." *XVIIe siècle* no. 120 (July/September 1978): 157–70.

Martin, F. *Le Livre d'Enoch.* Paris: Letouzey et Ané, 1906.

Martin, W. "The Life of a Dutch Artist in the Seventeenth Century. Part III: The Painter's Studio." *The Burlington Magazine* 8, no. 31 (October 1905): 13–24.

Marx, Karl. *Capital.* Vol. 1 Edited by Frederick Engels. Translated from the third German edition by Samuel Moore and Edward Aveling. 1867. Reprint, New York: International Publishers, 1967.

———. *Capital.* Vol. 2. Edited by Frederick Engels. Translated by Samuel Moore and Edward Aveling. 1885. Reprint, New York: International Publishers, 1967.

———. *Grundrisse.* Translated by Martin Nicolaus. 1857. London: Penguin Books, 1973.

Meiss, Millard. "Light as Form and Symbol in Some 15th Century Paintings." *Art Bulletin* 27 (1945): 175–81.

Merkel, Ingrid, and Allen G. Debus, eds. *Hermeticism and the Renaissance: Intellectual History and the Occult in Early Modern Europe.* Washington, DC: Folger Shakespeare Library, 1988.

Meurdrac, Marie. *La Chymie Charitable et Facile, En faveur des Dames.* 1666. Edited by Jean Jacques. Reprint, Paris: CNRS, 1999.

Moffitt, John T. *Alchemist of the Avant-Garde: The Case of Marcel Duchamp.* Albany, NY: SUNY Press, 2003.

Montesquieu, Charles de Secondat, Baron de. *The Spirit of the Laws.* Amherst, NY: Prometheus Books, 2002.

Motz, Lotte. *The Wise One on the Mountain: Form, Function and Significance of the Subterranean Smith.* Göppingen: Kümmerle Verlag, 1983.

Müller-Sievers, Helmut. *Self-Generation: Biology, Philosophy, and Literature Around 1800.* Stanford, CA: Stanford University Press, 1997.

Nelson, Anitra. *Marx's Concept of Money: The God of Commodities.* London: Routledge, 1999.

Newman, William R. *Promethean Ambitions: Alchemy and the Quest to Perfect Nature.* Chicago: University of Chicago Press, 2004.

Obrist, Barbara. *Les débuts de l'imagerie alchimique: XIVe–XVe siecles.* Paris: Le Sycomore, 1982.

Ovid. *Metamorphoses.* Translated by Frank Miller. Cambridge, Massachusetts: Harvard University Press, 1977

Pagden, Sylvia Ferino, Francesca Del Torre Scheuch, Elisabetta Fadda, and Mino Gabriele, eds. *Parmigianino e la pratica dell'alchimia.* Milan, Italy: Silvana Editoriale, 2003.

Paracelsus. *The Hermetical and Alchemical Writings.* 1910. Edited by Arthur Edward Waite. Reprint, Whitefish, MT: Kessinger Publications, 1991.

Parker, Andrew. "Unthinking Sex: Marx, Engels, and the Scene of Writing." In *Fear of a Queer Planet: Queer Politics and Social Theory*, edited by Michael Warner, 19–41. Minneapolis: University of Minnesota Press, 1993.

Perelman, Michael. *The Invention of Capitalism: Classical Political Economy and the Secret History of Primitive Accumulation*. Durham, NC: Duke University Press, 2000.

Pernety, Antoine-Joseph. *Dictionaire mytho-hérmetique*. Paris: Bauche, 1758.

Philalethes, Eirenaeus [pseudo. of George Starkey]. *Introitus apertus ad occlusm regis palatium*. 1667. Translated as *Secrets Revealed or an Open Entrance to the Shut Palace of the King*. London: William Cooper, 1669.

Pincombe, Michael. "The Ovidian Hermaphrodite: Moralizations by Peend and Spenser." In *Ovid and the Renaissance Body*, edited by Goran V. Stanivukovic, 155–70. Toronto: University of Toronto Press, 2001.

Pinkus, Karen. "Hermaphrodite Poetics." *Arcadia: International Journal of Literary Studies* 41, no. 1 (2006): 91–111.

———. *Picturing Silence: Emblem, Language, Counter-Reformation Materiality*. Ann Arbor: University of Michigan Press, 1996.

Pinto-Correia, Clara. *The Ovary of Eve: Egg and Sperm in Preformation*. Chicago and London: University of Chicago Press, 1997.

Polizzi, Gilles. "La fabrique de l'énigme: Lectures 'alchimiques' du Poliphile chez Gohory et Béroalde de Verville." In *Alchimie et philosophie à la Renaissance*, edited by Jean-Claude Margolin and Sylvain Matton. Paris: Vrin, 1993.

Poovey, Mary. *A History of the Modern Fact*. Chicago: University of Chicago Press, 1998.

Principe, Lawrence. *The Aspiring Adept: Robert Boyle and His Alchemical Quest*. Princeton, NJ: Princeton University Press, 1998.

Rieken, Bernd. "Die Spinne als Symbol in Volksdictung und Literatur." *Fabula* 36, nos. 3–4 (1995): 187–204.

Ripellino, Angelo Maria. *Magic Prague*. Edited by Michael Heim. Translated by David Newton Marinelli. Berkeley: University of California Press, 1994.

Rosarium philosophorum. Frankurt: Jocaob Cyriacus, 1550.

Rossi, Paolo. *Logic and the Art of Memory*. Translated by Stephen Clucas. Chicago: University of Chicago Press, 2000.

Royle, Nicholas. *The Uncanny*. New York and London: Routledge, 2003.

Schama, Simon. *Rembrandt's Eyes*. New York: Knopf, 1999.

Scherér, René. "Nota sull'Homunculus di Goethe." Translated by Vito Bianco. In *Desiderio del mostro: Dal circo al laboratorio alla politica*, edited by Ubaldo Fadini, Antonio Negri, and Charles T. Wolfe, 247–53. Rome: Manifestolibri, 2001.

Schnapp, Jeffrey. "Bad Dada (Evola)." In *The Dada Seminars*, edited by Leah Dickerman and Matthew S. Witkovsky, 30–55. Washington, DC: National Gallery of Art, 2005.

Schneider, Jane. "Rumplestiltskin's Bargain." In *Cloth and Human Experience*, edited by Annette B. Weiner and Jane Schneider. Washington, DC: Smithsonian, 1989.

Schwartz, Jerome. "Some Emblematic Marriage Topoi in the French Renaissance." *Emblematica* 1, no. 2 (Fall 1986): 245–66.

Sendivogius, Michael (Michał Sędziwój). *Cosmopolite, ou nouvelle lumière chimique, divisez en douse traitez, avec un dialogue de Mercure, de l'alchymiste et de la Nature*. Paris: Jean d'Houry, 1569.

Shell, Marc. *Money, Literature, and Thought*. Baltimore, MD: Johns Hopkins University Press, 1982.

Silberer, Herbert. *Problems of Mysticism and Its Symbolism*. Translated by Smith Ely Jelliffe. New York: Moffat, Yard and Company, 1917.

Silberman, Lauren. "Mythographic Transformations of Ovid's Hermaphrodite." *Sixteenth-Century Journal* 19, no. 4 (Winter 1988): 52–63.

Sinclair, Upton. *The Jungle*. New York: Modern Library, 2002.

Smith, Pamela. "Alchemy as a Language of Mediation at the Habsburg Court." *Isis* 85 (March 1994): 1–25.

———. *The Business of Alchemy: Science and Culture in the Holy Roman Empire*. Princeton, NJ: Princeton University Press, 1994.

Smithson, Robert. *The Collected Writings*. Edited by Jack Flam. Berkeley: University of California Press, 1996.

Solomon, Elinor Harris. *Virtual Money: Understanding the Power and Risk of Money's High-Speed Journey into Electronic Space*. New York: Oxford, 1997.

Sonnenfeld, Albert. "The Poetics of Antisemitism." *Romanic Review* 76, no. 1 (January 1995): 76–93.

Stewart, Alison. *Unequal Lovers: A Study of Unequal Couples in Northern Art*. New York: Abaris Books, 1978.

Stoichita, Victor. *Brève histoire de l'ombre*. Geneva: Droz, 2000.

Strindberg, August. *Inferno / From an Occult Diary*. Translated by Mary Sandbach. New York: Penguin, 1979.

Sutherland, Keston. "Marx in Jargon." *World Picture* 1. www.worldpicture journal.com.

Teich, Mikulas. "Circulation, Transformation, Conservation of Matter and the Balancing of the Biological World in the 18th Century." *Ambix* 27, no. 1 (March 1981): 363–80.

Terrall, Mary. *The Man Who Flattened the Earth: Maupertuis and the Sciences in the Enlightenment*. Chicago: University of Chicago Press, 2002.

Tietze-Conrat, E. *Dwarfs and Jesters in Art*. London: Phaidon, 1952.

Tiffany, Daniel. "Lyric Substance: On Riddles, Materialism, and Poetic Obscurity." *Critical Inquiry* 28, no. 1 (Autumn 2001): 72–98.

Timpanaro, Sebastiano. *The Freudian Slip: Psychoanalysis and Textual Criticism.* Translated by Kate Soper. London: Verso, 1985.

Todorov, Tzvetan. *Eloge du quotidien: Essai sur la peinture hollandaise du XVIIe siècle.* Paris: Adam Biro, 1993.

Turba philosophorum. Translated by A. E. Waite. London: George Redway, 1896.

Urbigerus, Baro. *Aphorismi Urbigerani, or Certain Rules Clearly Demonstrating the Three Infallible Ways of Preparing the Grand Elixir.* London: Henry Faithorne, 1690.

Valentine, Basil. *The Triumphal Chariot of Antimony.* Annotated by Theodore Kerckring. 1685. Reprint, Whitefish, MT: Kessinger Publications, 1990.

Van Lennep, Jacques. *Alchimie.* Brussels: Crédits Commerciales, 1984.

———. *Art et alchimie.* Brussels: Meddens, 1971.

Varchi, Benedetto. *Questione sull'alchimia.* 1544. Reprint, Florence: Magheri, 1827.

Vickers, Brian. "Francis Yates and the Writing of History." *Journal of Modern History* 51 (June 1979): 287–316.

Vidal, Mary. "David Among the Moderns: Art, Science and the Lavoisiers." *Journal of the History of Ideas* 56, no. 4 (October 1995): 595–623.

Vilar, Pierre. *A History of Gold and Money: 1450–1920.* Translated by Judith White. London and New York: Verso, 1969.

Warburg, Aby. "Pagan-Antique Prophecy in Words and Images in the Age of Luther" (1920). In *Aby Warburg: The Revival of Pagan Antiquity,* translated by David Britt, 597–697. Los Angeles: Getty Research Institute, 1999.

Weart, Spencer. *Nuclear Fear: A History of Images.* Cambridge, MA: Harvard University Press, 1988.

Weber, Samuel. *The Legend of Freud.* Expanded edition. Stanford, CA: Stanford University Press, 2000.

Weschler, Lawrence. *Boggs: A Comedy of Values.* Chicago: University of Chicago Press, 1999.

Wheelock, Arthur K., ed. *Gerard ter Borch.* Washington: National Gallery of Art, 2004.

Wiesenfarth, Joseph. "Demythologizing Silas Marner." *ELH* 37, no. 2 (June 1970): 226–44.

Yates, Frances. *Giordano Bruno and the Hermetic Tradition.* Chicago: University of Chicago Press, 1991.

———. *The Rosicrucian Enlightenment.* London: Routledge, 1972.

Zinguer, Ilana. *Le roman stéganomorphique: Le voyage des fortunez de Béroalde de Verville.* Paris: Champion, 1993.

Zipes, Jack. "Spinning with Fate: Rumpelstiltskin and the Decline of Female Productivity." *Western Folklore* 52 (January 1993): 43–60.

Index